W9-BMX-099

The Joanne Kates

Toronto Restaurant Guide

by the restaurant critic for

CANADA'S NATIONAL NEWSPAPER

THE GLOBE AND MAIL

SOMERVILLE HOUSE PUBLISHING

TORONTO

To Leon, Max and Mara: partners in gluttony

Copyright © 1995 by Joanne Kates

Canadian Cataloguing in Publication Data
Kates, Joanne, 1949-
        The Joanne Kates Toronto restaurant guide
New ed.
Includes index.
ISBN 1-895897-47-5
1. Restaurants - Ontario - Toronto - Guidebooks
I. Title. II. Title: Toronto restaurant guide.
TX910.C2K3 1995   647.95713'541   C95-930921-7

Produced by Somerville House Books Limited
Printed in Canada

Design: Brenda van Ginkel
Editor: Ruth Chernia

The reviews published in this book are based upon ones written by the author for *The Globe and Mail*. Facts contained in them were checked and updated by researchers at the time of publication. However, there will inevitably be subsequent changes in management, chefs, menus and decor. This should be kept in mind by anyone relying on this book when choosing a restaurant.

Table of Contents

The Reviews

Index of Restaurants

INDEX OF RESTAURANTS

RESTAURANTS BY CATEGORY

Brunch

Cafe La Gaffe
Café Victoria
Chapeau (Sun.)
College Street Bar
   (Sat.-Sun.)
Cuisine of India (Sun.)
Delisle Restaurant and
   Wine Bar (Sat.-Sun.)
Jamie Kennedy at the Museum
   (Sun.-Thurs.)
Kuraya Restaurant
Marketta (Sat & Sun)
Matisse Restaurant and Bar
   (Sat.-Sun.)
Mezzetta Restaurant
O Mei
Pazzo's Restaurant and Café
   (in summer only)
Young Thailand on Church
   (Mon.-Fri.)
Young Thailand on Gerrard
   (Mon.-Fri.)

Joso's
Jump Café and Bar
Katz's Delicatessen and
   Corned Beef Emporium
Kit Kat Italian Bar and Grill
Le Passe-Partout
Lotus
Masquerade Caffé Bar
North 44
Officers 1893
Otago (fall and winter only)
Rodney's Oyster House
Sanona
Scaccia Restaurant
Scaramouche Restaurant,
   Pasta Bar & Grill
Shark City Athletic Club
   Bar & Grill
Thai Magic Restaurant
Tiger Lily's (in winter only)
Tojo
Truffles
Twiggy
Vanipha Lanna

Closed Sunday

Acqua Ristorante & Bar
Acrobat Bis
Arlequin Restaurant
Auberge du Pommier
Avalon
BamBoo
Caro
Centro Grill and Wine Bar
Da Dante
Gio's Italian Food
Iguana

Open for Dinner Only

Acrobat Bis
Avalon (in winter only)
Boba
Boujadi Moroccan Restaurant
Byzantium
Centro Grill and Wine Bar
Cities Bistro
Gio's Italian Food
Iguana
Lee Garden Restaurant

Lotus
Medieval Times
Michael Stadtländer at
    Eiginsinn Farm
North 44
Officers 1893
Otago
Positano Restaurant
Prelude Restaurant
Ristorante Grappa
Roof Restaurant Park Plaza
    Hotel
Scaramouche Restaurant,
    Pasta Bar and Grill
Shanghai Garden
Sotto Sotto Ristorante
Spiaggia Trattoria
Splendido Bar and Grill
Thai Magic Restaurant
Tojo
Truffles

Open Late

Acrobat Bis
    (1 a.m. Tues.-Sat.)
Alice Fazooli's Italian
    Crabshack Saloon
    (1 a.m. daily)
Anh Dao Restaurant
    (Midnight daily)
BamBoo (1 a.m. Mon.-Sat.)
Bar Italia (1 a.m. daily)
Bofinger Brasserie
    (1 a.m. Fri.-Sat.)
Chapeau (Midnight Tues.-Sun.)
Classic Chinese
    (Midnight daily)

College Street Bar
    (1:30 a.m. daily)
Commisso Fine Foods
    (Midnight Sun.- Thu.,
    1 a.m. Fri.-Sat.)
Dunn's Famous Delicatessen
    (open 24 hrs daily)
The Fish House (Oyster Bar
    only, midnight Sun.-Thu.
    1 a.m. Fri.-Sat.)
Giovanna Trattoria (Midnight
    Sat.-Sun.)
Kim Hoa (1 a.m. Wed.- Mon.)
Kit Kat Italian Bar and Grill
    (1 a.m. Mon.- Sat.)
Kuraya Restaurant (Midnight
    Tues.-Sat.)
Lakes Bar and Grill (1 a.m.
    Mon.-Sat.)
La Serre (1 a.m. Mon.-Sat.)
Lee Garden Restaurant
    (Midnight Sun.-Thu.,
    1 a.m. Fri.-Sat.)
Mandaloon (Midnight daily in
    spring, summer and fall)
Margarita's
    (Midnight Sat.-Sun.)
Masquerade Caffé Bar
    (Midnight Mon.-Wed.,
    1 a.m. Thu.-Sat.)
Milano Billiards Lounge
    and Bistro (1:30 a.m.
    Mon.-Fri., 2 a.m. Sat.,
    1 a.m. Sun.)
Montana (Midnight daily)
Mövenpick Marché
    (2 a.m. daily)
Palavrion

9

RESTAURANTS BY CATEGORY

(Midnight Sun. and Wed.-
Thu., 1 a.m. Fri.-Sat.)
Pan (1 a.m. daily)
Pazzo's Restaurant and Café
(Midnight daily)
Pearl (4 a.m. daily)
Primadonna (Midnight Sun.,
1 a.m. Mon.-Sat.)
Rodney's Oyster House
(1 a.m. Mon.-Sat.)
Sang-Ho Seafood Restaurant
(Midnight daily)
Sanona (Midnight Fri.-Sat.)
Senator on the Square
(Midnight Thurs.,
1 a.m. Fri.-Sat.)
Shark City Athletic Club Bar
& Grill (Midnight
Mon.-Fri., 1 a.m. Sat.)
Sotto Sotto Ristorante
(Midnight daily)
Sukhothai (Midnight Fri.-Sat.)
Vanipha Lanna (Midnight
Fri.-Sat.)
Wayne Gretsky's Restaurant
and Bar (1 a.m. daily)

Open for Lunch

Acqua Ristorante & Bar
Alice Fazooli's Italian
Crabshack Saloon
Anh Dao Restaurant
Arlequin Restaurant
Art Gallery of Ontario
Restaurant
Auberge du Pommier
Avalon (except in Winter)

BamBoo
Bar Italia
Bayview Garden
Browne's Bistro
Bofinger Brasserie
Café Asia
Cafe La Gaffe
Café Victoria
Caro
Cedars of Lebanon
Chopstix and Rice
Classic Chinese
Commisso Fine Foods
Cuisine of India
Da Dante
Delisle Restaurant and
Wine Bar
Dunn's Famous Delicatessen
Dynasty Chinese Cuisine
Ema-Tei
The Fish House
Forkchops
Grand Yatt Chinese
Restaurant (Downtown
Toronto)
Grand Yatt Chinese
Restaurant (Richmond Hill)
Giovanna Trattoria
Herbs Restaurant
Imperial Seafood Restaurant
Istria Taverna
Jamie Kennedy at the Museum
Joso's
Jump Café and Bar
Katsura Japanese Restaurant
Katz's Delicatessen and
Corned Beef Emporium
Kebab House Restaurant

Kim Hoa
Kit Kat Italian Bar and Grill
Kuraya Restaurant
Lakes Bar and Grill
La Serre
The Left Bank
Le Passe-Partout
Lotus Pond Vegetarian
  Restaurant
Lox, Stock & Bagel
Mandaloon (except in Winter)
Mandarin
Margarita's
Marketta
Masquerade Caffe Bar
Matisse Restaurant and Bar
Mediterraneo
Mercer Street Grill
Messis
Mezzetta Restaurant
Milano Billiards Lounge
  and Bistro
Mövenpick Marché
New Hunan Restaurant
O Mei
Palavrion
Pan
Pazzo's Restaurant and Café
Pearl
Pho-Hoa
Primadonna
Primi Ristorante
Rikishi Japanese Restaurant
Rodney's Oyster House
Sang-Ho Seafood Restaurant
Sanona
Scaccia Restaurant
Senator on the Square

Shanghai Garden
Shark City Athletic Club
  Bar & Grill
South Vietnam
Southern Accent Restaurant
  (summer only)
Spring Villa
Studio Café
Sukhothai Restaurant
Sun Sui Wah
Tiger Lily's
Twiggy
Vanipha Lanna
Victoria
Wayne Gretzky's Restaurant
  and Bar
Young Lok (North York)
Young Thailand (on Church)
Young Thailand (on Gerrard)

Open Sunday

Alice Fazooli's Italian
  Crabshack Saloon
Anh Dao Restaurant
Art Gallery of Ontario
  Restaurant
Bar Italia
Bayview Garden
Boba
Browne's Bistro
Bofinger Brasserie
Boujadi Moroccan Restaurant
Byzantium
Café Asia
Cafe La Gaffe
Café Victoria
Cedars of Lebanon

RESTAURANTS BY CATEGORY

Chapeau

Chopstix and Rice

Cities Bistro

Classic Chinese

College Street Bar

Commisso Fine Foods

Cuisine of India

Delisle Restaurant and
    Wine Bar

Dunn's Famous Delicatessen

Dynasty Chinese Cuisine

Ema-Tei

The Fish House

Forkchops

Grand Yatt Chinese Restaurant
    (Downtown Toronto)

Grand Yatt Chinese Restaurant
    (Richmond Hill)

Giovanna Trattoria

Herbs Restaurant

Imperial Seafood Restaurant

Inori

Istria Taverna

Jamie Kennedy at the Museum

Katsura Japanese Restaurant

Kebab House Restaurant

Kim Hoa

Kuraya Restaurant

Lakes Bar & Grill

La Serre

Lee Garden Restaurant

The Left Bank

Lotus Pond Vegetarian
    Restaurant

Lox, Stock & Bagel

Mandaloon

Mandarin

Margarita's

Marketta

Matisse Restaurant and Bar

Medieval Times

Mediterraneo

Mercer Street Grill

Messis

Mezzetta Restaurant

Michael Stadtländer at
    Eiginsinn farm

Milano Billiards Lounge
    and Bistro

Montana

Mövenpick Marché

New Hunan Restaurant

O Mei

Otago (in Spring and
    Summer)

Palavrion

Pan

Pazzo's Restaurant and Café

Pearl

Pho-Hoa

Positano Restaurant

Primadonna

Primi Ristorante

Rikishi Japanese Restaurant

Ristorante Grappa

Roof Restaurant Park
    Plaza Hotel

Sang-Ho Seafood Restaurant

Senator on the Square

Shanghai Garden

Sotto Sotto Ristorante

South Vietnam

Southern Accent Restaurant

Spiaggia Trattoria

Splendido Bar and Grill

Spring Villa

Studio Café
Sukhothai Restaurant
Sun Sui Wah
Tiger Lily's (except in winter)
Victoria
Wayne Gretsky's Restaurant
    and Bar
Young Lok (North York)
Young Thailand (on Church)
Young Thailand (on Gerrard)

Outdoor Dining

Acrobat Bis
Alice Fazooli's Italian
    Crabshack Saloon
Auberge du Pommier
Avalon
BamBoo
Bar Italia
Boba
Café Asia
Cafe La Gaffe
Chopstix and Rice
College Street Bar
Commisso Fine Foods
Cuisine of India
Ema-Tei
The Fish House
Giovanna Trattoria
Iguana
Istria Taverna
Jamie Kennedy at the Museum
Joso's
Jump Café and Bar
Kit Kat Italian Bar and Grill
Lotus
Lox, Stock & Bagel

Mandaloon
Margarita's
Mercer Street Grill
Messis
Milano Billiards Lounge
    and Bistro
Mövenpick Marché
Palavrion
Pan
Pazzo's Restaurant and Café
Roof Restaurant Park
    Plaza Hotel
Senator on the Square
Shanghai Garden
Shark City Athletic Club
    Bar & Grill
Southern Accent Restaurant
Tojo
Truffles
Twiggy
Wayne Gretzky's Restaurant
    and Bar
Young Thailand (on Church)

Introduction

There's one thing that's been really great about the recession: I am no longer an icon.

This is not to say that I know what it's like to be Jane Fonda or Madonna, but if my life during the crazy 80s was even one-twentieth as intensely scrutinized as theirs, then I feel mighty sorry for real stars. Because being perceived as the holder of the keys to an important and desirable kingdom got to be tedious really fast.

I spent the 80s on Canada's highest gastro-pedestal. If that sounds like a disease that might give you cramps in the gut, it is. It was not all the expense account food that made me sick, but rather the positively *religious* way that people approached eating, and the resulting anointing of me as some kind of avenging high priestess.

Does it really matter whether the truffles are black or white, and if tiny green beans and teardrop yellow tomatoes have been flown to Toronto from the tropics for the pluperfect garnish? The gourmania of the 80s reminded me of two oenophiles arguing over which side of the hill the grapes were grown on.

It was taking good eating (which is a *good* thing) too far. The excesses of the 80s turned good eating from an honest pleasure into a raging status war; and that made me want to puke. I hated the fact that fashionable people badly wanted to know me and were full of creative schemes to try to arrange dinners in my supposedly august company. (They don't any more.

I have sunk again to the level of the ordinary. Thank heavens.)

The upper middle-class interest in food became a bizarre obsession in the 80s. You had to talk the talk and walk the walk, or you were socially *outré*. Basic requirements included

• Knowing about a hot new restaurant well before it opened, being there within two weeks of its debut and being able to give a semi-professional analysis of its strengths and weaknesses.

• Reading at least one food magazine regularly (and displaying it/them conspicuously).

• Having a sophisticated kitchen equipped with some high class gadgetry and maybe even using it.

• Being able to name, and recognize on the plate, your basic gourmet lexicon—sun-dried tomatoes, chevre, various sushi, teardrop tomatoes, starfruit, kumquats, monkfish, jicama....

People who couldn't cut the mustard were *out*. Or poor. One hardly knew which was worse. I remember dining at Centro in the late 80s with an ambitious and successful couple from Winnipeg. They looked at the menu and then called for an interpreter. Although these people were self-possessed enough to make the appropriate self-deprecating jokes about their ignorance of chevre and sun-dried tomatoes, their discomfort was palpable. They were out of the loop and it *mattered*. They knew it did and they were right. Until they moved to Toronto and got the gastro-lingo down, they were perceived to a certain extent to be yokels.

Thank goodness that's all over now. In bursting the bubble, the recession brought gourmands down from over the top. The status wars are over. Obsession has mellowed down into a long-term companionate

INTRODUCTION

relationship with good food. Hence my relief. It's so much more normal.

Part of the reason for this new level of relaxation about food matters is exemplified by the categories in this book. The last time I wrote a restaurant guide to Toronto (in 1989), Grande Luxe was a big category. Today it's almost an afterthought. I haven't done computer data analysis to prove this, but I have a strong feeling in my capacious gut that the average price of dinner for two in *this* book is substantially lower than it was in the 1989 book.

Some restaurants have dropped their prices. Some of the $100-a-couple restaurants have closed, and they have been replaced not by other grand establishments but by cheaper bistros. This is the wave of the future, and I welcome it.

I was tired of having to dress to the nines and act stiff and serious and important in order to eat well. I was tired of the formality and the rigour of the whole food experience. It's more fun now! The stakes are lower, the air is out of the balloon, the starch is out of the shirts. Hallelujah!

Has the quality of the food dropped? Perhaps slightly, in the sense that simplicity has replaced artifice, and expensive ingredients are not as evident. But we shan't lose the food knowledge we gained in the crazy 80s, and restaurants will always have to cater to an informed and demanding public. This is positive, and if the whole food experience is a little more relaxed and less frantic, that also is positive.

This book is a tool for having more fun in restaurants. To use it, you need some background. Most of the reviews in this guide have been collected and edited from those published in *The Globe and Mail* over the past two-and-a-half years. I have not revisited most restaurants to review them again for this book. However my day-to-day involvement and knowledge of the restaurant industry in Toronto allowed me to make changes when I knew the original review from the *Globe* was incorrect or outdated. Forgive my inevitable inaccuracies; my gall bladder would never have forgiven *me* had I dined in more than 100 restaurants over a short period of time.

The opinions expressed in this book are mine and mine alone. They represent my professional standards. I try hard to be anonymous in every restaurant I visit. I never reserve in my own name, and I avoid calling attention to myself. My goal at all times in restaurants is to have an average experience and be given the food and service that the *average* person eating in that restaurant gets, for better or for worse. I do not meet chefs or restaurateurs first, because that, of course, would result in their giving me special treatment and, second, because I believe that a personal relationship (however brief or unimportant) with the subject of a review would make impartiality impossible.

All of the prices, hours open, credit cards accepted, phone numbers and other information have been checked and are as accurate and up-to-date as possible at the time of this writing, but restaurants are by nature unstable creatures, as ephemeral as the humans who run them, and things change from moment to moment. More than 500 restaurants go out of business every year in Toronto. I have tried to include only those that are relatively stable, but changes may have occurred between the time of publication and the time you read this. When a price is indicated, it includes tax, tip, a moderate bottle of wine and dinner for two. I have established three price categories: a dinner for two (as defined above) costing less than $40 for two is rated **cheap**. The **moderate** category covers $40 to $70. If dinner for two costs more than $70, the restaurant falls in the **expensive** category. Of course, your bill could come to more or less than the indicated price range, depending on the number of extras you order and the amount and type of alcohol you order.

Please write to me at *The Globe and Mail* with your disagreements and suggestions of better places to include in the next book. We are all in this eating game together. Bon Appetit.

Bistros

Browne's Bistro

4 Woodlawn East (At Yonge, north of Summerhill)
416 924-8132
Moderate. All major cards.
HOURS: Lunch Tues.-Fri. 12 noon-2 p.m.
Dinner daily 6 p.m.-10:30 p.m.
Closed major holidays.
Wheelchair accessible. Licensed. Allergy aware.
Reservations necessary.

I see a lot of mink coats in this job, and the restaurant where I see them most is Browne's Bistro, Rosedale's home of the plain and the pure. I'm talking full-length, dark ranch. What does a person who spends $17,000 on a coat want in a restaurant?

Apparently they want comfort food. Browne's is an impeccable bistro, no more and no less. Unlike other Toronto restaurants (e.g., Bofinger) that ape Paris bistros, this one avoids the tarted up decor/tarted up food trap. Everything is breathtakingly simple.

The room is plain as plain could be: white paper on

BISTROS

the tables and small black and white ceramic tiles, à la Paris bistro. Coats hung on hooks on the pillars, do-it-yerself. A monochromatic room, coloured only by dark wood panelling (Is it mahogany or stained pine? Do we care?) and one fuchsia azalea at the bar. In the open kitchen hang aluminum pots. Fie on copper. Unpretension is elevated to art.

Cordon Bleu cooking teacher Beverly Burge had a reputation for strict adherence to "la cuisine classique." Breeding tells. Principles maketh the restaurant (along with 22-hour days, capital and luck).

Browne's pizza may be the best pizza in Toronto. The thin (but not emaciated) crust is crispy on the bottom, soft on the top and the toppings are perfect: home-made lamb sausage, fontina, tomato, chewy marinated eggplant and olives. Sigh. Melt.

Browne's offers superbly cooked and always unadorned meats and fish. The emphasis is on perfect freshness and correct cooking. Who can complain? A fat hunk of fresh grouper barely grilled and a bouquet of designer greens doth not a life make, but it's a helluva lunch.

There are pleasant pasta dishes, a herbed bruschetta with goat cheese and fine-flavoured soups. We are happily cossetted by Browne's warm and clever service, and when they bring that lighter-than-air crème brûlée at the end, we are theirs.

Cities Bistro

859 Queen Street West (Near Bathurst)

416 594-3762

Expensive. All major cards.

HOURS: Dinner Mon.-Fri. 5:30 p.m.-10 p.m.,

Sat.-Sun. 5:30 p.m.-11 p.m.

Closed Christmas Eve and Christmas Day.

Wheelchair accessible, except to washrooms.

Licensed. Allergy aware. Reservations

recommended.

Queen Street suffers more than its fair share of culinary chicanery. Artsy streets invariably do, thanks to the gullibility of tourists (both local and come-from-aways) whose eyes and critical faculties glaze over in the presence of Art. On Queen Street, in the main, gastro-schlock reigns in artsy clothing.

When a restaurant opens on Queen Street, serious eaters don't exactly line up. But they do for Cities. Eugene Shewchuk, a young man from Manitoba who lived in Paris for 17 years, spent the last three years of that sojourn abroad cooking in his very own bistro.

When chef Shewchuk returned to Canada, he went to work as a waiter at Auberge du Pommier in order to save money to open a restaurant in Toronto. He threw in his lot with Brian Heasman, another waiter on the Pommier staff, and together they worked and saved until they had enough money to open Cities.

You can tell from the decor that these fellows have

more taste than capital. The walls are persimmon, the lights halogen, and that's as far as it goes, in the design sense. They couldn't even afford a second coat rack. The kitchen is about the size you'd find in a Manhattan apartment. The prices are low for ambitious cooking and one would expect the quality to match.

But one is wrong. These are gentlemen of passion for their work—and they are driven by two abiding desires: keep it cheap and get it right. Mr. Shewchuk likely learned his passion for the taste of things in Paris: his cooking has a decidedly French bistro feel, with its strength of flavour and close attention to sauces.

One has the sense that every dish is cared for at Cities. From soup to dessert, there is not a plate that feels slapped together. This is not haute cuisine. Mr. Shewchuk's style is more plainspun than fine. But taken for what it is—bistro cooking that is the salt of the earth, the weekly restaurant fare for normal folk (as opposed to the Mercedes Benz and country club set)—Eugene Shewchuk's food is delightful.

His soups are strong-flavoured with nary a hint of powdered stock. His appetizers thrive on invention: one day a seafood sausage (shrimp mousse stuffed with lobster, wrapped in smoked salmon), goat cheese with sun-dried tomatoes baked in crispy phyllo packets and further explorations in the territory of the delicious. Another day there is a superb lentil and vegetable soup, a gooey creamy polenta cooked with camembert, tomatoes and mushrooms and home-marinated gravlax with piquant, herbed sour cream.

There is a steady coterie of regulars who come to Cities weekly, secure in the knowledge that the menu will have changed since their last visit, but the welcome will be unfailing. The warmth that Eugene

Shewchuk creates in the kitchen is easily matched by his partner on the floor.

Brian Heasman reminds me of the late Cecil Troy and his partner Lazlo Stibinger. Few will remember these men, but they were seminal in the birth of Toronto's dining scene. During the early 70s when Toronto was awakening, in the sensual sense, one of the first restaurants that helped our taste buds wake up and smell the coffee was Troy's. Cecil cooked, Lazlo served, they lived upstairs. One felt like a treasured guest in a very special home, which was the truth. Lazlo *cherished* every guest. Today there's nary a maître d'hôtel who communicates that message.

Brian Heasman does. He smiles when you arrive, he remembers where you sat last time and what you ate; he is the Jewish grandmother who set the ineffable chicken soup before us and then adored us for enjoying it. Cities is the home of his heart and we are invited in. Bottle Brian Heasman's warmth and a greasy spoon could print money.

It doesn't matter that the guinea fowl is overcooked and so is the seafood in the otherwise entertaining couscous. On the plate there are divine scalloped potatoes with a cheddar roof and a medley of al dente vegetables. For dessert, chef Shewchuk does a credible tarte tatin (the French classic upside-down pie involving caramelized apples in a carnal connection with buttery crust) and a superbly lemony lemon tart, the kind that puckers your mouth with pleasure. He does less justice to crème brûlée, which sometimes suffers from the heartbreak of syneresis (wherein excess heat has caused the egg protein to curdle).

But this is to quarrel about that which should be accepted. What's a little syneresis between friends?

Delisle Restaurant and Wine Bar

1560 Yonge Street (At St. Clair)

416 960-1707

Expensive. All major cards.

HOURS: Lunch daily 11:30 a.m.-3 p.m.

Dinner Sun.-Thurs. 5 p.m.-10 p.m.,

Fri.-Sat. 5 p.m.-11 p.m. Closed major holidays.

Wheelchair accessible. Licensed. Allergy aware.

Reservations recommended.

When Chris McDonald came home from Mexico in late 1993, he took a look around the Toronto restaurant scene and sighed deeply. One would have expected a chef of his stature to open and run an important new restaurant, having arrived home from two years doing just that in Zihuatanejo, Mexico. He would have expected to too. But it didn't take a rocket scientist to figure out that the economy was no friend to a new restaurant.

McDonald is a chef with a substantial résumé: he cooked at Centro, was chef at Santa Fe when it was delicious and then opened Massimo Rosticceria, the restaurant that (briefly) served superlative table d'hôte dinners with Tuscan wood-roasted chicken as their centrepiece. McDonald also enjoys a creative association with Mark Miller, the chef who made Coyote Café in Santa Fe and, more recently, Red Sage

Delisle

But the celebrity chef circuit doth not a life make: a guy—especially such a fine cook as McDonald—needs roots. Toronto is home and this is where the roots go down. Given McDonald's reluctance to risk a new restaurant, he chose instead to set himself up as a restaurant consultant and to play a supporting role in a friend's place.

The place is Delisle Restaurant and Wine Bar, the friend is its owner, Steve Campbell, and the mission was to bring the Delisle kitchen up to the level of its wine cellar, which the *Wine Spectator* called one of the best restaurant wine cellars in the world. The world! The Delisle wine list sports a booklet's worth of significant bottles and half bottles, but what's more important for oenoslobs like me, you can buy a three ounce glass of Châteauneuf du Pape, chardonnays of lengthy pedigree and other thrills in a glass.

Until McDonald arrived on the scene and revamped both kitchen and menu, the food needed help. His new menu is French bistro, with no entrée costing more than $14.50 and most far less. But Chris McDonald is not the Delisle chef: he is executive chef, which makes him responsible for what goes on the table, but he's not the person putting it there. That job is in the hands of chef David Van Den Driesschen, who had the same role at Massimo's Rosticceria and nobody complained about the food there.

The Delisle menu is so simple that mistakes are visible from far away. And they are few. Rabbit terrine is a splendidly tasty loaf, happily garnished with spiced stewed prunes. French lentil salad is a classic of the legume world, served with sweet little goat cheese croutons. The mussels are plump and pretty. And potato, bacon and chard soup is full of flavour and, hurrah, has no cream.

Somehow that soup personifies French bistro cooking: its three key ingredients could not be more ordinary. Potato and bacon are both plain, but each offers the smart cook oodles of taste. Chard, a humble green, is an important fall vegetable because it stands frost in the field. Only a kitchen that values local ingredients in their season will bother with chard, for it is not chic.

The main courses at Delisle hearken back in that same jolly way to meals some of us have been lucky enough to enjoy in the French countryside: steak frites with aioli, here a tender little loin, cooked perfectly, married to crispy sweet frites. Perfectly cooked salmon with a herb butter. An only slightly overcooked chicken breast (tsk-tsk) with full-flavoured ratatouille and properly lumpy Yukon gold mashed potatoes. Tasty pasta dishes for $8.95. Pleasantly pink roast lamb served with wonderful creamy scalloped potatoes and barely wilted spinach the colour of emeralds. Duck confit, cooked till it falls off the bone, served with one of the kitchen's few false moves: a pancake made by frying mashed potatoes. Feh!

The desserts are also in the French country mode. My favourite is caramelized apple tart, but plum tart with a fresh custard filling is a close runner-up and flourless chocolate cake is not exactly a punishment either. The Delisle's desserts are a metaphor for its totality: this is a seemingly simple, not-very-ambitious little restaurant. But underneath the unassuming exterior lies an endlessly entertaining heart.

Delisle

Herbs Restaurant

3187 Yonge Street (Near Lawrence)

416 322-0487

Moderate. All major cards.

HOURS: Lunch Mon.-Thurs. 11:30 a.m.-2 p.m.

Dinner Mon.-Thurs. 5:30 p.m.-10 p.m.

All-day menu Fri.-Sat. 11:30 a.m.-11 p.m.

Dinner Sun. 5:30 p.m.-10 p.m. Open some

holidays; telephone ahead.

Wheelchair accessible, except to washrooms.

Licensed. Allergy aware. Reservations necessary.

Herbs is on Yonge Street north of Lawrence, in a world full of faded blonde Havergal old girls out with their still boyish husbands, who wear Burberry's and play squash at lunchtime. To say that the good burghers of Lawrence Park are homogeneous would be crude. Let's just say that life has been kind to them, and that they can afford to drop 60 bucks for two on a casual midweek dinner.

Herbs is the ultimate neighbourhood restaurant: hang up your own coat and then sit down in downscale Splendido, complete with the peachy colour scheme, high ceiling and lovely flower paintings on the walls.

A good neighbourhood restaurant offers both stability and change, in balanced proportion. The stability is required for comfort. One wants to see the same friendly faces each time, to be recognized and cherished and coddled. One seeks comfort also in the food. It oughtn't be the same all the time or boredom would set in. But there needs to be a sameness of both subject matter and approach.

To wit: it's pleasant to know that your neighbourhood spot always does a cream soup, a poached fish and a grilled steak. That they change the soup's base, use different fish and buy varying cuts of beef are all salutary: one doesn't wish to eat the same thing week after week. But the feel and style of the food are stable: Herbs doesn't veer from Thai to Italian or from spring rolls to baba ghanoush.

The cream soup might be beet or spinach or something else; the vegetable changes but the integrity does not. Herbs' soups are full of the flavour of good stock and fresh vegetables. Other appetizers change with the whim of both chef and daily market. On our first visit chef Tony Nuth seduces us with mussels poached, removed from their shells and reclining on a bed of barely wilted spinach with little jewels—red pepper, zucchini and onion—for dazzle.

And that's only the foreplay. He goes in for the kill with a plump pink beef tenderloin sitting on a Stilton croute, with wild mushroom glaze. And beside it he puts a splendid bouquet of perfect vegetables—a segment of corn on the cob, snow peas, red pepper, a broccoli floweret, one poached white radish and a new potato. Breast of duck is rare and juicy, and everything comes with that splendid rainbow of vegetables, which speaks of effort and generosity and passion. Are you breathing harder yet? No? Then try the little seafood stew in a delicate fennel and spinach broth.

Chef goes in for the kill with chocolate crème brûlée for dessert. I am his.

The people have spoken, and they are, as usual, not

wrong: Herbs is a wonderful neighbourhood restaurant, a model bistro. So what if the raspberry trim framing persimmon and mustard walls is a lapse of taste? Who cares if the chocolate pâté is too dense? The tarte tatin has slightly soggy pastry but someone has taken care to caramelize those apples into sweet gilded submission.

The word around town is that Herbs is a scion of the beloved Cities Bistro on Queen Street. It is, but only in the most limited sense. Cities chef Eugene Shewchuk is a silent partner in Herbs, which is owned by its chef Tony Nuth and maître d' Richard Marshall. All three men are alumni of Peter Oliver's Auberge du Pommier, where they learned a thing or two about value for money and how to show the people a good time. Herbs is like grownup love, slightly blemished but delicious.

Jump Café and Bar

Commerce Court East (Yonge and Bay)
416 363-3400
Moderate. All major cards.
HOURS: All-day menu Mon.-Fri. 11 a.m.-11 p.m.
Bar open till 1 a.m. Dinner Sat. 5 p.m.-11 p.m.
Closed Sun. and major holidays.
Wheelchair accessible. Licensed. Allergy aware.
Reservations recommended.

In Sleepless in Seattle, two men, the lonely widower and his helpful friend, are sitting in a bar. Having enlightened the widower about the basics concerning dating à la 90s, his friend delivers the *coup de grâce:* the widower needs tiramisu in his romantic arsenal.

BISTROS

"What's tiramisu?" asks the hapless widower, who obviously sat out the 80s. His friend isn't telling. The widower blanches. "What if a woman expects me to do that to her, and I don't even know what it is?"

If our widower wanted a crash course in tiramisu and associated practices, he could do no better than Jump, which is the child of unlikely partners, Peter Oliver and Michael Bonacini, with Martin Kouprie cooking. Peter Oliver is the dynamo who owns Oliver's, Bofinger and Auberge du Pommier, prosperous and well-run restaurants that are not targets for serious epicures. Michael Bonacini was chef at Centro (and before that, the Windsor Arms Hotel) until Peter Oliver lured him away from there. Martin Kouprie cooked at Pronto.

Bonacini and Kouprie are both serious food men. They have cooked in fine kitchens, and made them what they are. Both chefs are strangers to compromise. These are not the kind of cooks who squirt store-bought mango purée out of ketchup containers and call dessert a gourmet experience. Peter Oliver, on the other hand, built a restaurant mini-empire by catering, with finesse, to the market that appreciates that sort of thing.

One would not, therefore, have expected Mr. Oliver to go wooing a demanding chef like Michael Bonacini. Perhaps success (especially sweet during difficult times) allowed Peter Oliver to indulge in the luxury of becoming a purveyor of fine food. To make matters more complicated, Michael Bonacini wasn't about to stay in the kitchen. This exodus is common among successful chefs: having proven that they can do something very well, they then stop doing it and begin doing something for which their training and background have not prepared them in the least—managing the whole restaurant.

Jump

BISTROS

Under normal circumstances, none of this works. But these are not your run-of-the-mill guys. Peter Oliver had not previously chosen to *bother* that much about good food, but he is a restaurateur of formidable talent and drive. His restaurants do exactly what he wants them to do; they do it well and at a healthy profit. Michael Bonacini is more than a cook. He is the chef, the leader, who could wrestle the wild beast of Centro's kitchen (250 people for dinner) and win every night. The combination is electric: Oliver and Bonacini, with a terrific cook like Martin Kouprie to do their bidding in the kitchen.

Bonacini and Kouprie remembered all the lessons learned at the Windsor Arms, Centro and Pronto, and wrapped it up with a downscale bow for Jump. The most expensive entrée is $20, but the lessons of 80s gastronomy have not been forgotten. Any epicure who can tolerate the noise and the bustle of Jump will be rewarded with food that is robust and honest and full of flavour.

At dinnertime place yourself in chef Kouprie's fine hands and start with the chef's appetizer platter. It will include sweetly grilled squid, mahogany glazed quail, barely charred tuna, grilled endive and other splendours of the Cal/Ital lexicon. That is, if you can resist the crispy spring roll served with cucumber mango salsa and sweet and sour plum sauce. And the huge but appealing plate of goat cheese on a crisp potato rössti with watercress and bacon. Salivating yet? And I haven't even mentioned the black bean soup with crispy fresh asparagus and sweet little corn bits in it. Or the corn-fried squid. Or the olive oil with coriander that comes one day with the bread instead of butter. Or the olive paste that comes another day in its stead.

BISTROS

Among main courses, some are merely pleasant (most of the pastas) while others demand hosannas. In a casual bistro such as Jump, one hardly expects the perfect risotto. But here it is, long-stirred rice with al dente kernels and creamy sauce, blessed with flavour and garnished with perfectly cooked shrimp, scallops and vegetables. The rack of lamb, with a piquant mustard crust, turnip purée (horseradish-spiked) and greens, is perfect. Rare duck breast with drunken sour cherries and root vegetables wouldn't be such a bad last meal before a diet either.

Desserts are the expectable extravaganzas: banana coconut cream pie is a tropical cloud that goes down like a dream, tiramisu is exactly what the young widower needs for foreplay and apple tart is a wickedly sybaritic remake of mom's.

Jump is the 90s, downscale with a smile. Jump is mashed potatoes and waitpeople in custom t-shirts, Jump is minimalist decor, risotto and banana coconut cream pie. Jump is jumping.

Lakes Bar and Grill

1112 Yonge Street (Near Macpherson)
416 966-0185
Expensive. All major cards.
HOURS: All-day menu Mon.-Fri. 11:30 a.m.-1 a.m.
Dinner Sat. 6 p.m.-1 a.m., Sun. 6 p.m.-11 p.m.
Closed Christmas Day.
No wheelchair access. Licensed. Allergy aware.
Reservations recommended.

The room is long and narrow, with an open kitchen not five feet from the nearest table. This is an unforgiving arrangement, relentlessly demanding on kitchen staff. God forbid the chef should lose his cool or spill the soup: the whole of Rosedale will know. For this is Lakes, the neighbourhood bistro of very particular folks.

Lakes has been around for years, ever tasteful. But with the recent loss of Suzanne Baby at the stoves, it suffered a gastronomical downturn. However, downturns are relative: Lakes' location on Yonge Street between Roxborough and Macpherson determines its clientele; at lunchtime we see two groups: the ladies who lunch (lots of blonde hair and serious jewellery. But understated, my dear) and advertising people from nearby Vickers and Benson and other ad agencies. Neither of these two groups suffers bad food.

Lakes' menu continues in the Cal/Ital lexicon, with a dash of old-fashioned comfort food: steak and liver for comfort, warm salads and grilled fish for pizazz. Although the sauces have lost their sparkle and there is the occasional heinous sin of overcooking, the Lakes' kitchen is generally user-friendly.

Marketta

138 Avenue Road (Near Davenport)
416 924-4447
Moderate. All major cards.
HOURS: All-day menu Mon-Wed. 10 a.m.-10 p.m,
Thurs.-Sat. 10 a.m.-11 p.m., Sun. 10 a.m.-5 p.m.
Closed on major holidays.
Wheelchair accessible. Licensed. Allergy aware.
Reservations recommended.

In the spring of 1995, Marketta catapulted from its bottom-of-the-heap position as midtown's most tasteless pretty face to being the most delicious all-day diner between the lake and Eglinton. Mark McEwan of North 44 picked up Marketta for a song, added a little garden statuary to warm up the good-looking but cool room, and and installed Jason Nesbitt, a smart young cook from North 44, to cook up PoMo diner delights.

Marketta is on the splendid little strip of Avenue Road just south of Davenport where flowers bloom year-round on the cramped, cheerful sidewalk. Its looks have always been divine: a trendy verdigris sign and, at the front, an antipasto counter with assorted antipasti (both for consumption in the restaurant and to take away), which are now up to North 44 standards. There is a tall space in the back decorated with huge, old French posters for eating in.

McEwan's commitment, on buying Marketta, was that nary a black sesame seed would enter its kitchen. Meaning that the food would be unpretentious, down-home, the opposite of exotic. His goal was to create a laid-back neighbourhood diner—but with standards.

He has done it, in spades. We are enthralled with the grilled calamari on toast, all mixed up with tomato, celery, olives, red onions and a sassy, balsamic vinaigrette. Seduced by the fresh cranberry juice. Bedazzled by al dente risotto with fresh sweet peas, grilled corn and quality parmesan cheese. Bowled over by house-made duck sausage served with fresh (!!!) green fava beans and mellow barley risotto.

Marketta is a true satellite of North 44 and, clearly, McEwan can handle the killing pace of managing two restaurants. Only a fool would commit to working that hard; his foolishness is our delight.

Matisse Restaurant and Bar

90 Bloor Street East (Near Church)

416 920-6500

Expensive. All major cards.

HOURS: Lunch Mon.-Fri. 11 a.m.-4 p.m.

Dinner daily 5 p.m.-11 p.m.

Brunch Sat.-Sun. 7 a.m.-4 p.m. Open holidays.

Wheelchair accessible. Licensed. Allergy aware.

Reservations necessary for lunch,

recommended for dinner.

Fee fie *faux* fum. I smell the scent of a theme overdone.

Matisse is a restaurant decorated in homage to the artist. But to call it "decorated" may be like saying Barbra Streisand carries a tune. The floors, the ceilings, the walls (egad, even the coat closet!) are covered in slavishly accurate paintings of Matisseland and copies of the great man's *oeuvre*. Is that a window looking out onto a bay with sailing boats, complete with open shutters and drapes hung on a rod and pulled back, or is it all painted on the wall? Will fire burn in the fireplace and do chatchkas perch on the mantle or is that all painted too?

This is not to be finicky about *faux*. *Faux* is fun. But it sets up *expectations*. Take, for example, our earliest dining experiences with *faux*. Recall the seafood

Matisse

36

restaurants of yesteryear that were generally festooned with fishnets and lobster traps and decorated with ship's wheels and other insignia of the sea. The idea was to suggest another world. It worked (sort of) because of the congruence between theme and food.

We hear the name Matisse, we think of his beloved Mediterranean, of the Matisse chapel in Vence (near Nice), which was his last work. Is it too much to expect a restaurant bearing the name (and the look) of Matisse to serve French food?

As if a menu littered with the detritus of trendy Cal/Ital were not enough insult to the great man, why is there a television playing nonstop over the bar? Is there a deep symbolic connection (awaiting deconstruction) between "Hockey Night in Canada" and Matisse's paper-and-scissors nudes? Quick, pass my smelling salts. I feel faint with anticipation at the mere thought of what a PoMo art critic could do with this.

But until that great moment comes, we mere mortals will have to content ourselves wondering why a restaurant called Matisse serves Oriental dumplings, quesadilla, pork chops and chili linguini. And lousy ones at that.

One could suspend one's disbelief if the Cal/Ital lexicon were beautifully executed. But to betray the artist's legacy for lobster enchilada with a lemon chutney sauce that recalls lemon Jell-O? Please. To wrap what tastes like Chinatown storebought barbecued pork and duck in a tortilla and slather on both hoi sen sauce and cranberry relish? This is a marriage made in hell. To serve a huge pork chop so overcooked it resists the knife?

Is an overcooked pork chop homage to a French artist? Is an Oriental dumpling that's too big and kind of tough? Is a thick bland tortilla soup? Is a pedestrian Caesar salad? Is a fairly flavour-free stir-fry of chicken with coriander? Is an Atlantic salmon sandwich served with curly fries that have that dreadful McCain's frozen feeling? (Funny, I never met a salmon in the Mediterranean...)

This is not to suggest that the Matisse menu completely neglects the land of foie gras and salade niçoise. There is bouillabaisse with overcooked fish. There is deep-fried mozzarella cheese. There is salmon in a very French chive cream sauce. For dessert there are deep-fried chocolate truffles (??!!) sitting on a mountain of icing sugar. And a huge frozen Bailey's soufflé with the delicacy and finesse of Whip 'n' Chill.

Is *faux* still fun? Can we believe in an illusion that causes chocolate truffles to be deep fried? It's a stretch. Just like the valet parking the sign outside promises. You pull in, expecting the white carpet treatment and who's there to take the car? Nobody. Maybe they took the *faux* too far.

Matisse

Messis

97 Harbord Avenue (At Robert Street)

416 920-2186

Expensive. All major cards.

HOURS: Lunch Tues.-Fri. 12 noon-2:30 p.m.

Dinner Mon.-Fri. 5:30 p.m.-10 p.m.,

Sat.-Sun. 5:30 p.m.-11 p.m.

No wheelchair access. Licensed. Allergy aware.

Reservations recommended.

We desperately want Messis to be tasty. It is politically correct, in the best sense. Messis is like the kindest, sweetest, most principled person you know. You *want* to like that person. And sometimes there's just not enough there.

Messis' physical presence is full of warm fuzzies: Harbord Street west of Spadina is about as unsnobby as you can get, artistic enough to be interesting and minus the Attitude that makes Queen Street less than fully appetizing. Inside, the restaurant is equally pleasant: sponged yellow walls, simple wall sconces that act as vases to hold flowers, a persimmon ceiling and a little bit of decorative wrought iron.

In the kitchen all is warm and non-hierarchical: there is no actual *chef* but, rather, a team of people who cook together as equals. Renée Foote, who was dessert chef at North 44 and also cooked at Byzantium, is kitchen manager. Eugene Shewchuk, who owns Messis (and Cities on Queen Street), cooks too.

When the restaurant opened in 1994, it had a chef in

BISTROS

the conventional sense. Danny Griesdorf (who is now cooking amazing dinners at the Senator Diner, after a very brief stint at The Four Seasons Studio Café) gave Messis its gastronomical jump start. Since he left last fall, the kitchen has not quite recovered. Which doesn't seem to matter to Messis' happy fans. The restaurant is tremendously popular with people who appreciate fancy food when the price tag for an appetizer never goes above $7 and most expensive main courses cost $15.

Who am I to quarrel with happiness?

You cannot get better food for those prices, but that still begs the question: must I content myself with boring Asian noodle salad with barbecued duck and coriander pesto because the price is right? Or less than flavourful risotto of tomato, spinach and fennel because nobody else sells an appetizer portion of risotto for $7?

The food is kind of, well, limp. All these very entertaining sounding PoMo dishes taste as if they were produced by a...committee. The word on the street is that part of the reason Danny Griesdorf left Messis was because owner Shewchuk couldn't stomach a star in his kitchen. A cooking committee is more egalitarian, but is it as creative?

If Renée Foote were the chef, with full power to make (or break) her own menu, would the food have more flavour? We'd love to know. Right now things feel pleasantly fuzzy. There is the feeling of too many elements on each plate, with insufficient passionate attention to individual tastes and textures. With the pleasant lamb there is a crowded collection of indistinguished add-ons. The Brazilian seafood stew is slightly overcooked seafood and there is weird, white goop on Portugese corn bread, which might be the ginger aioli listed on the menu. We can't tell.

Messis

We are also unhappy with the crème brûlée, which has the scent of sweetened condensed milk. We are depressed by the soggy crust under tarte tatin. But everybody else in the restaurant is happy. High standards do not always bring pleasure.

Scaramouche Restaurant, Pasta Bar and Grill

1 Benvenuto Place (At Avenue Road, south of St. Clair)
416 961-8011
Expensive. All major cards.
HOURS: Dinner Mon.-Sat. 6 p.m.-11 p.m.
Closed Sun. and all statutory holidays.
Wheelchair accessible. Licensed. Allergy aware.
Reservations recommended.

For a combination of breathtaking view, superb food and good prices, nothing beats the Scaramouche Pasta Bar. It is a radiant room that lets in the light and the leafiness of outside. Like everything Morden Yolles does, the excesses are there in impeccable taste: a master carpenter has rounded the edge of the fat piece of oak that is the bar, until it is a sensuous bullnose. It is matched by the round-edged tables in laminated birch broken by dark grey pinstripes. Money whispers in dulcet tones here.

BISTROS

Some clever designs scream at you; this one talks softly. Everywhere there are parallel horizontal lines: in the tables, the stained pine strips on the tall windows, the sea foam turquoise banquettes and the overgrown capitals mushrooming from the single fat column, with their hidden lights speaking softly and pinkly to the room as dusk turns the wall of windows midnight blue.

By nine o'clock on a Saturday night medium-sized Toronto money is stacked up five deep at the bar waiting for tables. Big money eats in the main restaurant, but those in the know stick to the Pasta Bar, which gives more bang for the buck and is far more relaxed. There are even, on slower nights, a few yuppie lonelyhearts who actually *eat* at the bar with a view of the open kitchen. It is the way to proclaim that you're a) single and b) a serious gourmand.

The food could hardly be better if one had died and gone to heaven. There are dazzling antipasto plates (fresh goat cheese, perfectly grilled and dressed vegetables, the best dried meats and olives), delicate salads, crispy fresh deep-fried calamari and perfect little pizzas. The pizza crust is as thin as it could be without having an identity crisis.

Main courses are, if that be possible, even more bursting with salutary flavours. Tender tiny gnocchi made from Yukon gold potatoes are flavoured with very smoked chicken, wilted spinach and sautéed oyster mushrooms. Bow tie pasta comes with a splendidly toasty tasting tomato sauce full of seafood and capers, with a grandly fragrant bouquet of fresh basil on top. Meat and fish dishes are handled with equal élan. Desserts come from the stellar Scaramouche dessert kitchen. Have we died and gone to heaven?

Scaramouche

Senator on the Square

5150 Yonge Street (At North York City Centre)

416 250-7234

Moderate. All major cards.

HOURS: Lunch Mon. 11:30 a.m.-3 p.m.

All-day menu Tues.-Wed. 11:30 a.m.-8 p.m.,

Thurs. 11:30 a.m.-12 midnight,

Fri.-Sat. 11:30 a.m.-1 a.m. Dinner Sun. 4 p.m.-8 p.m.

Closed major holidays.

Wheelchair accessible. Licensed. Allergy aware.

Reservations recommended.

First you drive. Which is not in and of itself an offense against humanity. After all, suburbanites have been doing it for years if they want to get anywhere civilized. So why not turn the tables for once? The existence of the Ford Centre for the Performing Arts provokes dining in the 'burbs on the part of many people who previously developed the vapours if forced to go north of St. Clair, let alone eat during the expedition.

The suburbanites have us by the short and curlies. When they come downtown, we are courteous enough to offer such amenities as road signs and, should they park underground, signs indicating where to find the elevator, the stairs and most of the other things a person in that situation needs. What happens when we

BISTROS

migrate northward towards the performing arts centre?

We enter the underground parking lot of the North York City Centre (so-called). The place is deadly quiet, eerily empty. Anyone with any sense has long ago fled to their split-level haven in a heartless world. God forbid we should get mugged here. At least downtown there'd be somebody to hear you scream. Having parked, we go in search of Senator on the Square, Bob Sniderman's effort to capitalize on the new arts centre.

We know it's there. We think it's there. We just can't find it, because there are no helpful signs and there's nobody around to ask. And people say downtown is scary.

When we do finally track down Senator on the Square, it is not clear that diligence is rewarded. Someone has made a half-hearted attempt to bring the patina of the downtown Senator Diner to a huge suburban barn, but their hearts were clearly elsewhere. Downtown, perhaps?

Save for the wonderful nubby geometric print banquettes, the decor is awful. Here and there a reference to traditional dinerdom, a little pressed tin and some dark wood, but in the main, the Senator's aesthetic took some heavy downers when it went north. On one wall is an embarrassing "sculpture": overgrown musical notes attached to saplings. The contradiction between the cosiness of the traditional diner (à la downtown Senator) and the huge chilly suburban room is so sad it's almost funny.

The food is on the same ride as the visual aesthetic: finding the flavour is like finding the restaurant. We could buy frozen salad shrimp at Loblaws and thaw them, but they'd probably have more flavour, and we wouldn't call them "Matane Shrimp" and charge $9.10 for an appetizer. The grilled vegetables suffer a similar

Senator on the Square

44

fate—the flavour of the vegetables has gone A.W.O.L., camouflaged by too much vinegar.

But one is thankful for small mercies: at least the waitperson wears deodorant. I know that because whenever she delivers food to the person beside me, she saves steps by passing it in front of me instead of walking around the table. Perhaps Senator north has committed to green values, including a new motto: Waste Not, Want Not. Effort and words both. The waitperson doesn't tell me that the rotisserie chicken had lost its advertised potato pancake. It comes instead with potato strudel. Any chef who puts mashed potatoes inside strudel dough deserves thumbscrews.

Was it the same cook who dumped a salt shaker on the chicken, and managed to produce designer pizza with no taste, badly overcooked seafood with the linguine and an acrid dark brown sauce, redolent of chemicals, on the calves' liver? When dessert arrives, our confusion intensifies: you would have thought that nobody can destroy apple crisp. You thought wrong. The rice pudding might be all right, but it is served too cold to tell.

This is too big to be the cook's fault. We're talking bad ingredients, bad aesthetics and bad intentions here. Is somebody trying to put something over on the suburban rubes? Given the competition in the neighbourhood, we'll probably be back.

Twiggy

232 Queen Street West (At McCaul)

416 977-6969

Expensive. All major cards.

HOURS: Lunch Mon.-Sat. 11:30 a.m.-4 p.m.

Dinner Mon.-Tues. 4 p.m.-11 p.m.,

Wed.-Sun. 4 p.m.-1 a.m. Closed Sunday.

Wheelchair accessible. Allergy aware.

Reservations recommended on weekends.

One hates to be caught (even if only by oneself) cherishing a prejudice. Do you know anyone who proudly holds the title of bigot? Meet me.

I have trouble with Queen Street restaurants. Usually within five minutes of sitting down in one, I am plunged into deep irritability. It's one of those here-we-go-again sensations, wherein prejudice no doubt plays a role. And I can't help it.

Certain key factors trigger the malaise. They all fall under the general heading of unprofessional service. Which makes sense, when you realize that Queen Street is the hippest place in town for waitpeople to work, and lots of artists and actors wait table in order to survive. Where do you find them? Serving (if you can call it that) dinner on Queen Street.

Which is not to imply that *all* Queen Street servers are artists. But *Attitude* sneaks in. The very notion of service (giving it, that is) likely is not attractive to

Twiggy

46

artists. And perhaps the servers, who are neither artists nor actors, are influenced by the values of the street, where wearing black and being Artistic are more important than other things. Which might explain a lot. Like the bad service.

Thus Twiggy, a recent addition to the Queen Street café dining scene. One evening at dinner we don't get bread. Not too surprising. Our server has trouble remembering the names of the wines, and has to come back to the table to ask what we ordered. But boy can she dress! In black, of course, and it's a micromini into which she has been poured. Bread comes midway through the main course. With a big smile. Do we tip for sweet ditzyness?

There is another woman, who was sitting at the bar smoking when we arrived, also wearing a slinky dress. She cruises the dining area looking vaguely supervisory, but she doesn't seem to notice the absence of bread on our table. She smiles a lot too. Maybe we should be thankful. Smiling is good for Queen Street. The service is as awful as usual on the street, but at Twiggy, at least they're sweet. Elsewhere on Queen Street we often meet surly Attitude as a substitute for service. As in the tacit message: I'm too good for this job (and to serve you).

The second oft-encountered Queen Street problem is smoke, of the second-hand variety. Apparently it's hip to smoke. (Is lung cancer cool?) Our experience at Twiggy was by no means unique. One evening we had reserved a non-smoking table and were seated (we thought) in the non-smoking section. After a while, a couple sat down at the next table and lit up. The restaurant staff did not appear to notice. We waited the requisite long time for our server to appear, and asked him to deal with the problem. He disappeared for five minutes.

Upon returning, he said there was a poetry reading that night, and people had been told they could smoke in the non-smoking section. Hurrah. That makes it really all right for us. Our server said he would tell the people to stop smoking until we left. It was a Pyrrhic victory, given that they had already done a job on the air. And given also the amount of smoke in the air from the (real) smoking section.

But what, you ask, about the food at Twiggy? Are we to hear only about the irritants? Some of the food is very strange, or wondrously original, depending on your perspective. Chestnut gnocchi with shrimp, and a sauce scented with Grappa and red currant oil, are pleasantly foreign. Brown (from the chestnuts) gnocchi have an unfortunate tendency to resemble dog kibble, but they taste kind-of nice.

Pizza ranges from the normal (tomato, pesto, etc.) to the bizarre. Imagine pizza with shrimp, lemon oil, bitter chocolate, spinach, peppers and shaved daikon. I thought of it as *mole* pizza (from the Mexican chocolate-based mole sauce) with a Japanese influence (from the white Japanese daikon radish), and found it mildly entertaining. Not bad, just weird.

Ditto the strawberries in the risotto (!!) that came with the pleasantly grilled salmon trout. I would not choose to have strawberries interfere with my risotto, but they were not gruesome.

When the chef restricts himself to the more ordinary Cal/Ital lexicon, he turns out pleasantries. His soups are well put together and nicely flavoured, his lunchtime sandwiches exuberant and full of flavour, and his normal pasta dishes also blessed with much

Twiggy

flavour. (My personal favourite is pearl pasta with sautéed chicken livers and a Port wine sauce.) The only big blooper is chocolate soufflé, which is uncooked in the middle, and cries out for crème anglaise custard sauce to cut the sweetness. The other desserts (of the tiramisu school) are all just fine.

If they could get the servers into normal clothes, teach them how to wait on table and do something about the second-hand smoke, Twiggy might actually be a pleasant restaurant.

Wayne Gretzky's Restaurant and Bar

99 Blue Jays Way (Peter and King)

416 979-7825

Moderate. All major cards.

HOURS: All-day menu daily 11:30 a.m.-1 a.m.

Closed major holidays.

Wheelchair accessible. Licensed. Allergy aware.

Reservations recommended.

Everywhere you look, there are the insignia of The Great One. Even an unrepentant hockey ignoramus cannot fail to notice. Where the front door handle is normally found, you grasp a skate blade. Hanging from the ceiling of the open kitchen are strands of hot red chilies and His hockey gloves. Imprisoned in a plexiglass display case in the middle of the restaurant are His hockey sticks *avec* pucks. On the walls are portraits of Himself. At the entrance are framed magazine cover pics of Him.

Even the food is a study in hero worship. His number, 99, is branded on the hamburger bun and they call it The Great One. Perhaps they know it's apocryphal, and that their restaurant is just an upscale sportsbar, for good ole boys grabbing a bite in the shadow of the Dome. Maybe it's only Wayne who has to be The Great One, and as long as he is, what's on the plate doesn't matter too much.

In which case, why did the Bitove Corporation (owners of Wayne Gretzky's) hire themselves a name chef? Although Chris Klugman's last two restaurants have gone down in fiduciary flames (King Ranch & Spa, and Winston's), he is still a chef to notice. His signature at the bottom of a menu leads an eater to expect a certain level of excellence. Especially when he writes on that menu that "our food is cooked to order" and this may mean a preparation time and a wait of up to 20 minutes. Okay Chris. We'll bite.

Then howcum we order The Great One very rare and it arrives well done, kinda brown and tough and resembling the Canada Packers patties we hate at summer camp? Why are the black linguine as gummy as Wrigley's and their seafood heinously overcooked? Ditto the calamari, which are supposed to be crispy crackly in their fried cornflour jacket, but are instead hard on the inside and mushy on the outside, as if they had spent too long in not very hot frying oil.

We're trying really hard to figure out if any of this *matters* to any of the apparently happy customers at Wayne Gretzky's. After one particularly inedible lunch (mushy pizza crust, watery soup and the weakest espresso I've ever met), we wonder if all the other

Wayne Gretzky's

customers in the quite crowded restaurant feel so good about Wayne Gretzky that they don't notice the food. Perhaps, to a fan, the mere proximity of The Great One's paraphernalia is enough. It must be nice to be a committed fan. Sort of like being strapped to a TV set tuned to the soaps, but not minding because of your prefrontal lobotomy.

Everything we eat at Wayne Gretzky's speaks of carelessness: one evening they actually cook a chicken properly; it has moist flesh and a sweet cinnamon-scented marmalade. But helter-skelter on the huge plate with it are messy not-quite-cooked potatoes and equally ugly hunks of not very carefully cooked squash. And, again, appalling espresso, which has all the depth of Nescafé.

Another day the Venice Beach sandwich (chicken breast with sour cream, guacamole and salsa) contains chicken so overcooked you might be able to walk on it. And the barbecued ribs are a tad stringy, with too much too sweet sauce that recollects the texture of those flour and water 3-D maps we used to build in grade four. You got a better mark if they were mounted on plywood and painted. Maybe there's a future for The Great One's barbecue sauce. They could bottle it under His name and sell it to elementary schools for use in school projects. Imagine that: another spinoff! You've enjoyed Paul Newman's salad dressings. Now let your small fry benefit from Wayne Gretzky's "cooking."

And spinoff is the name of this particular game. You call 979-PUCK for reservations at the restaurant located at 99 Blue Jays Way (a.k.a. Peter Street). A store at the restaurant's entrance sells hockey clothing and memorabilia. This is sports' fan chatchka-land, a happy homage to one of Canada's few genuine heroes, a man of action, not a man of the kitchen. And don't we know it.

Brunch

Café Victoria

King Edward Hotel

37 King Street East (At Victoria)

416 863-9700

Expensive. All major cards.

HOURS: Breakfast Mon.-Fri. 6:30 a.m.-11:00 a.m.,

Sat. 7:30-11 a.m., Sun. 7:30 a.m.-10:30 a.m.

Lunch Mon.-Sat. 11:30 a.m.-2:30 p.m.

Brunch Sun. 11 a.m.-2:30 p.m. Dinner Mon.-Thurs.

5 p.m.-9 p.m., Fri.-Sun. 5 p.m.-11 p.m.

Wheelchair accessible. Licensed.

Reservations recommended.

Weep for the dowager betrayed. Any long life has its ups and downs, but we think that an *éminence grise* born so elegantly, in 1903, deserves better. I speak, of course, of the most beautiful hotel in Toronto—the King Edward Hotel on King Street East. The Four Seasons may be gorgeous, but it's *nouveau riche,* and nothing can disguise the cultural pallor of your basic modern skyscraper. The King Eddie owns the architectural grace of yesteryear: the classical columns, the gracious proportions of the lobby. And, my goodness me, the plasterwork in the Café Victoria is so lovely one can hardly stop craning one's neck. It's Toronto's very own homage to the Paris Opera. As if that were not enough, the Café Victoria's 20-foot ceilings and tall, lace-clad windows are grace incarnate.

When brunch is good, it represents an extravagance of pleasure, for its own sake. And when it's just so-so, it's what has happened to the grand old dowager of King Street. They charge $34.50 for adults and $17.50 for children, which buys all you can eat at the buffet.

It begins well, with three fresh juices that they keep on pouring: fresh orange, grapefruit or grape juice.

But once we begin to plumb the depths of the buffet, we feel like actors on a stage set: it all looks so right and tastes like so...little.

The smoked salmon is flavourless; the crab claws have that wet, previously frozen texture; the salads are ordinary; the cold salmon is overcooked; and the fish pâté has the bloodlines of seagoing Spam. The meat pâté is equally uninviting, and we are not amused by tiny, watery shrimp.

The hot foods are somewhat better: beef Wellington, that classic of another life, is made from the tenderest beef wrapped in good puff pastry with a tasty mushroom layer. The cheese blintzes are credible and the pheasant stew is pleasant. The eggs Benedict won't offend anyone, although their hollandaise sauce is so lacking in lemon as to be almost soporific. And the so-called veal, clad in egg batter, in a brown sauce, is a really horrific example of what sitting on a steam table can do to something that might once have been edible. We can't tell.

Café Victoria

Then there are the desserts, which, in the context of a buffet brunch, ought to be the ultimate in decadence. They're trying hard here. Sort of. Crème brûlée is authentic, as are madeleines, chocolate pecan tarts and shortbreads. Marinated berries are very good. But the key lime pie (an acrid green colour) is flavourfree with a godawful soggy crust, and Lord preserve us from bland chocolate mousses in little chocolate cups.

La Serre

Four Seasons Hotel, 21 Avenue Road (North of Bloor)
416 964-0411
Price category not applicable to La Serre;
menu focuses on light snacks, cheese plates
and the like. All major cards.
HOURS: All-day menu Mon.-Sat. 11:45 a.m.-1 a.m.
Brunch Sun. 11 a.m.-2:30 p.m.
Open most holidays.
Wheelchair accessible. Licensed. Allergy aware.
Reservations recommended.

I often want to run away from home. There are those special moments in life: the children are attacking each other with weapons, the macaroni and cheese is burning and the spouse is either out at a meeting or being a complete jerk. I ask myself then: is this what life is about? I close my eyes and imagine something a little easier on mind and body: a hotel. Alone. A fancy hotel where your every whim is their fondest desire, where the word "pamper" has no limits and is not a reference to a brand of diapers.

It costs, but a weekend at a grand hotel is cheaper than divorce, which can happen to people who never run away from home together. As an old hand at this game, I have some advice to give: postponement is not smart. Do it now. And make it unscheduled time; plan on doing nothing beyond eating, sleeping and re-capturing the mysterious skill of relating.

Except for people with a tin palate or a professed scorn for the world of gastronomy, the eating part of the getaway is very important. Eating in a nice restaurant serves a number of purposes: it places the diners across a table from one another for at least an hour and forces them to talk to one another. It sets the scene for sensuality. And it slows you down from overdrive to pleasure mode. By the time Sunday brunch rolls around, mellow will be your middle name.

If it's going to bear the burden of accomplishing all that, a restaurant had best be pretty sharp. The food needs to be fun, but for these purposes we need some very intense cosseting, and the two (TLC and fine food) are not necessarily found in the same locations. For example Lotus, which serves some of the best food in Toronto. Pampering is not the word that comes to mind when you think of Lotus.

No one can give TLC better than a grand hotel. Even if you're not staying in the hotel, if life has been cruel lately, consider a little upscale TLC. In Toronto the best place for that is the Four Seasons. First they take your car. In a town without pity, where parking is a contact sport, anybody who whisks my car away is fine with me. In theory, valet parking costs $16 for an hour-and-a-half. But in practice, they give you free valet parking if you eat at one of the restaurants.

The Four Seasons' kitchen doesn't make mistakes. The flavours are subdued but they're never *wrong*. La Serre is the Four Seasons bar, where Sunday brunch is served for $28.50 per person ($13 for children under 12). Here we have an all-you-can-eat buffet of some distinction. Concentrate on the cold seafood table and you could probably best the hotel in the economic sense. It would be a happy challenge. There is unctuous smoked salmon, fresh crab legs, lovely poached shrimp and smoked sturgeon and trout. Then there are the breads (superb), the salads and pâtés (excellent), the desserts (competent) and the hot dishes (terrific, for steam table breakfast).

Here we have the kind of tender loving service that helps us to believe—if only for an afternoon—that life is not an uphill portage in a rainstorm. Eating at the Four Seasons is like a holiday. They should send out Seasons' tickets to everybody.

Cajun/Creole

Southern Accent Restaurant

595 Markham Street (Bloor and Bathurst)

416 536-3211

Moderate. All major cards.

HOURS: Lunch Tues.-Sat. 12 noon to 3 p.m.,
during summer only. Dinner daily 6 p.m.-11 p.m.
(all year). Open most holidays.

No wheelchair access to washrooms.

Private dining rooms available. Licensed.

Allergy aware. Reservations necessary
for Fri. and Sat., recommended for other days.

Southern Accent is the city's longest-running Cajun restaurant, and recently a staunch and delicious supporter of Knives & Forks Organic Farmers' Market every Saturday morning. The restaurant offers the market an indoor venue when it's bitter cold and, as well, hosts monthly organic lunches to promote the organic way of eating.

CAJUN/CREOLE

The entire upstairs of the restaurant is a non-smoking area—Hallelujah! Downstairs houses the bar and is equally funky. There are stained glass windows, old Acadian signs, diverse flowered tablecloths, artsy young servers and hip zydeco music—the hot pulsing sound of New Orleans. Southern Accent is the opposite of slick, not an iota of postmodern, but lovely in its own cramped manner.

Cajun food is an honourable cuisine that deserves far better than the nasty dried-out overcooked abomination called blackened fish that is served in so many Toronto restaurants. At Southern Accent when they blacken something they do not aim to compete with the fossil kingdom. Blackened means spiced and seared, melting in the middle and with sensual surrender ensured by lemony beurre blanc on top. When it's right.

But Southern Accent has suffered a reduction of quality lately, which has perhaps been occasioned by the change of chefs. Blackened used to mean melt-in-the-mouth. Now it means kissin' cousin to petrified. They used to do very appealing "bronzed" fish and chicken, which meant less heat than blackened, more delicate. Bronzing has disappeared from the menu.

The appetizers too have suffered. We find the crunchy hush puppies (deep-fried corn fritters) dry now. The gumbo, that Cajun classic based on a dark roux, has lost its distinct flavours. Proper gumbo is a dream from the bayou—highly flavoured pork sausage (called *andouille*) and other meats in a strong broth based on roux, with okra, and topped with a snowy hill of rice. These days the rice is dry, the broth weak.

Most Cajun cooking is based on the roux, which is a paste of flour and oil cooked over exceedingly high heat.

Then they will often *étoufée* the meat or fish, which literally means 'smother' it, usually with onions, tomatoes and peppers. Gumbo and other dishes are thickened with *file,* fragrant powder made from ground young sassafras leaves.

The queen of the Cajun kitchen is jambalaya, from the French *jambon,* 'ham,' the African *ya,* 'rice,' and the Acadian language, which calls foods *à la.* Jambalaya is the paella, the stew, the chow mein, the major complex statement of Louisiana cooking. It is rice-based, with andouille, smoked ham, beef, chicken, bacon, vegetables and shrimp in Cajun spices. Southern Accent's jambalaya, which used to be a proud Cajun, has deteriorated into something that feels like mush more than spicy rice.

The Cajuns are descendents of the French who lived in Acadia (today's Nova Scotia) and were expelled by the British in the 1750s. These were the people who were sent or fled South and settled in Louisiana where, despite all efforts to the contrary, they never melted into the homogeneous American pot. They clung to their Cajun identity ("Cajun" comes from "Acadian") and, to this day, they celebrate it, especially in the kitchen. We know Southern Accent can do that too: we await its renaissance.

Cheap 'n' Cheerful

BamBoo

312 Queen Street West (East of Spadina)

416 593-5771

Moderate. All major cards.

HOURS: Mon.-Sat. noon-1 a.m.

Closed Sun., statutory holidays and

Mon. after holiday closings.

Wheelchair accessible. Licensed. Allergy aware.

Reservations recommended for large parties.

Now that the gastro-bubble has burst and Toronto has survived the 80s glitz and settled down to being a normal city, the BamBoo seems less exotic. You enter an alleyway guarded by a booth that represents the hybridization of a stand of bamboo and the Beverly Hillbillies. Thence into a funky little inner courtyard decorated (if such is the word) by a bohemian hand: fishnets on the walls. A stand of Muskoka bamboo (a papyrus-like grass) standing guard over an empty stone fountain filled with small boulders of raw glass, surmounted by two red flags. A little junk heap crowned with a bicycle. Fading signs offering the pleasures of patio grazing. And all bordered by a thatched roof, à la South Pacific, and on it, a tall sculpture, a multi-coloured crazy quilt of found objects.

Welcome to BamBoo. It is the relentlessly low-tech club-cum-restaurant that rebukes Toronto, with a smile up its sleeve.

People who are pushing 40 and sometimes forget to wear at least three items of black clothing (preferably somewhat tattered) can be forgiven for sometimes avoiding Queen Street. It is not that Queen Street lacks charm, but rather that we non-artsy types fear that the denizens of Queen Street will find *us* lacking in charm. People who think that 10 o'clock is the time to watch the news, not to boogie, and who have never had a blue Margarita get nervous about going to a restaurant that's in a club that has waiters who wear more than three earrings and do not necessarily think that shaving is next to godliness.

Isn't it ironic that Torontonians who dine out seriously are less intimidated by luxurious pleasure palaces than we are by downtown bistros where the mean annual income of the customers is probably around $20,000? Indeed, the BamBoo does not ask that prospective clients seek prior approval from the Bohemian Central Committee. They're nice to everybody, especially those who manage to find the place.

Which can be difficult, given the narrowness of the alleyway entrance and the absence of a conventional sign. From SoHo Street, however, the BamBoo proclaims itself: with a tall yellow industrial stack, that euphonious crazy quilt sculpture poking its head above

BamBoo

the neighbouring building and a mural of otherworldly creatures bopping to the beat.

More and more Ordinary People are going to the BamBoo for one purpose only: to eat. They get in their ordinary cars well north of Queen Street and drive downtown to eat food that jumps up joyously on the tongue. The equally delicious bonus is the BamBoo human mosaic. Unlike the Centros and the Prontos of this world, where one could get bored by upscale homogeneity, BamBoo collects a variety of shapes, sizes, colours and styles.

When BamBoo was opening in 1983, Wandee Young, who was chef and co-owner (with her husband Andy Young) of the beloved Young Thailand on Eglinton, was at loose ends because she and Andy had ended their partnership, both marital and epicurean. Patty Habib and Richard O'Brien, who were busy renovating a wicker warehouse (ex-Chinese laundry) to make the BamBoo, had never run a restaurant before.

They had both worked for the CBC; Patty helped organize some pretty terrific parties at the Palais Royale, and the two partners had run an after hours private club catering to musicians. But the only liquour licence they could get required a dining lounge. So they hired Wandee Young, wizard of Thai, and Vera Kahn, a Trinidadian cook, to produce a Thai/Caribbean menu that remains in place to this day, even though its creators moved on.

At BamBoo you can eat in the club area (240 seats, barn-like but warm) or the small funky dining room off to the right. Beware: no reservations are taken and most nights by 6:30 the dining room is full. In the summer, two levels of patio sizzle and snap. It all adds up to more than 500 dinners sold on most Saturday nights—at about $10 per dinner for some of the most fun food in Toronto. Weekends they line up for both the food and the live Caribbean music, which starts at 10 p.m.

The BamBoo makes a hot and sour soup that has more oomph than anything I've had in Chinatown in years. The kakai, a soup of coconut milk, lemon grass, ginger and chilies, is ineffably delicate, with an unforgettable citrus wake-up. Much of the food is spicy. The callalloo, a creamed spinach and coconut soup, is the very weapon that blocked sinuses require.

The BamBoo's single most popular dish, Thai spicy noodles, comes in three modes, mild, medium and Yow! I cannot vouch for Yow! but mild is a superlative ungreasy wok-fry of rice noodles with peanuts, bean sprouts, chicken, shrimp, tofu, egg, Vietnamese fish sauce, chilies, sugar, garlic and fresh lime juice. Not Yow! but Wow! Chicken wings are marinated overnight in ginger, mustard, soy sauce, oyster sauce, sesame oil, pepper and paprika, deep fried into hot juicy submission and served with a pretty spectacular garlic chili vinegar dipping sauce.

This is not detailed artistic Thai cooking. Things are more casual—and more multi-ethnic—at the BamBoo. The portions are large, the flavours assertive and the cooking rather like the best of fresh home cooking. Beside charcoal-sweet satays and earthy curries, there are burgers and yummy fresh-cut fries.

And lately they have added a dessert called squirrel pie, which is a seductive re-make of Reese Peanut Butter Cups, not sophisticated, but one wants more. The BamBoo is like that too—so refreshingly, adultly countercultural that it hardly seems to be in Toronto—which is perhaps its most endearing aspect.

Bamboo

Cafe La Gaffe

24 Baldwin Street (Beverley and McCaul)

416 596-2397

Moderate. Visa and Mastercard.

HOURS: Lunch daily 11:45 a.m.-4 p.m.

Dinner daily 6 p.m.-11 p.m.

Closed Christmas Day and New Year's Day.

No wheelchair access. Licensed. Allergy aware.

Reservations necessary for first seating

at lunch and dinner.

One hates to be forever harping on one's advanced age, but there are times when it does seem a determining factor. Like whenever one dines at Cafe La Gaffe on Baldwin Street (itself home of youth and counterculture). Everybody else there is happy, and there are so many of them. The place always seems full to bursting with such happy people. And they're all eating!

Which is why I invoke age. Food that seems delicious to the under-30 set might be rough 'n' ready to the more jaded palate of middle age. Maybe service is even more in the eye of the beholder. Aging makes us persnickety. I am a middle-aged codger who doesn't suffer fools gladly, especially when they're waiting on me. Mediocre service that would have seemed cute (or maybe even my fault) 20 years ago is now intolerable.

It's like that at Cafe La Gaffe. So you asked for another glass of wine. Who cares? Apparently they don't. You've been sitting a long time with neither food nor drink for succour? Don't get cantankerous. It won't help. And besides, everybody else in the restaurant is having fun.

They like it because the cooking is exuberant, and it has that gourmet *feel,* while avoiding both formality and high prices. In theory this is a winning combination. In practice it reads like a charm and tastes like something nobody would have to apologize for at home. But, when you're paying money....

The pizza is the best example. It all sounds very designer, *très* 90s: curried goat cheese pizza, vegetable pizza. But the crust is thick and tough (in the manner of footwear) and the toppings sophomoric. Dumping supermarket curry powder on goat cheese is not an act of kindness to the dairy industry. There is something equally graceless about the grilled vegetable pizza, having to do with not very carefully grilled vegetables.

Am I sounding like a broken record? A querulous oldster who might perhaps be happier at the Arcadian Court? Do forgive me if I get ill-tempered when served the likes of mussels Marius, a huge serving of overcooked mussels drowned in obnoxiously thick tomato sauce. And seafood salad brimful (oh yes they're generous here) with overcooked mussels, squid and shrimp, and dressed in that same unpleasant tomato sauce that is no friend to salad greens.

Almost anybody could make Cafe La Gaffe's chicken Dijon at home. Here's how I'd do it. Take a chicken. Cut up the white meat. Sauté it until it's somewhat overcooked. Stir in whipping cream and a great wad of Dijon mustard. Stir and simmer for three minutes. Serve. Would people pay $60 for dinner for two in your house to eat that? Maybe if you had a pressed tin ceiling, a terrace on Baldwin Street for sunny lunches and artsy stuff on the walls.

Cafe La Gaffe

Kit Kat Italian Bar and Grill

297 King Street West (Near John)

416 977-4461

Moderate. All major cards.

HOURS: All-day menu Mon.-Fri. 11:30 a.m.-1 a.m.

Dinner Sat. 4:30 p.m.-1 a.m.

Closed Sun. and major holidays.

No wheelchair access to washrooms.

Licensed. Allergy aware (will customize dishes).

Reservations recommended.

Taking shots at beloved neighbourhood restaurants is not my idea of a good time. A small businessperson is selling comfort. People want it and need it. Who am I to butt in on their good time? I am the person who noticed the restaurant's growing popularity, ate there a few times and found cold comfort.

Kit Kat is the name. Cool is the game. In more ways than one. Kit Kat started life as a variety store cum coffee shop almost four years ago and has grown, like Topsy, into a full-fledged restaurant. Because bits and pieces of the restaurant (in terms of both building and menu) have been added over a few years, there are certain areas of, to put it kindly, incoherence.

CHEAP 'N' CHEERFUL

Such as the heating system. Sit at the front table in the front room and you are alternately blasted with heat (from the heater under the table) and cold (from the too-close front door that is funky and hard to close). Say you wish to read the menu (not an unreasonable assumption when you're going out to eat). It's on a blackboard. But where? Find the nearest blackboard, which is not necessarily readable from your seat.

So why am I bothering with this place? Because it's fun to bitch? No. Kit Kat, flawed as it is, possesses more street-style charm than any other restaurant serving food in Toronto today. First the look: the front room (non-smoking) is one long line of tables and a display case of antipasti, with cooks doing the full-tilt gastro-boogey behind it at the stoves. High ceiling, walls crammed with old movie posters, counters overflowing with bottles of olive oil, wine vinegar and the other signs that an Italian sensibility is presiding here.

Walk to the end of the front room, past the antique dental chair, and you enter the back room (smoking). The back room is wider, possessed of tall black wooden booths and decorated with a hybrid of funk and whimsy. Every table is set with a diversity of Italian hand-painted ceramic plates, the beautiful kind that chip easily, which most have done.

Both at lunch and dinner, Kit Kat is heavily populated with Queen Street types who don't seem to mind draughts, chipped crockery or inconveniently located blackboards. It's only middle-aged fogeys from uptown, like me, who are addicted to our bourgeois comforts. Since Kit Kat has been, for all its life, a restaurant in process rather than a finished product, one awaits and believes in all needed improvements.

From cappuccino and muffins came the slow, step-

Kit Kat

wise metamorphosis. First came takeout salads and sandwiches. Then they added soups. Then they installed summertime seating on the patio out back, and Al got a stove and set up a real (sort of) kitchen, and year-round seating inside.

Al is an exceedingly charming maître d', and his instincts are basically sound. The Italian trattoria core of Kit Kat's menu is based on those perennial delights— olive oil, eggplant, zucchini, pasta and tomato sauce— with which one cannot go too far wrong.

So stay with those, because when the Kit Kat kitchen starts grilling, all hell breaks loose. They can turn squid into rubber, fresh tuna into a travesty resembling well-done round steak and shrimp into dust. Chicken on the grill suffers the same fate. The rule at Kit Kat is: eat antipasto and pasta with any tomato-based sauce. The sauce is robust and sweet, and antipasto is always full of niceties. If they offer salad with artichoke hearts for $7.95, resist. Do you really need canned artichoke hearts on underdressed romaine?

Steer clear of edible uptown glitz at Kit Kat and all will be well. For dessert there are familiar pleasures from Dufflet. And for Kit Kat's future, there is the promise of continued improvement. Such is the beauty of a permanent work-in-progress.

Chinese

Classic Chinese

330 Highway 7 East, Units 106-109

(Near Chalmers)

905 771-9393

Cheap. Visa and Mastercard.

HOURS: All-day menu daily 10 a.m.-12 midnight.

Open all holidays.

No wheelchair access. Not licensed.

Allergy aware. Reservations recommended.

Just like its near neighbour, Shanghai Garden, Classic Chinese will let you choose live sea creatures from the seafood store in the mall. You make your seafood needs known to the server and then hotfoot it over to the seafood store (with server) to salivate and choose. Swimming in big tanks are lobsters, scallops, geoduck (giant clams), oysters, finned fish and other delicious denizens of the deep. All there for your delectation. Choose which you want, discuss cooking method with the server and then walk back to the restaurant to await the crustacean parade.

Classic Chinese is far more formal dining than Shanghai, and the staff seem less enthused about going to the fish store and foraging for dinner. The Classic Chinese cooking of the seafood, while competent, is less sensitive. The scallops and clams are sometimes slightly overcooked, and the service can be slow. Nonetheless the fresh seafood experience, from tank to table, is nothing to sniff at.

Dynasty Chinese Cuisine

131 Bloor Street West (East of Avenue Road)

416 923-3323

Moderate. All major cards.

HOURS: Mon.-Fri. 11 a.m.-11 p.m.

Sat.-Sun. 10 a.m.-11 p.m.

Wheelchair accessible. Allergy aware.

Reservations not necessary.

Sinophilia had become such a labour-intensive habit in the last few years that we had almost talked ourselves out of our previously constant craving for Chinese food. Having to drive to Highway 7 to get a decent lobster with ginger and green onion is not perhaps everyone's idea of hardship.

Given my ennui with having to schlep to the suburbs for good Chinese food, I was elated when Dynasty opened on Bloor Street near Avenue Road. So what if they're capitalist roaders with white tablecloths, fancy china and French service? We've learned to put up with that at the great Chinese restaurants in Richmond Hill. Although Chinese food seems to taste better amid the cold draughts amid the grunge of Spadina, everybody knows you don't judge a restaurant by the decor.

So, with an open mind, we went to Dynasty on the second floor of the Colonnade. Here is the scent of money: the lobster tank is a suave built-in, the decor says "luxe" all the way to the Villeroy and Boch plates. The menu is impressive (shark's fin, abalone and the like) and the servers are forever whisking away dirty plates in favour of clean, fresh ones.

But there's many a slip 'twixt the standard of pretension and the lip. One evening we order the glamorous sounding sliced fresh fruit with abalone and chicken. It never arrives. We ask the servers to discuss the edible possibilities of the seafood tank. They appear not to understand and they ignore the request. Here we are on politically thin ice. It would not be politically correct to complain about the linguistic limitations of waitpeople who are immigrants. But....

In cheap and cheerful Chinese dives we *expect* linguistic limitations. But when mixed seafood with vegetables costs $13, and the restaurant looks like a country club, are we not allowed to expect to be able to communicate with the servers?

Which shortcoming wouldn't matter if the food were better. But Dynasty has been attacked by the forces of gastro-evil: it's all bland and boring, except for lobster with black bean sauce; the delicate flesh has been annihilated by too too much sauce, which is too too acrid.

The good news at Dynasty is the dim sum, which is fresher than the petrified products of downtown dim sum and includes a selection of noodle soups. Seafood noodle soup Japanese style is expensive for lunch ($14) but it is a huge serving of mostly pristine seafood (the one exception being a stick of fake crab) in delicate broth.

Grand Yatt Chinese Restaurant
(Downtown Toronto)

Westin Harbour Castle (Bay and Queen's Quay)

416 869-3663

Moderate. All major cards.

HOURS: Lunch Mon.-Fri 11 a.m.-3:30 p.m.

and Sat.-Sun. 11 a.m.-4 p.m. Dinner

daily 5:30 p.m.-11 p.m. Closed some holidays.

Wheelchair accessible. Licensed. Allergy aware.

Reservations not necessary.

The bad news is that Grand Yatt downtown, appropriately situated in the Westin Harbour Castle Hotel, is less delicious than its parent for dinner. The good news is the dim sum at lunch.

Ahh! In an era of terrible dim sum deprivation, Grand Yatt brings it back downtown. Their basic beloved dumplings are carefully and freshly made: the sticky rice has the requisite quail egg, shrimp dumpling has a whole shrimp on top, soup dumpling is fragrant with black mushrooms and, wonder of wonders, the steamed chive dumpling comes in an emerald green rice-flour wrapper, dyed with chives.

For dinner, however, get thee to the DVP.

Dynasty

Grand Yatt
Chinese Restaurant
(Richmond Hill)

9019 Bayview Avenue (Richmond Hill)

905 882-9388

Moderate. All major cards.

HOURS: Dim Sum Mon.-Fri.

All-day menu Sat.-Sun. 10 a.m.-11 p.m.

Wheelchair accessible. Licensed. Allergy aware.

Reservations not necessary.

I have given in to four-lane blacktop. I, who formerly experienced acute suburbophobia if forced to venture north of Eglinton, have become an habitué of the Don Valley Parkway at dinnertime. It's really swell to be hurtling north (or crawling, if you go too early), knowing that you're going to spend $50 on the only decent Chinese dinner for two that money can buy in Toronto or environs. But, why would any sane person want to fight her way northbound at dinnertime, when Toronto is not exactly under-supplied with restaurants?

The answer, my friends, lies in the lobster. And the geoduck. And the shrimps. And the noodles. And the addiction. For many Toronto folk who are now enduring the trials of middle age, the pleasures enjoyed in early adulthood are unprintable; but for an entire generation of Torontonians, these were punctuated by frequent Chinese meals on Spadina between College and Dundas.

Over hot and sour soup we marked the beginnings

and endings of relationships, extramarital affairs, moving from apartments to houses, impassioned political moments. We measured the days of our young lives in eggplant with garlic sauce, and thereby learned to crave a certain kind of taste.

Long after the adventures of youth have faded into scrapbook memories, we still crave Chinese food. No other cuisine offers such definite flavours and such clean, crisp textures. I *need* Chinese food.

And almost every time I eat it downtown, it's disappointing. Sometimes greasy, sometimes not so fresh, sometimes overcooked. When the shrimps smell musty, and dim sum wrappers separate from their contents and stick to the steamer, you know you're in the land of day-old bread. Hence the great northward trek.

Where money goes, there goeth good food, and where is the Chinese money in Toronto today? Richmond Hill. *Vide* Grand Yatt, where they can sell geoduck for $28 a plate (enough for six or seven good bites) and shark's fin soup for $9.50 per serving.

Grand Yatt is a large, plain room with the look of a very nice gymnasium. Which fact becomes insignificant when the aesthetics of the kitchen assert themselves. Every platter comes with a border of vegetable decoration, which is a small touch that speaks of much caring. This is a kitchen that pays attention to detail.

So-called crystal prawns (a fat shrimp by any other name...) are served in a delicate Cantonese sauce with the thinnest slivers of barely cooked onion. Geoduck (giant B.C. clam) is poached for about half a minute, just long enough to tenderize it slightly and bring out its sweetness, and served on ultrafresh greens. Boneless chicken is steamed till its juices run golden, and served with small slices of pungent smoked ham. Fat noodles are sautéed with a minimum of grease. It costs almost twice what they charge on Spadina, but what the hell, we're middle aged.

Kim Hoa

332 Spadina Avenue (Near Dundas)

416 971-9719

Cheap. All major cards.

HOURS: All-day menu daily Mon., Wed.-Fri.

11 a.m.-1 a.m., Sat.-Sun. 10 a.m.-1 a.m.

Closed Tues. Open all major holidays.

Wheelchair accessible. Beer only.

Not allergy aware. Reservations recommended.

Kim Hoa B.B.Q. & Seafood House is alive, delicious and grungy in the splendid Spadina tradition of yesteryear. They do a pretty mean steamed pickerel (firm sweet flesh falling off the bone), and big fresh oysters come on a sizzling platter, braised with ginger and green onion.

After seafood, Kim Hoa's *pièce de résistance* is its barbecue. Hanging in the window is the evidence: ducks, chickens and various pig parts with the mahogany sheen of the Chinese barbecue treatment. Along with the chopped up barbecue meats, which are juicy and fine, comes a tiny saucer of lightly pickled garlic for dipping. We have happy taste buds.

Lifting chopsticks downtown again feels like

homecoming. After too many years of having to dress up to dine, it's time to mellow out, as they used to say in the days when there was only one Avenue in town and it was called Spadina.

Lee Garden Restaurant

331 Spadina Avenue (At Dundas)
416 593-9524
Moderate. All major cards.
HOURS: Sun.-Thu. 4 p.m.-12 midnight,
Fri.-Sat. 4 p.m.-1 a.m.
Wheelchair accessible, except washrooms. Beer
and wine only. Allergy aware.
Reservations not necessary, but recommended.

Okay, so I was wrong. Spadina isn't all washed up. There are still gastronomical diamonds to be mined on the Avenue. Having sustained countless salivary wounds in the search for the remaining decent Chinese food downtown, I can now happily report that my gall bladder survived (but just barely), and that when Lee Garden moved across the street to more genteel premises it recovered its lost glory.

The move across the street has been salutary. There is just the right amount of *je ne sais quoi* in the silver-flecked turquoise wallpaper, and the crinkle of many layers of white plastic tablecloth is comforting. One of

Kim Hoa

80

the things I can never get used to in the new upscale Chinese restaurants is the tablecloths. They aren't plastic and they don't *crinkle*.

Damask and French service are fine for yuppie bistros where you're getting an ego massage with the dinner, but Chinese food seems to require a more earthy experience. I like having seven different flavours of grease compete for space on the plate.

The fancy new Hong Kong-style Chinese restaurants in the 'burbs generally feature very correct waiters who take away one plate as soon as you've mussed it, and they won't bring more food until they've cleared the prior course, with its plates. This is elegant but antiseptic. One wants the culinary equivalent of simultaneous orgasm, all the food on the table at once.

Let's face it, nothing has replaced the hurdy-gurdy of eating Chinese on Spadina, and I've missed it. Lee Garden is a seafood house. Order lobster, Vancouver crab, soft shell crab and live grouper (which they still spell "garoupa"). Within two minutes of your ordering, the kitchen is populated with live sea creatures. The waiter nets a swimming grouper from the fish tank in the dining room. A cook brings live soft shell crabs, live lobster and live Vancouver crab from the fridge, and lays them on the counter. Many tentacles wave in the air. We are in seafood heaven.

They steam the grouper with julienne of black Chinese mushroom, ginger, green onion, oil and a touch of soy. It is perfection incarnate. The Vancouver crab and lobster are done either with ginger and green onion (subtle) or black bean sauce (salty). Soft shell crabs are deep fried in gossamer batter, hallelujah. Lee Garden also offers the slightly smoky fun of grandfather smoke chicken, and some pretty intense pleasure in the form of fresh fat oysters in hot pot (i.e., casserole) with ham, vegetables and thick unctuous brown sauce.

Lotus Pond Vegetarian Restaurant

3838 Midland Avenue (South of Steeles)

416 412-3140

Cheap. Visa.

HOURS: All-day menu daily 11 a.m.-10:30 p.m.

Open all holidays.

Wheelchair accessible. Not licensed. Not allergy aware. Reservations recommended.

For eaters who believe in cholesterol counts and high fibre, there is a splendid all vegetarian restaurant in Scarborough—Lotus Pond Vegetarian Restaurant. The dishes have wonderful names like Mercy to All (vegetable chop suey with mock duck's kidney, cured vegetable stem and peanuts), reunion of eight saints (fried vegetables) and paradise (mushrooms et al.).

For eaters accustomed to excesses of meat and seafood, this food will seem bland and repetitive. But it is wonderfully delicate, lacking both the grease that comes with meat and the heavy feeling attendant upon eating too much protein.

Lotus Pond makes much use of textured vegetable protein (a.k.a. TVP), a postmodern manipulation of

Lee Garden

82

vegetable matter that tries to imitate meat. Hence mock chicken with cashew nuts (pleasant, but we're not fooled), mock ham with bean sprouts, vegetables and peanuts and mock fish in the corn soup (feh!).

We prefer unashamed just plain vegetables to ersatz meat. For example fried spicy eggplant is divine, in the Szechuan mode. Double freshness in nest is a crispy golden deep-fried potato nest cradling an emerald ring of broccoli florets, with two kinds of fresh mushrooms in the middle. The good thing about eating just vegetables is how good you feel afterwards: virtue is its own reward.

Mandarin

2200 Yonge Street (Near Eglinton)
416 486-2222
Moderate. All major cards.
HOURS: All-day menu Mon.-Fri. 11:30 a.m.-9 p.m.,
Sat.-Sun. 11:30 a.m.-10:30 p.m. Lunch buffet daily
12 noon-3 p.m. Open major holidays.
Wheelchair accessible. Licensed.
Allergy aware (will customize dishes).
Reservations not necessary.

The people are abandoning the cheap Chinese restaurants of yesteryear and flocking to uptown chinoiserie with white tablecloths and (oh horror of horrors) clean bathrooms. For example, the Mandarin, a suburban chain with a city branch at Yonge and Eglinton.

CHINESE

We tried the Mandarin, thinking that the people cannot be wrong. Perhaps not wrong, but maybe gastronomically lobotomized. The Mandarin's key attraction is its all-you-can-eat buffet. Pretty much every Chinese dish is on that buffet, from hot and sour soup through Szechuan eggplant to fried shrimps and Singapore noodles. Whether it could pass the blind taste test is another matter. My guess is that with eyes closed, I couldn't tell the Mandarin's shrimp from its chicken. The Mandarin is an equal opportunity kitchen: everything is equally overcooked.

If matters Chinese were better elsewhere, one would be less pessimistic. But they aren't and I am. Losing the regular pleasure of great cheap Chinese food feels like losing a friend.

New Hunan Restaurant

4907 Yonge Street (Near Sheppard)
416 730-9398
Moderate. All major cards.
HOURS: All-day menu Mon.-Fri. 11 a.m.-10 p.m.
Dinner Sat.-Sun. 4 p.m.-10:30 p.m. Closed
Christmas Day. Open for lunch only Boxing Day.
No wheelchair access. Licensed. Allergy aware.
Reservations recommended.

How much bad Chinese food can a gourmandising sinophile eat before getting jaded? How many greasy spring rolls, how many aging dumplings with dessicated skin? How many flaccid bok choys and gristly spareribs? How many bowls of soup with thin stock? How many overcooked shrimp and rubber squid? Does it matter to the world that my faith (heretofore endless) in Chinese food is wavering?

And if I lose my faith, what will replace it? Surely not Thai, whose spicy excesses are not quite the thing for regular indulgence? And not Vietnamese, which is so ill used and inconsistent in these parts. Cal/Ital à la Splendido and Centro? Nothing to sneeze at, but the bastions of haute gastronomy will never fill the comfy, casual niche that Chinese restaurants occupy.

Oh for the wintry solace of a rich, hot and sour soup and garlicky eggplant to clear the sinuses. Like Diogenes, ever searching, I fetched up twice recently at New Hunan (hard by the Ford Centre for the Performing Arts). On the first visit to this unassuming *boîte* the dumplings were aged and the noodles a tad greasy, but we were deeply pleased by mo si soup, a Hunan specialty rich with shredded pork and vegetables in a strong chicken stock.

The fine scent of toasted sesame oil floated up from the food; it was all homespun but of good flavour, especially the chewy/tender house-smoked ham, which appears in several dishes, and the thin, fried green onion cake.

O Mei

5150 Yonge Street (North York City Centre)

416 222-2300

Moderate. All major cards.

HOURS: All-day menu Mon.-Thurs. 11 a.m.-10 p.m.,

Sat. 11 a.m.-11:30 p.m., Sun. 11 a.m.-10 p.m.

Open all holidays.

Wheelchair accessible. Licensed. Allergy aware.

Reservations recommended for Sat.

At O Mei we're standing in line on a Saturday night with folks who look just like us. How depressing. Aging yuppies don't die; they go to Richmond Hill and order lemon chicken.

O Mei is an exceedingly popular suburban chain operation, with three restaurants (in Downsview and Thornhill, in addition to Richmond Hill). Here we have the usual dusty rose draperies, with a menu that celebrates Szechuan and Peking, and a style suited to people who would still be eating at Lichee Gardens if they hadn't moved north of the 401.

Perhaps if they knew better.... But these are people who either never experienced Spadina in its heyday, or they always felt squeamish there because of the bathrooms. O Mei has nice bathrooms.

And tough fried dumplings. And too-sweet chicken with cashews. And greasy fried noodles. And overcooked sliced sautéed grouper. And overcooked dried, fried

O Mei

scallops. And musty shrimps. And not very fresh soft shell crabs. And when you order eggplant with shrimps in spicy garlic sauce, the eggplant comes battered and deep fried and greasy. Where, oh, where is the garlic eggplant of our youth? Gone to the place where our youth went. Somehow over the rainbow.

Pearl

110 Bloor Street West (West of Bay)
416 975-1155
Moderate. All major cards.
HOURS: Lunch daily 10:30 a.m.-4 p.m.
Dinner 5 p.m.-11 p.m. Open major holidays.
Wheelchair accessible. Licensed. Allergy aware.
Reservations recommended on weekends.

The dim sum is superb at Pearl, where the dumplings circulate on carts. This is a veritable festival of dim sum. There are the usual shrimp and chive, pork and vegetable affairs in rice flour, but Pearl also excels in less common deep-fried flaky pastry dumplings. Melt-in-the-mouth puff pastry pinwheels have a heart of sweet barbecued pork. Deep-fried bean curd wraps round cloud ear mushrooms with crunchy celery and carrot. There is deep-fried eggplant with shrimp, and shrimp with garlic. Egg noodle "purses" are tied up with chive ribbons, with shrimp, scallops, cloud ears and broccoli inside. The parade never stops.

Dinner at Pearl is a different story. One evening

everything we ask for is sold out. The stir-fried beef seems tenderized, and the vast majority of its touted "two kinds of mushrooms" are the supermarket Canadian kind. Prawns with hot chili give us the blahs and are less than plentiful for the price ($15.50).

We have discovered only two deep pleasures there: sliced chicken sautéed with home-made hot and black pepper sauce is moist and crispy and garnished with splendid candied walnuts. And baked chicken with tea leaves is moist and slightly smoky, in the manner of lapsang suchong tea.

Sang-Ho Seafood Restaurant

339 Spadina Avenue (At Baldwin)
416 596-1685
Cheap. Visa.
HOURS: All-day menu daily 11 a.m.-12 midnight.
Open all holidays.
No wheelchair access. Beer only.
Allergy aware (dishes customized on request).
Reservations not taken.

It seems forever ago that we used to debate how to change the world and which was the best hot and sour soup on Spadina. Nowadays there isn't any hot and sour soup worthy of the name downtown, and we're too busy changing diapers to change the world. Half of the

Pearl

good Chinese restaurants are gone. The Great Wall and many others are now Vietnamese restaurants. Those that remain have lost their sparkle.

There's nothing wrong with Vietnamese food. But the world's great cuisines are French and Chinese. Others have their great moments—the Japanese have sushi, the Italians have pasta and the Vietnamese have their astonishing soups. But for breadth and depth nobody comes up to the French and the Chinese and that shows on Spadina. Both the departure of so many Chinese people for the greener pastures (?) of Scarborough and the economically privileged position of so many recent Chinese immigrants have contributed to the withering of the Spadina Avenue Chinese restaurant scene.

So it is with delight that I report the renaissance of Sang-Ho. Finally—again—a decent Chinese restaurant, in the grungy and grotty style, on the Avenue. Here are the hundred plastic tablecloths on every table, here are the bathrooms from hell, here is the grease-encrusted kitchen, and here too are the succulent "twofer" lobsters and the fresh oysters steamed with black bean sauce, the greaseless Singapore noodles, the whole fresh flounder steamed with ginger and green onion.

Sang-Ho is not exactly undiscovered. On Saturday nights the lineup is in place by 6 sharp. In this situation it helps to have the instincts of a piranha. Stand in the freezing cold doorway and stare at the people sitting at tables, making it clear to them that failure to vacate in short order will result in their being cannibalized.

Having captured a table, insist on fresh scallops in black bean sauce, which come in the shell, their coral still attached. Or fat shrimp in lobster sauce, that wonderful misnomer that's decorated with pork bits. It's safe to eat everything on the back page

"Supplementary Menu" except the hot and sour soup, which has the hots but no taste. The claimed specialty of the house is seafood. Believe it.

I would be overjoyed to tell you about seven more like Sang-Ho, but the sad truth is I haven't found them yet, and it's not for lack of looking. I and my army of unpaid but voracious research assistants go out trolling for decent Chinese restaurants. You should see the one that got away.

Shanghai Garden

328 Highway 7 East (Richmond Hill,
Chalmers Gate in Golden Plaza)
905 886-3308
Expensive. Visa only.
HOURS: Daily 11 a.m.-11 p.m. Open on all holidays.
Wheelchair accessible. Licensed. Allergy aware.
Reservations recommended on weekends.

In the fat red books called the *Michelin Guides,* which have been the bible to two generations of epicurean travellers in western Europe, there is a special category of restaurant. Although the term "three star restaurant" has been borrowed and bastardized by people unaware of its genesis, it has a specific meaning. The *Michelin Guide* bestows its highest accolade, the three stars, on restaurants that are "worth a special journey."

In France that means planning one's holiday around one or two dinners in sacred temples of gastronomy and

Sang-Ho

then driving for days to get there. But that's France, the country where a chef once committed suicide when Michelin demoted him from three stars back down to two. Here in Canada, we've never been big on going too far out of our way to get grub. There's a McDonald's in every neighbourhood, eh?

But as our food tastes grow more sophisticated, and as it becomes harder to get certain of our cherished favourites near home, we acquiesce to the Michelin model of fine dining. Hit the road, Jacques.

And so we find ourselves in Richmond Hill, on Highway 7 east of Bayview, in the Golden Plaza, home of *eight* Chinese restaurants, one Chinese supermarket and one Japanese fish store. As the experience unfolds, the reference to the *Michelin Guide* becomes much stronger than mere coincidence.

We enter Shanghai Garden, a modest restaurant in the middle of the modest mall. We ask if they have lobster. No, they don't. We look unhappy. They say, don't worry, we'll go get some at the store. We ask questions. Is it fresh? Yes. Is it alive? Yes. The woman responds to our obvious skepticism by inviting us to go with her to the store and choose our own lobster.

So we follow her a few doors down to Unique Fishery. There are lobster swimming in one tank, bass and black cod and flatfish in others. Live scallops open and close their shells langorously in another tank. Giant BC crabs wave their antennae in another. There are live clams (both large and small) swimming in tanks, and oysters too. The woman turns to us and inquires: "What do you want to eat?"

Have we died and gone to gastro-heaven?

This is an experience related to the great rural eating moments in Europe, which are great in large part because the ingredients come from the farmer down the road or the wild food forager or angler who comes to the back door of the restaurant every day. This is a dining experience that will be determined by the freshest possible ingredients. Finally, for once, the horse is going before the cart. Hallelujah.

We go happily berserk.

We choose big oysters. We point to fat scallops. We choose a hefty lobster. We choose a cute little snapper. As the fishmonger nets each choice and begins to commit ritual murder, the woman asks how we would like it cooked. We talk steaming, we talk ginger and green onion, we talk garlic, we talk black bean sauce.

We return to Shanghai Garden bathed in the bliss of erotic anticipation. And the parade of delights begins. The scallops that were so recently swimming are barely steamed, with their coral, with garlic and wine. The oysters are similarly anointed. The lobster, also cooked perfectly, comes slathered with ginger and green onion. The snapper is supernal, perfectly cooked, perfumed with coriander and Chinese wine.

There are other dishes too, and they are excellent. The servers are deliciously pleased to be giving joy and the atmosphere is entirely unpretentious. But nothing compares to the gastronome's moment of discovery upon entering that fish store, seeing the denizens of the deep in the tanks and realizing what's to come.

Young Lok
(North York Branch)

4955 Yonge Street (Madison Centre)

416 225-8818

Moderate. All major cards.

HOURS: All-day menu daily 11:30 a.m.-11 p.m.

Pre-show buffet Wed.-Sun. 5:30 p.m.-9 p.m.

Open major holidays.

Wheelchair accessible. Licensed.

Allergy aware (all dishes 100% MSG-free).

Reservations recommended.

Young Lok north is big: 450 seats. We like Young Lok downtown. Although not setting any gastronomical fires, it is consistently good. But where have all the flavours gone?

We don't get it. Take, for example, Mandarin seafood chowder: downtown it is a delicate but flavourful chicken broth brimful with high ticket seafood and entertaining vegetables. Here in the 'burbs the broth has no flavour and the seafoods seem low rent. The crispy spring rolls aren't so crispy up here and the garlic shrimp have lost their edge. The Mongolian mixed grill (shrimp, chicken and beef) suffers from too much—too much marinating and too much cooking. And the potstickers—a Young Lok dumpling classic—seem doughy and tired, as if they were made well in advance.

Textures are flaccid and flavours meek. Dinner is

depressing at both restaurants. Is it because branch plants are invariably awful, given the inability of even the sharpest restaurateur to be in two places at once? As for Young Lok, if Chinese food in the suburbs were always terrible, we would perhaps be mollified and call this normal. But you can get a fine Chinese meal in Woodbridge, Markham and Richmond Hill. Even in Scarborough. So why not North York? Because Mel Lastman spent $48 million to build a performing arts centre that looks like a grain silo, but he couldn't give North York culture. Not even with $48 million to spend.

Young Lok

Dim Sum: Bayview Garden and Spring Villa

Bayview Garden

350 Highway 7 East (East of Leslie Street)

905 882-8333

Moderate. All major cards.

HOURS: All-day menu daily 11 a.m.-11 p.m.

Open all holidays.

Wheelchair accessible. Licensed. Allergy aware.

Reservations recommended.

Spring Villa

7301 Woodbine Avenue (South of Dennison)

905 940-2888

Moderate. All major cards.

HOURS: All-day menu daily 11 a.m.-11 p.m.

Open all holidays.

Wheelchair accessible. Licensed. Allergy aware.

Reservations accepted.

When you read a restaurant menu in China, it has most of the usual categories as we expect to see them: appetizers, hot; appetizers, cold; seafood; chicken; duck; seafood; fish; pork; vegetable dishes; beef; desserts. But there is one additional category: food. Under this heading are listed noodles, rice, buns, dumplings and breads. These foods form the foundation of the Chinese diet, a reality that is underlined by the traditional progression of dishes at Chinese banquets and celebrations—the rice and noodle dishes are never served until the end, in order to emphasize the luxury of the event, and the fact that it is about pleasure, not necessity. Words tell the tale too. The Chinese word for rice, *fan,* also means both food and meal.

Rice and grains are the heart of Chinese cooking, and they often appear in forms not instantly recognizable. If poverty forces you to eat rice three times a day, you'd best figure out how to produce a variety of results with it as a starting point. As with other aspects of Chinese cuisine, necessity has been the mother of invention. They cut up their food into small pieces prior to cooking because of the permanent shortage of fuel. Exposing more surfaces to heat also exposes them to flavourings.

Rice often becomes a noodle, a porridge, a limpid, translucent dough. It has more lives than the proverbial cat. Soybeans, the other staple of the Chinese diet, are altered with equal invention. Soybeans are used so extensively in China because acre for acre, dollar for dollar, they are the world's most inexpensive source of protein. But eat a soybean or, indeed, plain tofu (soybean curd), and you will be overcome by the blandness of it. No food is in more dire need of metamorphosis than the soybean.

The most exciting thing that Chinese cooks do to soybeans, rice and wheat is to make them into dough. And what does dough do? Dough becomes dumplings, a favourite food from the coast of Canton in the East all the way to the mountains of Szechuan in the West.

In Canton they eat dumplings for breakfast and call them *dim sum.* Dumplings are another of China's answers to fuel economy. Cooks pile anywhere from five to ten nesting bamboo steamers (each containing four or five little dumplings) atop one another, for a high-rise breakfast requiring only one burner to cook. Centuries of economy have inspired so much creativity using so little: one marvellous dim sum is a symphony of chopped pork and vegetables, wrapped in several layers of thin, smoked bean curd dough (smoked tofu is a specialty of Chengdu, capital of Szechuan province).

But there is little marvellous dim sum in the city of Toronto. A decade ago we were inhaling coriander and other fragrances in our little dumplings. Today, dim sum downtown is, for the most part, an adventure in grease management.

But drive along Highway 7 westward from the 404: you will sight more Mercedes, BMWs and other vehicular extravaganzas than in either Forest Hill or Rosedale. On weekend mornings, guess where they're going. Not to church, but to the temples of gastronomy on Highway 7 East and nearby, in the many small malls, each with its mirrored postmodern office building anchoring a collection of upscale Chinese shops. Welcome to Chinatown Five! By 11 a.m. on Saturdays and Sundays there are long lineups outside the most popular dim sum restaurants. Is it better than downtown, worth a special journey to the nether 'burbs? Is the pope Catholic?

The two best dim sum parlours are Spring Villa and Bayview Garden. At Spring Villa, a uniformed waiter stands behind your table to do your every bidding. Each dumpling comes as its own course. Eat it, they whisk away that steamer and bring the next. The greasy unpleasantness of downtown fades into dim memory under the onslaught of delicate dumplings. Spring Villa and Bayview Garden serve the same dim sum, with minor exceptions.

CHINESE

Both serve evanescent steamed shrimp and pork dumplings, fragrant with barely cooked chives. Both serve pan-fried onion cake, a tiny turban of ungreasy, fried flaky pastry envelopping sautéed onions in sauce. Both serve superb assorted seafood and shark's fin (the symbol of significant affluence and insignificant flavour) dumpling in very fine chicken stock soup. Both serve bean curd rolls. Spring Villa's use many thin layers of smoked tofu for a more sophisticated effect. But Bayview Garden has a pretty classy pan-fried fish puff made from many layers of *kamoboko* (Japanese fish paste).

On balance, Bayview Garden's dim sum are slightly fresher and more interesting. Like its decor, which is Asian Deco: on some walls, a forest of verdigris bamboo stalks. A large room cleverly divided by pillars and great curving shapes, some in burled wood, others made from brushed aluminum with peekaboo holes in it.

Spring Villa and Bayview Garden both serve dim sum seven days a week. Weekends they start at 10 a.m. and serve dim sum till 4 p.m. To avoid lineups, get there before 11 a.m. or after 1:30 p.m.

Delis

Dunn's Famous Delicatessen

160 Adelaide Street West (Near University)
416 869-3866
Moderate. All major cards.
HOURS: All-day menu daily, 24 hours a day.
Open all holidays.
No wheelchair access. Licensed. Allergy aware.
Reservations recommended for lunch.

Indelicate Deli: Dunn's Famous Delicatessen of Ottawa has a Toronto branch plant (160 Adelaide Street West). Having fressed our fill, we're still trying to figure out what Dunn's is famous for. First came the matzoh ball soup. Had the chicken merely passed briefly over the pot, or was this a real chicken soup, as the waitperson claimed? If so, either the chicken had a problem, or roasted chicken bones were used in the soup, as opposed to whole raw chickens.

Then there was borscht. Mrs. Manishewitz has

nothing to fear from Dunn's version, which would be pleasantly mediocre if not for the ludicrous pile of not very hot potatoes (and butter!) on a plate beside it. Both of my grandmothers would often put a potato in the borscht—a sweet, warm, just boiled potato. To put a pile of aging potatoes on the side of borscht is a crime against Jewish cooking.

Dunn's serves passable blintzes and grease-laden latkes, as well as pleasant enough Montreal smoked meat sandwiches. Someone who did not grow up on the soothing pleasures of Jewish cooking might even enjoy it. Ignorance is bliss.

Katz's Delicatessen and Corned Beef Emporium

3300 Dufferin Street (At Lawrence)

416 782-1111

Cheap. All major cards.

HOURS: All-day menu 8:30 a.m.-10 p.m.

Closed Sun. Open major holidays.

Wheelchair accessible. Wine and draft beer only.

Allergy aware. Reservations not accepted.

My favourite ancestral holiday (thanks to both the latkes and the lights) is Hanukkah. It is the holiday that celebrates the ancient Jews' liberation from Greek

Dunn's

domination and the Jews' renewed religious freedom. Every religious holiday needs a symbol: Hanukkah's symbol is oil, to recall the miracle of the lamp. When the Jews recovered their destroyed temple and sought to re-dedicate it, they found only enough oil to burn the sacred eternal lamp for one day. While someone fleet of foot ran to get more oil, the sacred lamp inexplicably burned for eight days, until more oil arrived. Hence the eight days of Hanukkah, and our burning of eight candles to commemorate the miracle.

And hence Hanukkah's special food, latkes. Like Diogenes on his quest (also lamp-related), I have often gone in search of honest latkes (which are potato cakes fried in oodles of *oil*). Neither his quest nor mine was easy. Take, for example, Katz's Deli on Dufferin Street. This is a *haimische* Jewish restaurant.

Don't be fooled by the huge windows and the fuchsia and purple paint job. That's just like when my Boba got her hair dyed the same hair colour as the Queen of England. Katz's is still a nice Jewish deli, with a fancy-shmancy decorator. They make a pretty good corned beef sandwich (although not to hold a Hanukkah candle to the Montreal smoked meat at Center Street Deli in Thornhill). But the latkes at Katz's? *(Oy vay.)* My Boba would have turned over in her grave at the mere thought of those warmed-over grease-sodden patties. Feh!

Eastern Europe

Istria Taverna

303 King Street West (Near John)
416 598-5656
Moderate to expensive. All major cards.
HOURS: In summer, all-day menu
Sun.-Thurs. 12 noon-11 p.m.,
Fri.-Sat. 12 noon-1 a.m. In winter, all-day menu
Sun., Tues.-Thurs. 12 noon-10 p.m.,
Fri.-Sat. 12 noon-12 midnight.
Closed Christmas Day, Easter Sunday
and January 2-3.
Wheelchair accessible. Licensed. Allergy aware.

Before the country that was Yugoslavia cracked apart, it had quite wonderful food. Not a major cuisine though. A thousand years worth of assorted wars, insurrections and other political *Sturm und Drang*, with resulting food shortages, prevented the Balkans from becoming culinary heavy hitters like France and Italy. It takes both stability and a wealth of ingredients to develop sophisticated foodways.

Although limited by its political history, the former Yugoslavia enjoyed the fruits of both seacoast and agricultural interior. The result has been a simple, fresh market cuisine, full of exuberant, sharp flavours. As you get closer to Italy, the cooking of the former Yugoslavia becomes increasingly recognizable to Italophiles. Eating at Istria, the King Street West restaurant named for the Croatian peninsula that juts into the Adriatic Sea south of Trieste and Italy's eastern border, is thus an exercise in Italo-Balkan cultural cross-pollination.

From the antipasto to the palacinka, from the chevapcici to the tiramisu, Istria is an Italian experience spiked with influences from Dubrovnik to Vienna. The panoramic sweep of geography is met and raised by the prettiest bistro to open in Toronto in a long time: hand-painted flowered ceramic dishes sit on pine-slatted tables painted in bright colours. *Faux* mosaic pillars hold up the splendidly high ceiling. Light pours into the front of the restaurant through two glass garage doors, ready to open onto King Street during warm summer days and nights. Near the back, high on a brick wall, are the words BAR ISTRIA in scarified paint.

At first we are mystified by the food, which veers from the sublime to the ridiculous. One day there are superlative mussels barely stewed with crunchy vegetables, and grilled chicken breast so badly overcooked that maybe they forgot to take it off the stove from my brother's Bar Mitzvah. Another day there is mouth-watering chevapcici (grilled sausage of

Istria Taverna

lamb, pork and beef with sweet red pepper dip) and grilled red snapper that has been cooked long enough to qualify it for fossildom.

Is this the kitchen that grills oyster mushrooms so fast they melt? That makes a mean pizza with crispy crust and fine toppings? How do we make sense of sweet little grilled calamari dressed in balsamic vinegar and seafood salad made with powdery shrimp and scallops that taste as if they were already leftovers yesterday? How do we add up piquant pasta in tomato sauce with veal that resembles the Swiss steak of my college dorm (They tenderized dead cow with a machine that chewed it up.)?

The answer is economic. Money talks.

You can't sell a big piece of veal for $12.95 in downtown Toronto; pay rent, waiters and cooks; and stay in business. The same goes for a whole fresh fish and a seafood salad and the other items Istria sells for bargain prices. It's sensible to keep the price down on pizza and pasta and calamari and mussels, because the cost of making those foods is so low.

But a kitchen that dares to discount the high ticket items is in dangerous territory. Two choices present themselves. You can chintz on the basic ingredients. Use less than impeccable veal and seafood. Covering them up with great lashings of sauce (especially tomato sauce) sort of helps. But not a lot. The more challenging option is to buy the best, expensive ingredients and use them sparingly, in the French manner. Put a small piece of good veal on the plate, surrounded by lots of interesting vegetables. (Not very carefully fried eggplant and zucchini, à la Istria, wouldn't count.)

When Istria sticks to the peasant foods that its name suggests, all is well. You can't get a better grilled calamari or grilled sausage in Toronto, and the pizzas and pastas are also lovely. But if they're going to grill fish and anoint it with balsamic vinegar, peppers and onions, it had better be with reference to the other local outposts of the Adriatic that also do that.

Joso's and Sotto Sotto both cook in the Adriatic mode. Both charge at least 50 percent more for the grilled fish than Istria charges, but neither is taking the extra money to the bank in a wheelbarrow. It *costs* that much to buy the freshest fish, to absorb the cost of throwing it away if it goes unsold, to train and pay enough good cooks so that they're not babysitting five other entrées while your fish is overcooking—that is an expensive challenge.

Istria isn't in that league and it doesn't need to be. It is a perfectly charming, inexpensive downtown restaurant that would be brilliant if it knew its limits. Like most of us.

Istria Taverna

French

Arlequin Restaurant

134 Avenue Road (South of Davenport)

416 928-9521

Moderate to expensive. All major cards.

HOURS: Lunch Mon.-Sat. 11 a.m.-3 p.m.

Dinner Mon.-Sat. 5:30 p.m.-10 p.m.

Closed Sun. and major holidays.

Wheelchair accessible, except to washrooms.

Licensed. Allergy aware. Reservations

recommended for lunch, necessary for dinner.

Here is a cautionary tale of the times, with resonance to spare: in 1978, Robert Sidi opened Patachou, a French patisserie, at Bathurst and Eglinton. He used the traditional tools of the real French baker: butter, eggs, cream and the lightest touch this side of the Champs Elysées. The people (who are smarter than some restaurateurs think) could tell, and they flocked to Patachou, for the little almond paste tarts, for the croissants so flaky they melted to butter on the tongue, for the dangerous chocolate confections.

FRENCH

Success stuck to Robert Sidi like glue. Soon came a Patachou branch, in the food store block on Yonge Street south of the Summerhill liquor store. In 1984, in partnership with Jean-François Casari, a former hotel chef, he opened Arlequin, a restaurant of the Mediterranean, on Avenue Road at Davenport.

Arlequin prospered. It was a sweet, beautiful room: pinky coral walls festooned with harlequin masks and beautiful bunches of dried herbs and flowers, à la Provence. Robert had always said that 10 years in the business would be enough for him. He wanted to get out before he burned out; in April 1989, he sold his share of Arlequin to Jean-François and entered a joyous early retirement.

His days were filled with the pleasurable minutiae of family life—taking care of his children (then ages 5 and 14), doing carpentry around the house and at his cabin near Wiarton, travelling and playing with ideas about starting a design business.

The design business went nowhere and, by 1992, that's where Arlequin was going too. Jean-François had fallen very ill and was increasingly less able to manage the business; but there were additional factors contributing to Arlequin's troubles and those factors were painfully universal.

Business was just plain awful. Avenue Road and Davenport is a corner that distills what Toronto is, and was, about, in the 80s. Many interior designers are located near there. As Toronto's fortunes rose in the glitzy 80s, so their's rose. And thus prospered the services they bought—with restaurants, florists and bars enjoying their plastic sprees. The people running those services believed the bubble was forever and they forgot their thrifty ways.

Arlequin

Over-spending led to a heavier debt load. When the recession hit, the design business fell apart and the bubble burst at Ave and Dav. Restaurants dropped like flies. Jean-François sickened; at the same time his business was declining; the payments were too big to handle.

Many restaurateurs have gone down that road in the past few years. It usually leads to a dead end. But Robert Sidi (like Herbert Sonzogni at Babsi's) wasn't about to see his creation die, so he took the restaurant back from Jean-François and dedicated himself to its regeneration.

Robert spruced up the room to be a little lighter and less formal and he dropped the prices substantially. (Main courses at dinner now hover around the $15 mark.) A new chef put his straightforward, exuberant *imprimateur* on both the restaurant menu and the takeout counter. The theme is Mediterranean, but the flavours are much stronger and more vibrant than they had been for years.

Dinner is a carnival of great ideas, almost all executed with joie de vivre and skill. Sautéed shrimps (perfectly cooked) with tahini and designer greens. Awesome lentil soup scented with cumin, garlic and tomato. Polenta with melted cambozola and tomato basil sauce.

The main courses have that same Mediterranean colour and exuberance, each plate a riot of colour and flavour: spaghetti with many grilled vegetables. Rabbit braised with tomatoes, capers and fresh rosemary and served in a pretty little white casserole. Lamb grilled with olive paste, served with tabbouleh and sweet skinny frites. Fish and shellfish in a highly flavoured broth.

The desserts come from our old friend Patachou and

are still some of the best pastries in town. From blackcurrant mousse to apple tart with almond paste, this is quality baking à la française. And so a cautionary tale ends, not in bankruptcy, but in a man making his own good luck in the only way that happens, by blood, sweat and tears.

Auberge du Pommier

4150 Yonge Street (At York Mills)

416 222-2220

Expensive. All major cards.

HOURS: Lunch Mon.-Fri. 11 a.m.-2:30 p.m.

Dinner Mon.-Sat. 5 p.m.-10:30 p.m.

Closed Sun. and major holidays.

Partially wheelchair accessible (three steps to

main floor). Licensed. Allergy aware. Reservations

recommended; necessary on weekends.

If Toronto has one perfect restaurant for romantic trysts, that place is Auberge du Pommier, Peter Oliver's sentimental homage to the French country inn. From the big terra cotta floor tiles to the rough plaster walls, the Auberge whispers romance. Before Mr. Oliver lured French chef Jean Pierre Challet from the Founders Club, the restaurant was like a bad novel with a beautiful cover. Peter Oliver knew he had a problem: he went chef-hunting from Vancouver to Lyon and, finally, waited five months in 1994 while chef Challet served out his contract at the Founders Club in SkyDome.

Arlequin

Jean Pierre Challet came late to cooking. He was working in architecture in his dad's construction business in Lyon when he heard the call. Classical chef training was the logical next step, but chef Challet's background in building makes itself felt in every plate that comes from his kitchen.

Some chefs seek to reveal the essence of an ingredient. Michael Stadtländer, the wizard of Collingwood, is that breed of chef: he studies an ingredient, strips away all the extras and struggles to reveal its very essence to the eater, in the simplest possible manner. He is one extreme. Jean Pierre Challet is the other: his is the architectural school of cooking, wherein a chef takes an ingredient and literally *builds* on it.

The ingredient is the foundation, the starting point, for a statement that can be a high-rise confection, a multi-layered event, a symphony for full orchestra. If Challet were a bad cook, we would not even be having this discussion. I would dismiss him as a pretentious charlatan. But he's quite a nice cook, who simply needs a little bit of the simple.

If he worked for me, I'd sentence him to Collingwood for a month. (It's not that far.) I'd force him to absorb Michael Statdländer's dogma. He'd come back with shorter shopping lists and a longer attention span for the nature of things.

The man has promise, drive and skill. He just needs direction. Take, for example, the appetizers: goat cheese and sun-dried tomato ravioli and escargot potato canneloni with a creamed leek sauce. That's *one* appetizer! I can barely comprehend it on the page, let alone the plate. Or golden beet consommé with truffled grain-fed chicken wings and lemon boursault cream lasagna. Same problem: too many elements and not enough attention to the flavour of each individual ingredient. Nothing is bad. It's just too complicated.

We feel the same way about the main courses: great long lashings of prose go in winding curlecues around the main event. We get confused. Where, oh, where is the guinea fowl under marinated baby shiitake mushroms, sun-dried tomato pistou and puff pastry cross-hatching? We are tempted to send out a search party. A fat hunk of striped bass has been perfectly baked, but we are irritated by the fixings. The white beans under it are undercooked and the carrots under it are overcooked, but we think the ginger aioli is nice. Or is that the tahini we're tasting or maybe the shrimp flour?

We feel the same way about the lobster and the beef. Confused. Things aren't bad; they are merely un-straightforward. This tendency to over-build reaches orgiastic proportions with the desserts. Great foldings of phyllo surmount things, for no good reason. Gratinée of blood oranges garnished with basil ice cream filled with blood orange sorbet is a cautionary tale: the best French chefs would be content to serve the gratinée without the gewgaws. Their goal would be to find perfect fruit, cut it just before service for ultimate freshness and bathe it in the most silken light custard, which is barely gilded under flames before being whisked into the dining room. Huge spheres of bizarre sorbet are beside the point. We want M. Challet to make a more delicate custard, and to cut his fruit *à la minute*. Do less, but do more with it.

That is the anthem of Auberge du Pommier: less is more. Any fool can complicate matters, but it takes talent to simplify. Chef Challet shows glimmers: now he needs to make his final break with the world of building. He must revel in revealing rather than constructing. It's time to fall in love with naked food.

Bofinger Brasserie

1507 Yonge Street (At St. Clair)

416 923-2300

Expensive. All major cards.

HOURS: All-day menu Mon.-Thurs. 11:30 a.m.-11 p.m.,

Fri.-Sat. 11:30 a.m.-1 a.m., Sun. 12:30 p.m.-11 p.m.

Open most holidays, but closed Christmas Day.

Wheelchair accessible (by ramp). Licensed.

Allergy aware. Reservations recommended.

Peter Oliver is not a man of small moves. He is six foot four; he drives a large, aging Mercedes; and he owns five big restaurants (Oliver's, Oliver's Bistro, Bofinger, Auberge du Pommier and Jump). Bofinger opened in 1986. The next year Peter Oliver's daughter, then aged seven, got diabetes. In 1988, he hired a guy to run the company, and turned his own energy to diabetes fund-raising, full-time, for almost four years.

While Nero fiddled, Rome burned. Diabetes research prospered, but the food in the restaurants....

Mr. Oliver said: "I'm not satisfied with 75 percent. Before it might have been 75 percent. Before, I would hold back my criticism.... This guy was running the company. You can't just say the bread's not good enough or this dressing needs to change. You have to be there."

FRENCH

In 1993, Peter Oliver got back into the driver's seat. Bye bye paid manager, hello big gestures: "I'm 45 years old, and for the next five years I'm going to dedicate everything I've got to making the restaurants the best they can be. We've gone back and defined a vision for each restaurant for the 90s. Bofinger is a bar café, much hipper than it was, more contemporary, in terms of influences from Asia and California."

In 1994, Bofinger got a new sign, a new chef (formerly number three chef at the Royal York) and a slightly more open look. But it is still a remake of a Parisian brasserie (which, visually, is nothing to complain about). The green marble fireplace, the small white tiles, the stained glass, the belle époque paintings on the walls, the deco lights: this is *faux* at its most tasteful.

Monsieur Oliver has always been a master of *faux,* but it wasn't only on the walls. And he knows it. Having acknowledged that his restaurants were indeed performing only at "75 percent" in terms of food quality, Peter Oliver has decided to go for the brass ring, and not just on the chandeliers: "It's about the kind of chef you have, and the chef's commitment."

For an organization man like Peter Oliver, that has always been a hard nut to crack. The best chefs don't work for big, controlling corporate guys. They don't like working in a bureaucracy where their methods are scrutinized and controlled by senior managers. They are *artistes* who insist on buying what they want when they want, and using it how they want, without reference to formal decision-making systems.

Hiring chefs like that is a challenge for Peter Oliver. Keeping them is another *vide* chef Bob Bermann who was hired to revamp Oliver's Bistro but quit precipitously, having seen the inside of life in a large organization. But to Mr. Oliver's credit, he is struggling to accommodate the artist-chef.

The menu at Bofinger is living proof of that struggle. Mr. Oliver held his breath and jumped: the chef went hog wild. There are enough ingredients in the dinner menu to entertain a gross of epicures for a year.

Pancetta and goat cheese is a slab of smoked cheese wrapped in a lot of pancetta (like a birthday gift), with a whole bouquet of designer greens on top of it, under which is hiding some kasha salad, a purée of eggplant (off to the side) and sliced marinated tomatoes. That's one appetizer. There is also jerked shrimp (very nice) that are garnished with grilled cocount, banana and papaya salsa, rhubarb relish and more designer greens.

Order the grilled salmon and you get a bowl containing the salmon (perfectly cooked), pink peppercorns, pimento, asparagus, potatoes, corn and about seven other vegetables, all swimming in a beige broth. Agnolotti are stuffed with asparagus, sun-dried tomato, ricotta and corn. They are similarly garnished. Is this a bad trip? The duck breast, which is pleasantly sautéed, has puddles of black currant sauce, salad of grapefruit and lemon, designer greens and salsa made from wild rice, corn, red peppers and the kitchen sink.

At least it feels that way. This is a chef running amok, a monument to the folly of unbridled artistic freedom in a setting where a) the chef is untested at the helm and b) people pay money to eat. Some of the food at Bofinger is evidence that the chef is skilled and is the proud possessor of taste buds: his brie and parsnip soup is a velvet taste sensation (note the unusually small number of ingredients). His jerked shrimp are properly cooked and tasty. The salmon has fine flavours. He can roast a quail.

FRENCH

The french fries, which are dreadfully overcooked at lunch, are sweet and fresh at dinner, but perhaps chef takes a break at lunchtime. With the exception of shoe-leather pizza crust, at dinner there is evidence of a skilled hand whose wrist needs slapping. Has Mr. Oliver eaten every single dish on the Bofinger menu?

For he cannot but agree that the chef's shopping list needs emergency amputation. If that chef worked for me, I would make a rule that every dish on the menu (save the soup) is to have 75 percent fewer ingredients and garnishes. Today.

I would also get grumpy about the service. Everybody is trying hard (lots of smiles, very friendly) but some days dinner is fraught with delays, and one evening they bring our main courses while we're still eating appetizers. Too many people are waiting on one table (a waitperson, a runner, a maître d'), which creates confusion. We really don't need to be asked for our wine order three times and then have the mineral water forgotten.

As a work in progress, Bofinger is at an interesting stage. It has been roused from its torpor, but the tuning will tell.

Chapeau

2433 Yonge Street (North of Eglinton)

416 485-1041

Expensive. All major cards.

HOURS: Dinner Tues.-Sun. 5 p.m.-12 midnight.

Brunch Sun. 11 a.m.-3 p.m. Closed Mon.

Open major holidays.

No wheelchair access. Licensed. Allergy aware.

Reservations recommended.

A kitchen is the cruellest master in the world. It takes no prisoners. The best chef in the world is only as good as the salad cook in the cold kitchen whose inattention allows brown-edged radicchio to sneak onto one plate—yours. Superchef Paul Bocuse would sink like a stone if his lowly cooks on the line overcooked a piece of salmon.

And they do.

And that is why even a superb manager like Peter Oliver can't make a fine restaurant. He has been struggling to bring his restaurants—including the recently re-done Chapeau—up to serious gastro-standards. He has been putting money and effort into hiring real chefs. He has been trying a little bit of the Franco Prevedello formula (*vide* Centro, Splendido) wherein a chef becomes a stakeholder and therefore more committed to the excellence that produces positive financial outcomes.

Making Michael Bonacini his partner in the Jump

venture produced Peter Oliver's first good-tasting (as opposed to just good-looking) restaurant. He generalized from that experience and gave chef Bonacini a bigger chunk of the action to oversee: the food in the entire company.

Thus, when the upstairs at Oliver's was re-decorated in late 1994 and re-christened Chapeau, it was the Bonacini *imprimateur* that was to determine the direction of the kitchen. Peter Oliver chose Lili Sullivan (sous-chef at his Auberge du Pommier) to be Chapeau's chef; Michael Bonacini then trained her and her team and supervised the creation of Chapeau's new menu, which debuted at the end of 1994.

On the surface it's a sensible arrangement: a godfather, a young professional ready for her first kitchen and a facelift. Chapeau is very pretty, in the impeccable Peter Oliver mode: pale lemon, rough plaster walls, wood-burning fireplaces, supercomfy banquettes and cobalt blue lights. The menu is equally tasteful, *très* postmodern and full of flourishes.

But where, oh, where is chef Bonacini when we need him? Well, he could be at Jump or at Auberge du Pommier or at Oliver's downstairs or at Bofinger or, maybe, at Chapeau. But they've killed the goose that laid the golden egg. Michael Bonacini knows how to supervise one kitchen so that it puts out terrific food. So they promoted him to taking care of five of them.

The guy is only human. He has not yet perfected the art of being in two places at once and, until he does, the food at Peter Oliver's restaurants is still in trouble. This is the nature of the beast: in every superb restaurant that I know, the presiding chef (by definition both a cook and a team leader of some stature) still works hands on every night and works 14 hours every day, most of those

Chapeau

hours in the kitchen. It's never the same when the chef isn't there. The chef can show the cooks 50 times how to do something, but it will not be done exactly the right way—not every time—without the chef's eyes and hands ever present. Why is Lotus great? Because Susur Lee stands behind the stove every night.

This is not to suggest that Susur Lee is a better cook or a smarter team leader than Michael Bonacini. Susur too can only run the kitchen that he physically occupies. This limitation seems to be generic to the craft.

The second impediment to the taste of Chapeau's food is the physical law of inertia. It's very hard to stick even the greatest chef in an existing organization and expect the team to start playing by the new rules. It takes a very strong and impassioned leader to change how people work, and it takes a long time to change the habits of every cook in the kitchen, so that the back of the house has the necessary strength to make food visions happen. You don't just write a fancy new menu, practise it a while with Michael Bonacini and then open the door.

The food at Chapeau tastes precisely as one would expect under these circumstances: it varies wildly from not-very-good to showing promise. The so-called wilted spinach salad is so wilted and watery one is tempted to request a sponge to mop up. The house signature appetizer, smoked salmon brûlée (a savory takeoff on crème brûlée) is one of those interesting notions that has too little flavour and should have been euthanized after the second draft. We feel similar about the pumpkin-seed crusted goat cheese with many a garnish. Smoked pear sounds great on the page but is too weird on the tongue.

There is life in this kitchen: the hot and sour

shrimp and coconut soup is Thai fire and velvet. A lunchtime turkey breast sandwich with avocado and cambozola melt takes turkey to previously unimagined sybaritic heights.

The big main courses are equally inconsistent, which is not happy news when dinner for two is heading towards $80. At lunch we wish for a chainsaw to get through shoe-leather overcooked marlin. Crackling roast chicken could be more crackling and less cooked. Poached salmon piled high with a mountain of trout mousse and three butter sauces is *de trop* and overcooked. But the mustard-crusted perfectly pink rack of lamb is heaven-sent, with a large serving of oozingly buttery, rosemary-flavoured bread pudding.

Talent in the kitchen is the prerequisite for good food. Talent makes the splendid soft-style warm gingerbread cake with cooked apples and warm cider sabayon. Talent does a seductive cornbread pudding with berries. But something grittier and more powerful than talent is required to make sure nobody ever has to eat pumpkin ginger crème brûlée with a caramel roof so thick and hard it needs that chainsaw. That something is the finicky, demanding control freak—the omnipresent, know-it-all, see-it-all, do-it-all, long-term chef.

Gastro-Stars

Avalon

270 Adelaide Street West (At John)
416 979-9918
Expensive. All major cards.
HOURS: Dinner Mon.-Sat. 5:30 p.m.-10:30 p.m.,
Lunch Tues.-Fri. 11:30 a.m.-2 p.m.
Closed Sun. and major holidays.
No wheelchair access. Licensed. Allergy aware.
Reservations recommended.

Avalon: the word conjures dreams. Avalon sings of wishes and glory, of plans woven at 2 a.m. under a full moon. The word bespeaks fond hopes of getting it right.

All of which is logical: Chris McDonald never had his own restaurant before. The man had spent a decade readying himself for this. His chef résumé is impressive for both depth and breadth. Earlier in his career he cooked at Centro, and was chef at Santa Fe when it was delicious.

McDonald was chef at Massimo Rosticerria on Yonge Street when it opened in late 1990, and there (briefly) he produced some of the most authentic and excellent back-to-basics Italian cooking that Toronto has ever eaten. Inspired by the wood-roasted chicken at Zuni in San Francisco, McDonald bought a wood-fired rotisserie and used it to impeccable advantage at the Rosticerria.

Epicurean Toronto flocked to Massimo. Gastronomes genuflected before his Tuscan bread salad, his artichokes, the unctuous flesh of his chicken. But this triumph was short-lived. The owner changed the restaurant's orientation before it was three months old. McDonald fled. He spent almost two years cooking at a resort in Zihuatanejo, Mexico, and came home in 1993 talking tamales, seduced by ceviche. He then began to search for a restaurant of his own.

Meanwhile it was necessary to earn a living and keep his hand in at the stoves, so McDonald became a toque temp, a top gun for hire on a short-term basis. In late 1993, when Delisle Restaurant and Wine Bar owner Steve Campbell decided to get serious about food, he hired Chris McDonald to invent and implement a new menu. In the spring of 1994, Michael Bonacini and Peter Oliver were getting ready to open the summer terrace at their new restaurant Jump in Commerce Court. Seeking a zippy menu for the terrace, they hired McDonald to provide upscale Mexicana.

In 1995 his own moment arrived: McDonald rented the corner space at Adelaide and John streets. It had housed several restaurant failures, including Cocco Lezzone and KL Malaysia. McDonald brought his wood-fired rotisserie from the Rosticerria and opened Avalon on that corner. His menu is a small careful compendium of everything he holds dear about cooking.

McDonald's Italiana is as far from the pasta-and-tomato-sauce school of cookery as penguins are from parrots. There is no menu in Toronto quite like Avalon's, and it is not through fancy flourishes or oodles of gewgaws and garnishes that McDonald achieves uniqueness.

To wit, his opening lines at Avalon: as soon as you arrive, the friendly waitpeople bring the current McDonald signature spread: a smoky splendour of eggplant puréed with red pepper. It comes with house-made breadsticks, tailored for dipping. Finish that and the server brings sourdough baguette with sweet butter. Confess to liking the eggplant-pepper concoction and more of that arrives, even if you try to resist. We are putty in their hands.

Which is not to say McDonald is perfect. Risk-takers make mistakes. He does a ho-hum white bean soup, and the shrimp in the ceviche taste too cooked. We are also unhappy to be served an antipasto plate comprising slightly overcooked broccoli, roasted peppers and salt cod and potato salad.

Having gotten his errors out of the way, let us now praise Chris McDonald. Who else in Toronto would dare to make sauce of carrot broth (tamed to orange silk) for barely seared scallops with toothsome fresh artichoke hearts?

When McDonald roasts a chicken on his wood-fired rotisserie, all is well in the world. Crisp skin, melting juicy flesh and porcini gravy would be more than enough pleasure for one night. Add buttery mashed potatoes. I swoon. The man has a fair way with fowl. He braises duck leg until it becomes ungreasy tenderness and serves it with sweet red cabbage and lightly fried apple slices.

Who else dares cauliflower croquettes, deep-fried little nuggets of veg and crispness, which go splendidly with ascetic perfectly steamed salmon, whose sauce is a light lemon froth? His throwaway lines are small art, that which lesser cooks would fumble: braised endive is the attractively bitter Belgian endive cooked perfectly (until tender but not falling apart) and gentled by the sweetness of good brown stock. Creamed spinach is a nursery dream—perfectly cooked spinach with just enough cream to smooth its edges. His gnocchi are plump little pillows in a seductive sea of gorgonzola cream.

In the past, McDonald has followed the Italian tradition and been a dessert maven. (At Massimo's, cheese, fruit and biscotti were as good as it got.) But Avalon's desserts are divine. He caters to the sweet tooth without capitulating to the tiramisu generation. My personal favourite is the warm ricotta cake (the lightest cheesecake in these parts) with blood orange segments, tiny pieces of candied blood orange peel and a lace cookie studded with pine nuts. On the other hand, one could hardly ignore the warm flourless chocolate cake hiding in its cream robe and sitting in a pool of espresso *crème anglaise*. This is a dessert that probes the erotic potential of chocolate. For real grownups, McDonald serves room-temperature farmhouse cheeses—a restrained morbier and an oozing rich époisse. There is also perfectly poached pear with vanilla ice cream and superb biscotti. We are entranced. Can you tell?

Boba

90 Avenue Road (North of Bloor)

416 961-2622

Expensive. All major cards.

HOURS: Dinner daily 5:30 p.m.-10:30 p.m.

Closed major holidays.

Wheelchair accessible, except to men's washroom.

Licensed. Private party room available.

Allergy aware. Reservations necessary.

In the summer of 1994, when I found out that Barbara Gordon and Bob Bermann were seriously considering opening a new restaurant where Auberge Gavroche, L'Avenue and L'Entrecote used to be (not all at the same time), I was worried. Good people don't deserve to fail, and the location at 90 Avenue Road has been a killer. You know what they say in the restaurant business: three factors determine a restaurant's success: location, location and location.

The location at 90 Avenue Road is too far north of Bloor to benefit from pedestrian traffic and has no obvious parking. There is a lot behind the high-rise across the street, but you have to know it's there. I was afraid the Bermann/Gordon duo were cruising for a bruising, and after watching them struggle for survival on John Street since 1986, first as Beaujolais and then as The Avocado Club, I wanted success for them. The problem on John Street (I think) was another issue of location: they were only steps north of Queen Street, but being *off* the strip, and also on the second floor of a building, their restaurant suffered from location blues.

I don't know these people personally, but I've been following their cooking since Barbara opened La Cachette in Vancouver, where she cooked some of the best food in Canada. While running La Cachette, she took in (to her heart as well as her kitchen) a young apprentice chef named Bob Bermann. Together they moved to Toronto and opened Beaujolais in that nasty second floor warehouse space where The Cow Café and Stadtländer's had recently failed. At the time I figured that Barbara's move from the kitchen to the front of the house was designed to cede turf to Bob in his new role as Chef de Cuisine.

I was sorry about that. Bob is very fine cook, but Barbara is too. I longed for her amazing appetizers and for the stellar "duck two ways" from La Cachette. And there it was on the Boba Menu: duck "La Cachette." Barbara is back in the kitchen!

Boba opened at the end of 1994, with both Barbara and Bob in the kitchen. The hired hands out front could use a bit of a boost in the warmth department, but perhaps they are simply overwhelmed by the crowds.

Yes, I was wrong. Again. (I always thought Beaujolais and then The Avocado Club should do well, which didn't happen.) Getting a table at Boba isn't easy: they were mobbed from the get-go. And small wonder: redecorating has brought the already charming house at 90 Avenue Road into the 90s, with light and whimsy. The colours are lavender, yellow, green and blue, with vaguely oriental grace notes. And the menu is ambitious, with back-up, meaning they have both bright ideas and the ability to execute them.

Boba

Sautéed seafood cakes are what happened when crab cakes gave up fake crab and met real seafood. Chunks of scallops and shrimp are mixed with puréed fish in a light fried cake to be eaten with divine tarragon-scented tartar sauce. Barbara makes tasty vegetable sushi and serves them with barely seared tuna and steamed soy-flavoured rapini. The daily soups are long on flavour and short on cream. This is dangerously addictive food.

We find the main courses slightly less exciting than the appetizers, but still head and shoulders above most of what passes for fine food in this town. My favourite is duck "La Cachette," which Barbara used to call "duck two ways," in wise recognition of the different cooking requirements of the duck breast and leg. We are given the duck breast cooked rare, sliced and fanned out on the plate like an edible rose, with splendid plum wine sauce. The leg meat has been braised at length and formed into a small and wonderful edible edifice: the top layer is fried celery root in slices. Under it is purée of celery root (which is a sweet lovable winter vegetable) with tiny carrot chunks. And under it is the perfectly braised duck leg meat, in very good company indeed.

We are less than happy one evening with a bland gummy pasta dish, but find ourselves much mollified by great scads of crispy red onion rings on top of the filet mignon, which also arrives with glorious roast garlic bread pudding (ah, the comforts of winter). We would like the chicken to have been cooked slightly less, but this may be like finding little zits on the Mona Lisa, when you consider the pineapple black rice and the piquant vinegar sauce, reminiscent of points far East.

When dessert time comes, I counsel fortitude: resist the two big dessert plates (the grand dessert and chocolate blackout). Both are overwhelming. Less is more. Double chocolate paradise with double espresso sabayon gives all the kick a chocoholic needs. And then some. Neither mousse nor cake, it is chocolate velvet incarnate. Get a life. Get a chocolate life. At Boba.

Café Asia

370 King Street West

(Concourse level of Holiday Inn, at Peter)

416 408-2742

All major cards.

HOURS: Lunch Tues.-Fri. 12 noon-2:30 p.m.

Dinner Tues.-Sat. 5 p.m.-11 p.m.,

Sun. 5 p.m.-10 p.m.

Closed Mon. and major holidays.

Wheelchair accessible. Licensed. Allergy aware

(please call ahead to request customized dishes).

Reservations recommended.

It couldn't happen to two nicer guys. Andrew Chase and Camilo Costales have paid their dues. From 1989 until 1993 they slaved at the Berkeley Café, serving Thai food with an Italian accent. It made them loved but not wealthy: it's hard to make money on 22 seats (Berkeley Café had a 16–seat patio, so in the summer they had some pin money).

When their lease ran out and the rent went sky-high in 1993, Andrew and Camilo opened a new place: Pine

Boba

and Bamboo Grill on Yonge Street between Bloor and Davenport. That was a bad call on two counts: one, that strip of Yonge Street is restaurant hell. Two, their menu was ill conceived: the idea was half East (bamboo), half West (pine), to reflect the partners' ethnic origins (Costales is Filipino, Chase is from Boston). But the Chase/Costales team's strength is all in the East. They do not excel at European cooking: Asia is their spiritual home. Pine and Bamboo didn't make it and closed after less than a year.

And then along came a sugar daddy with deep pockets, although the route was roundabout: first the Holiday Inn at King and Peter streets hired Costales and Chase to manage their Matsura restaurant, because the restaurant's tenants had decamped and the hotel had gotten stuck running the restaurant. Then along came the backers (insisting on anonymity), who were enthralled by Chase and Costales' cooking, and wanted to give them great lashings of money to run a restaurant. So Costales and Chase leased the space from the Holiday Inn, with the backers' money. As Chase said: "We didn't come into this with a whole lot of money. So we can't lose. We can only win."

It couldn't happen to nicer guys or better cooks. Having been chastened by the abject failure of Pine and Bamboo Grill, the partners wisely decided to restrict themselves to the subject they know best: Oriental cuisine. Café Asia is Thai, Filipino, Japanese, Korean and Vietnamese, all filtered through the carefully exuberant Costales/Chase lens. The restaurant is absurdly huge, with 230 seats but broken into separate diverse rooms, each with its own decor and menu. From 22 seats to 230. Rather a leap.

In the grill room, you grill your own dinner,

Korean-style, on gas-fired grills in the centre of each table. The main dining room features the all-Asian menu, and in the sushi bar two young sushi chefs are learning to blend the art of traditional sushi with Chase/Costales PoMo notions.

The main dining room is a shadowed understatement in pale oak and fat bamboo, with a trans-Asiatic menu that ranges from the delicious to the astonishing: green mango salad with shrimp, (real) crab and crab roe and just a hint of coriander. Raw tuna in soy dressing with starfruit, white radish, kumquat and sesame for added dazzle. Juicy little tea-smoked quails, à la chinois. Thai raw beef salad with more than the average flavour. Steamed Thai-spiced fish sitting in velvet coconut custard. Duck liver is poached in Chinese wine and served sitting on a little "mat" of woven chives, so that it has the look of art and the texture of silk. Oyster mushrooms and tofu are steamed with seaweed and shrimp roe.

And the sushi! The execution is classic but the ideas take flight: there are handrolls of raw tuna (or cooked shrimp) with mango and basil. Raw salmon is wrapped on the outside of rolls with seaweed and rice in the middle. A dot of sea urchin roe sits on top of other rolls. Sesame seeds and rice form the outside of some rolls. All the fish is impeccably fresh.

Main courses have an equally splendid eastern range, from Indonesia (satay) to Japan (sushi, sashimi, noodle dinners, yakitori), Vietnam (incredibly moist and citric-scented grilled chicken) and Thailand (strong and smooth seafood curries garnished with the likes of deep-fried basil, toasted peanuts and starfruit).

In the grill room, a spare yet elegant place with oil-burning ceramic lamps and great brush-strokes of

Café Asia

burnt sienna on the walls, the specialty is Korean-style grilled dinners. In the middle of each table is a gas-fired grill on which you cook your own dinner. (Is this Palavrion revisited? No. Here you don't have to stand up to get your dinner.) You choose your main course—essentially chicken, assorted meat or seafood. The server turns on the gas grill and brings Korean appetizers (kimchee, the fiery cabbage pickle, chili-spiked daikon and greens and soy tofu).

Then comes a huge platter of raw fixings. There are oyster mushrooms and regular mushrooms, green onions and regular onions, zucchini and summer squash, sweet potato and sweet peppers. On the flesh front there is chicken in soy marinade, thin-sliced beef tongue, meaty beef ribs, steak, fresh fish, fresh squid and/or big fat shrimps. It's all raw and impeccably fresh, and you don't need to be Julia Child to cook it on the grill. Having grilled each item, you then dip it in sauce (sweet spicy marmalade for the tongue, sweet soy for all else) and then munch. Think of it as fun with chopsticks, a.k.a. East meets foodfest.

Jamie Kennedy
at the Museum

Royal Ontario Museum, 100 Queen's Park (At Bloor)

416 586-5578

Expensive. All major cards.

HOURS: Brunch Sun.-Thurs. 11:30 a.m.-4 p.m.,

Fri.-Sat. 11:30-3 p.m.

Dinner Fri.-Sat. 6:30 p.m.-10 p.m.

Closed major holidays.

Wheelchair accessible. Licensed. Allergy aware.

Reservations recommended.

To follow a chef whither he goest and strew roses in his path are my deepest pleasures. Do I struggle through snowstorms in the middle of nowhere (Collingwood area) to eat at Michael Stadtländer's farm? This guy doesn't even have a sign on his (unplowed) driveway, but still I go. Following Stadtländer's best friend Jamie Kennedy has been easier. The two were co-chefs at Scaramouche when it opened. Then, while Michael bounced from pillar to post, Jamie opened Palmerston and stayed put, save for a brief and unsatisfying interregnum at the Founders Club in Skydome.

When Jamie left Palmerston this fall to take over the restaurant at the Royal Ontario Museum, one could easily see why he had had enough. No matter what you put on the table at College and Palmerston, the people

Jamie Kennedy

who routinely spend $100 on dinner for two are not going to come. Money doesn't like College Street. Jamie lowered his prices and changed to a more bistro-style of cooking, but it was an uneasy balance. His cooking is too fine to survive slash and burn budgetary measures and Palmerston felt too serious for the bistro set.

Jamie Kennedy needed a new challenge and a more appropriate venue. The ROM needed better food in its very beautiful but heretofore inedible restaurant.

It is the duty of a real fan not only to follow the peregrinations of the chef, but to take his *oeuvre* seriously enough to notice its highs and lows. Mindless gushing is insufficient and should be mistrusted. A real fan cares about the chef's art enough to be his conscience.

Jamie Kennedy is still one of the best we've got in a white toque. His particular gift is to understand the nature of things and to reveal it. Woody Allen cooking (21 ingredients on a plate, with a description as long as your arm) is not his way. Culinary obfuscation was never his game. As one of the founders of Knives & Forks, the farmers and chefs' organization to promote organic foods, Kennedy laid his cards on the table: ingredients *matter.* Using local and organic ingredients is worth starting an organization. Jamie's art has been the splendour in simplicity, which can only be demonstrated by a chef in consummate control of technique.

A fan has to tell it like it is. Having explored the menu at J.K. ROM from soup to nuts and back again, we have found inconsistencies. The beef consommé is a soup no one could match—crystal-clear, bursting with flavour. But Jamie's cabbage borscht? He should have stayed off my Boba's ethnic turf, cause his borscht can't pack a punch. The curried baked squash soup is autumn incarnate, rich with flavour, but the parsley soup is only firing on one cylinder.

His pâté with celery root salad is splendiferous, a boozey velvet loaf. He makes a tart with the most delicate possible pastry and fills it with a veritable cloud of whipped Ontario goat cheese. One longs for more. He grills vegetables—perfectly—and serves them with tomato-flavoured risotto.

Jamie Kennedy is probably one of the five chefs in Toronto who does not overcook chicken: he grills a flattened chicken breast until it is just barely cooked, still oozing juices, and he serves it with a symphony of green delights: broccoli, fresh artichokes and wondrously bittersweet braised Belgian endive. The subtlety of the three green vegetables, each cooked differently, is set off by a small pool of cheese-flavoured beurre blanc. This is a grown-up painterly plate. Other chefs throw colours at a plate. Jamie Kennedy *thinks* before he makes a move.

But how can the man who did the chicken give us badly overcooked and sadly greasy, deep-fried fish with Moroccan spices? We are also lost in bewilderment when he overcooks guinea hen. The sauce is lots of fun, a play on the traditional coq au vin, with red wine, *lardons,* glazed baby onions and mushrooms. But was it a bad day for the maestro?

Excising the Moroccan fish from the menu and taking more care with daily specials will likely vastly reduce the possibility of bad days. For now the restaurant is open only for lunch daily, with brunch on Sundays. One need not be a Museum member to eat there, or even to pay the Museum entrance fee. Simply state you're there to dine and you are granted free entry to the Museum.

The room is very beautiful, possessed of a quiet

Jamie Kennedy

grandeur that befits its home. Burnt sienna marble tables and floor-to-ceiling windows bring in art and light. The maestro has an artful home and the fan is in the audience, exercising the scrutiny required of a true fan.

Lotus

96 Tecumseth Street (King and Bathurst)

416 504-7620

Expensive. All major cards.

HOURS: Tue.-Sat. 6 p.m.-10 p.m.

Closed Sun.-Mon., Christmas Eve, Christmas Day,

Boxing Day and New Year's Day.

No wheelchair access. Licensed. Allergy aware.

Reservations necessary.

Superlatives are dangerous. If I say that Susur Lee is *still* cooking the most interesting food in Toronto, then tomorrow he will be either out of business or out of fashion. But there is no getting around the scrumptious reality: in 1995 Susur Lee is the best chef in Toronto.

Susur Lee was born in Hong Kong, but was sadly deracinated there by a culinary apprenticeship that dwelt only on French cuisine, at Hong Kong's fancy, shmancy Peninsula Hotel. Then he came to Toronto and did time at the Westbury Hotel, Le Connaisseur, Le Trou Normand and Peter Pan, before opening Lotus in 1987.

In spite of his very orthodox continental cooking background, Susur Lee was an Occidental tourist. He is an Oriental, and his food at Lotus has always been an expression of his training as a conduit to his culinary roots. Hong Kong is more than a birthplace: it remains The Source.

So it is that Chinese and Japanese ingredients are prominent on Susur Lee's plates, but always overlaid on his strong French base. The combination is extremely winning.

East meets West in astonishing lobster ravioli—a perfect al dente pasta base holding a pile of very fresh lobster spiked with ginger, sitting on a pool of soy sauce with hot chili oil. He does classic lobster, scallop and shrimp gratin but, instead of putting the sweet flesh to sleep with cream, Susur Lee uses a mousseline of black bean, à la chinois, to awaken it.

This suggests that Susur Lee is an intellectual chef who builds ideas. He is, but in lesser hands those cross-cultural notions would turn out badly. Mr. Lee has the technique to support his fantasies. Witness perfectly cooked house-made spätzle (thread-like dumpling noodles of south German extraction) made entrancing with smoked tomato sauce, fresh straw mushrooms and corn, artichokes, capers and parmiggiano cheese. Or the tenderest pork tenderloin I have ever eaten, marinated in Chinese spices and served with Chinese ratatouille (which means stewed tomatoes wrapped in thinnest skin of sautéed baby Chinese eggplant), sweet-tart rhubarb compote and a splendid piquant sauce of apricots and mustard. This is cooking to sigh for.

Susur Lee uses organic ingredients whenever he can and makes many dishes without any dairy foods. Aside from his outrageous desserts, grand creations often involving gossamer pastries, wicked custard sauces and magical mousses, he includes the idea of health in his cooking. Fats are avoided. Sauces are bound and

Lotus

thickened with vegetable purées. This too is part of the Oriental idea of food being good from the inside out.

Dinner at Lotus is very expensive ($170 for two) and very slow: a two-hour event. The maestro will not be rushed. Service is less than obsequious. The room is small and rather plain, but warm, with Chinese scrolls, jars of preserves, a small glass oil lamp on each table. Calm reigns.

Mercer Street Grill

36 Mercer Street (King and John)
416 599-3399
Expensive. All major cards.
HOURS: Lunch Mon.-Fri. 11:45 a.m.-2 p.m.
Dinner daily 5:30 p.m.-10:30 p.m.
Closed some holidays.
Wheelchair accessible. Licensed. Allergy aware.
Reservations necessary.

Simon Bower found the funky little spot on Mercer Street almost a year before he opened the restaurant. It wasn't for rent. But he knew that *this* was the place for his next restaurant, so he pestered the owner, who was planning to do a little restaurant there himself. Each month, Simon Bower presented himself for a chat and, suddenly, after many months of pestering, the long narrow room across the street from Wayne Gretzky's was his.

Simon Bower owned the redoubtable Bowers on

GASTRO-STARS

Eglinton. Bowers had one of the most creative and delicious menus in town, but Simon Bower couldn't make it on Eglinton. The problem wasn't an absence of moneyed clientele, but perhaps an absence of imagination. On their part, not his. Of course Eglinton and Avenue Road is a veritable breeding ground of good taste, but the locals tend to play it safe when on home turf (egg salad and bagels at Yitz's) and migrate downtown for thrills. Bowers was the victim of geographic ennui: it was too interesting for its environs. It folded.

Simon Bower spent the interregnum travelling in Central America and re-charging his entrepreneurial batteries. Then, in late 1994, he opened Mercer Street Grill, with six *(six!)* coats of urethane on the hardwood floor and a cool but user-friendly 90s design courtesy of Richard Eppstadt (who also designed Rodney's Oyster Bar, Enoteca and Byzantium). The chefs are Gordon O'Neill and David Eaglesham, both of whom cooked at Bowers.

And here is Simon Bower at his most welcoming. His chefs have clearly waited for this moment too. Their menu is full of flights of fancy but also anchored by solid technique, with frequent reality checks. This is cooking that sees the imagination as a key tool, but exotica is never allowed to gang up on common sense. Each plate has no more ingredients than a normal person can understand.

The most wonderful starter is squid grilled so carefully it's fork-tender, with a hint of soy glaze, and thinnest egg noodles wrapped up, sushi style, with little vegetables in a *nori* (seaweed) casing. The flavours are subtly splendid. There are also knock-em-out fresh corn and scallion *pakoras* (deep-fried fritters) served with tangy green curry vinaigrette and a wonderful fruit relish. And braised duck (also perfectly cooked) with Chinese greens, tiny sweet scallops and Chinese broth flavoured with five spices and star anise. And Rodney's steamer clams with mussels. And daily soups like purée of red pepper or purée of beet garnished with sour cream with smoked salmon and dill.

This is a kitchen that sings, that dances, that knows how to turn vegetables into erotic moments. Their vegetarian main course is called Mekong vegetarian bundle with grass noodles in *chipotle* broth. Chipotle are smoked chilies. Mekong means the flavours are Vietnamese (think coriander and lemon grass). The bundles are crispy vegetables enclosed in al dente noodle purses tied up with scallions.

Fish is another strength: tuna is barely grilled, crusted with scallions, served with basmati rice topped with black sesame seeds and an almost-sauce scented with sweet black vinegar. Salmon is also perfectly cooked, with its heart left soft and wet, and glazed with ginger. It comes with wehani rice (a fragrant brown rice from California and my personal favourite grain) and baby bok choy.

The kitchen's only weakness is chicken, which is overcooked, as are the accompanying sweet potato fries. One could, however, make a meal of the eggplant and tomato marmalade on that plate, so full is it of the sweet, strong flavours of the harvest.

But perhaps the kitchen's finest hour is the steak. It may be very politically incorrect, but Mercer Street Grill makes a small steak so tender it melts in the mouth, so pretty with its cross-hatched grill marks, and flanked by sautéed shiitake mushrooms. As if that were not enough, between the steak and the herbed greens there is a small piece of flan hiding: flan? Ho hum. Not this flan. Thin layers of Yukon gold potato and shiitake mushroom sit in a buttery flaky pie crust, baked with just enough cream to bring strong gourmands to their knees.

The steak is the French connection. So many PoMo cooks go gaga for Thai/Ital/Cal, and they decide to throw national identity to the winds. They think it's just fine to mix gastro-metaphors and countries, throwing together Thai basil and cream, or lemon grass and butter. Mercer Street Grill gives each plate coherence and harmony, taking heed of how things fit together.

Michael Stadtländer at Eiginsinn Farm

R.R. 2, Singhampton (20 kilometres
from Collingwood)
519 922-3128
Expensive. Credit cards not accepted.
HOURS: Dinner daily, 7 p.m. Closed Christmas.
No wheelchair access. Not licensed—bring
own wine. Allergy aware (vegetarian meals
available). Reservations necessary.
Minimum of four per party.

Mercer Street Grill

We are cruel to our artists. In times like these (when some would say we need them most) we call our artists a luxury and refuse to support them. After all, we say, what do they produce? Do they create jobs or consumer products? Do they nourish the economy? No, just the imagination.

Of all things to sacrifice in troubled times, surely the imagination shouldn't top the list. Without imagination, we lose vision, and without vision, we drift. We stop asking important questions about who we are, where we're going, and why we're going there. We become robotic. Eat, sleep, work, reproduce, defecate.

Am I talking about pictures on gallery walls? Not only. I am talking about food, which does not usually come under the august heading of "art" in people's minds. Guess again. If art is defined as that which unwinds and stretches the imagination, that which broadens the mind to see different visions, then why can't food be art?

Alice Waters, whose Berkeley, California restaurant Chez Panisse is a holy destination for gourmands, didn't get her star status by being a great cook. She is a wonderful chef, but her special place in the gastronomical firmament is thanks to *vision*. Alice Waters gave America the radical notion that cooks should pay closer heed to where and how food is produced. She turned the locally produced organic ingredient into a gourmet food.

Alice Waters was the first North American restaurateur to hire a full-time forager to find those products for her restaurant. She was the first to send her chefs out to the farm to pick their vegetables, so they could first feel and then strengthen the connection between the earth and the eater. The theory is that both our stewardship of the earth and the taste of our food will improve when we finally figure out that connection.

GASTRO-STARS

Canada has somebody like Alice Waters too. His name is Michael Stadtländer.

The difference between Michael Stadtländer and Alice Waters is that she has business and marketing skills as well as being a visionary, and he probably couldn't sell Popsicles on a Florida beach.

But Stadtländer is that precious resource, an artist in the world of food. By artist I do not refer to his talent as a cook, although he has that aplenty. Rather, I mean his vision. For Stadtländer, putting a perfect multi-course meal on the table is second nature. The challenge and the excitement for him comes in the grounding of that meal in the earth. He has always, in his various restaurants, used as many organic and local ingredients as possible. But that was minor league compared to Stadtländer's current adventure.

In 1993, Michael Stadtländer and his wife Nobuyo bought a 100-acre farm on a back road near Singhampton, which is 20 minutes south of Collingwood and just under two hours northwest of Toronto (north of Shelburne). They serve multi-course dinners for $80 per person, and also have small bedrooms upstairs for the bed-and-breakfast trade.

You don't go visit Michael Stadtländer for the sole purpose of dining. Even if he is one of the five best cooks in Canada (which he is), one is hardly motivated to drive two hours and pay $200 a couple for dinner in a draughty farmhouse, with no sign out front to help you find it. It will be a wonderful dinner, and Michael has made his dining room into a thing of beauty, but you go for the vision.

You go for the picture, so rare in these times, of food as *connection* to the earth and to history, both past and future. Nobuyo brings the first course: a big clam shell cradles a barely warmed oyster that sits on a bed of delectable seaweed. Nobuyo's mother gathers the seaweed on the seashore of her Japanese island home. She salts it and sends it to her daughter, and Michael then seasons and serves it.

The next course is scallop soup served in a handmade ceramic bowl that sits on a small tangle of driftwood. The medium is the message: the sea is our supermarket and we are its stewards—or else. The sole light in the room is from candles mounted on huge fungi attached to crimson walls. Light flickers off the gilt-trimmed coloured clouds on the ceiling. Warmth comes from the maple logs burning in the stone fireplace.

Next comes roast quail wrapped in lemongrass, with ginger carrot sauce good enough to warrant plate-licking. Then Georgian Bay trout in a sauce of salmon and whitefish caviar, garnished with organic greens. Then an apricot sorbet served in an ice ring in which are imprisoned small pine cones and field grasses.

While we eat the sorbet, Michael comes forth from the kitchen and puts a rack of organic lamb (from a nearby farm) on the fire. When it's ready, we have the lamb with paper-thin curls of crispy baked butternut squash, squash purée, fried potato and marjoram cake, and a trademark terrific Stadtländer brown sauce.

For dessert there is his rum raisin ice cream on a maple hazelnut crisp with plums in syrup on the side, and afterwards little bites of Statdtländer's preserved summer fruit marinated in rum and wrapped in marzipan paste. Nobuyo serves tea from their silver pot, in Michael's grandparents' translucent china cups.

On the table the candles flicker in their holders: old mattress springs sitting on flat Georgian Bay rocks. Under the window there are nascent vegetable seedlings, which will be planted in the spring to produce food for this table in the fall. Out back are three hairy pigs of the wild boar variety, and Michael is planning the smokehouse for their future (their loss, our gain).

From Nobuyo's mother's seaweed to the marzipan fruit that Michael preserves every summer, a Stadtländer farm dinner is an opportunity to share his dream of going back to the land and going forward to a visionary gastronomy.

North 44

2537 Yonge Street (North of Eglinton)

416 487-4897

All major cards.

HOURS: Dinner Mon.-Sat. 5 p.m.-11 p.m.

Closed Sun. and most major holidays.

Wheelchair access to main floor. Licensed.

Two dinner rooms for private groups available.

Allergy aware (information on menu).

Reservations recommended.

North 44, Toronto's latitude, is the restaurant's logo, and an oft-repeated visual refrain. It sneaks up on you—the points of the compass etched in glass at the entrance, expensively etched in more glass separating the open kitchen from the restaurant. There it is again in the custom-made broadloom—in the middle of the stairs up to the wine bar where light meals are sold (including a fine pizza and some very grownup

Michael Stadtländer

144

sandwiches). And in the stone fragments that make up the tabletops (another custom item) in the bar. In the brass and stone mosaic floor of the entrance.

Everywhere you look there is another Design Statement. The message is metallic, modern, more L.A. than Toronto: huge copper frames on big windows. Copper and steel bannisters and metal mesh on the wine bar balcony. Angled tops to the backs of the chairs, and halogen lights eerily illuminating great glass flower vases from below, bouncing the light off the bevelled mirrors that are their backgrounds. Money. Big money. Not just eating in the restaurant but also in the making of it. Mark McEwan spent $1.5 million to open North 44. Even the washrooms have The Designer Touch: in the men's, black enamel urinals, huge polished steel sink, a hunting scene. In the women's all is pink and pretty with floral wallpaper and pink marble.

As for the food, Mark McEwan has never been better. This is a man in love with the basics and in possession of the technique to give superb ingredients their due. Any idiot with a cookbook and a souschef can churn out complicated food that tastes of everything and yet nothing. Call that artifice, not good cooking. But revealing the nature of ingredients—that takes an artist of the stoves.

Mark McEwan is that artist. His soups are distillates of pure flavour, served from silver tureens with a *soupçon* of pomp. Other appetizers burst with flavour. Calamari have been grilled with hair-trigger timing, unto succulent tenderness. Beef carpaccio is sweetened with the mellowest of onions; tuna carpaccio is a red slab that melts in the mouth; tortilla spring rolls are crisp and ungreasy; salmon is smoked over cherrywood curls to bring out its inherent sweetness;

gnocchi have just the hint of a sauce made from charred leeks, radicchio and gorgonzola. The pizzas (which can be bought as a main course in the wine bar upstairs) are a splendour in the bakery: crunchy yeasty crust with fresh rosemary, fat fresh oyster mushrooms and other pizza-friendly treats.

Main courses from the McEwan kitchen also carry that stamp of caring for the nature of things, the comprehension that to reveal is divine, to obfuscate is devilry. Mark McEwan knows texture and flavour like the cat knows mice. For example, pristine sweetbreads roasted to bring out their tenderness and delicacy, partnered with the thinnest of crispy sweet potato fries, spring asparagus with a touch of lemon beurre blanc and fresh oyster mushrooms. Calves liver treated with equal sensitivity, served with high-flavoured wild mushroom risotto and fragrant roasted garlic. Scallops charred very fast to keep their hearts soft, served with thin strands of vegetables "à la fettucine," and a light little throwaway line of a coconut lime sauce. McEwan's only false move is Caribbean seafood stew, wherein he deserts simple cooking and the flavours muddle.

The endnotes are in harmony with McEwan's vision: the dessert chef crunches up crêpes with hazelnuts and stacks them with apples. Lemon mousse is a citric cloud, caramel cream an erotic rendezvous between burnt sugar and butterfat. Wash all that down with the sweet tingle from a glass of Ontario Riesling B.A. from Cave Spring. Drink a toast to chef Mark McEwan, the master of North 44.

North 44

Otago

1995 Yonge Street (North of Davisville)
416 486-7060
Expensive. All major cards.
HOURS: In fall and winter, dinner Mon.-Sat.
5:30p.m.-10:30 p.m. In spring and summer,
dinner daily, 5:30 p.m.-10:30 p.m.
Closed major holidays.
No wheelchair access. Licensed. Allergy aware.
Reservations recommended.

Much ink was spilled. Superlatives not heard in several years were dragged out for the occasion. "The Anglo-French avant-garde.... desserts of formidable pedigree." Another writer gushed: "Go soon. Go often." Pity the hungry hounds with nought but the scrawniest of foxes. 'Tis true. When the recession hit hard, covering restaurants in Toronto was a sorry task, low on inspiration, high on depression.

Pathetically few interesting restaurants have opened in the last few years. With few exceptions, our restaurants are on wartime rations, tightening their belts and simplifying their menus. The paucity of beurre blanc and silken sauces is enough to drive a food writer to fantasy. And that's just what happened to them when Otago opened, in the premises of the former Avec on Yonge Street north of Davisville.

GASTRO-STARS

Like any good fantasy, this one is based on a germ of truth. Otago's owner, New Zealander Vaughan Chittock, is possessed of an ounce of technique and a pound of imagination. He dares combinations and permutations that haven't been seen in this town since they stopped shaving white truffles on fettucine. (That was at least five years ago.) Chef Chittock's excesses have occasioned orgasmic responses from desperately starved scribes. His menu reads like Escoffier crossed with Michael Stadtländer and then gilded.

Chittock trained in England under the legendary chef Albert Roux; one would have thus expected him to learn to mind his peas and q's, in the technical sense. Maybe it was Mr. Chittock's sojourn as souschef at Auberge du Pommier that caused gastro-amnesia (especially in the lobe of the brain that governs restraint). Clearly the man has taste. Instead of the usual stale soggy hogtown breadbasket, we are greeted by Ace Bakery focaccia and raisin bread (both superb) and a little bowl of addictive oven-dried grapes (a grape on its way to being a raisin).

The menu is full of splendid ideas. For example, lime-cured duck timbale over creamed rice with light soy sauce. Slices of rare duck breast are marinated in lime juice and fanned like flower petals, but they lie on a bed of cold hard rice in a decidedly un-creamy bath. Add a soy-flavoured vinaigrette and you have a botched attempt at nouvelle cuisine. Wild mushroom and chicken liver cannelloni have that same sophomoric feel—too many elements, too much ambition.

We get the influences, we read the references. When Paul Bocuse put a puff pastry cap on a bowl of soup, no one could fault the man for what was underneath; that's how he got away with pastry hyperbole. But

Otago

148

when chef Chittock puts a puff pastry roof on his quail and thyme casserole, we say, "A for effort, and how about holding back some of the cream in that sauce?"

It is clear from chef Chittock's work that he knows how to cook: his beef fillet is a carnivore's dream, red and juicy. His soups are strong flavoured and not too creamy. His desserts couple short buttery crusts with marvellous fruit confections. Some of his sauces are superb—the beef comes with a translucent brown sauce of fine flavour.

The salmon is mucked up with all manner of tomfoolery, but has a faultless lobster sauce. This dish is a case in point: here sits a piece of properly cooked salmon. Atop it is a roof of fried shredded potato. Around it, in the moat of perfect sauce, are arranged small, badly overcooked lobster claws. Add to that the little tray of sautéed vegetables. This isn't dinner— it's a hallucinogenic nightmare that would be more appropriate in a Coleridge poem than on one's plate.

Quick, someone, give this chef some limits. He is a dizzy artist who can't seem to stop himself from going over the top. Here's the ticket: make chef Chittock a rule that every dish needs to have 50 percent of its elements removed. In the salmon dish: amputate the potato roof, excise the overcooked lobster claws. The duck appetizer: ditch the soy sauce and the yucky rice. The paupiettes of sole on scrambled egg with morel and tarragon cream: pay attention to the fish so that it's not overcooked. Forget the eggs, which seem curdled. Don't bother with morels, 'cause they don't go.

The theory is simple. Pay very close attention to fewer elements and they will be better executed. If chef Chittock were a ham-handed idiot, this wouldn't be worth saying because his cooking would be no more interesting pared down. But this guy can cook. When he doesn't set himself ridiculous challenges, things work just fine. So quick, somebody, throw him a lifejacket: simplify Vaughan Chittock's plates before he drowns his talent in excess.

Sanona

325 Queen Street West (Between John and Peter)

416 595-5585

Expensive. All major cards.

HOURS: Lunch Mon.-Sat. 12 noon-3 p.m.

Dinner Thurs. 5 p.m.-11 p.m.,

Fri.-Sat. 5 p.m.-12 midnight.

Closed Sun. and major holidays.

Wheelchair accessible, except to washrooms.

Licensed. Allergy aware. Reservations

recommended.

I like genuflecting, and not being a particularly religious person, I bow at the feet of chefs. I am craven. Chefs satisfy more creature needs than deities. And they get around, which makes life interesting. The very first gastronomical book I ever read was called *Blue Trout and Black Truffles, The Peregrinations of An Epicure,* by Joseph Wechsberg. It was published in 1966, when Mr. Wechsberg was writing for *Gourmet* and *The New Yorker.*

Otago

In those days, when an epicure had peregrinations, that meant he (for most of them back then were "he's." They still wore the pants—and the pants had the credit cards in them) travelled around in search of gourmet experiences. To experience fine food, an epicure had to make journeys. They were lengthy; indeed, an epicure didn't casually go out to dinner, he drove hundreds of miles to Lyon or southwest France to worship at the shrine of an important chef.

The chefs didn't move. They put down roots, cultivated gardens, waited for orchards to bear fruit. They got to know local folk who would come regularly to the kitchen door with wild strawberries and forest mushrooms. Anglers brought them the same fish year after year, nearby farmers fattened pigs and made cheeses for them; the fruits they preserved and the wines they laid down kept company on dusty cellar shelves. It was a life of stability. When you ate their food, you ate history and craft and local initiative. You ate their cousin's farmhouse cheese, and their wife's fresh herbs, and their brother-in-law's loin of pork, etc., etc. You could almost taste those deep, interconnected roots and that was satisfying.

Today where we live, the opposite is true. We enjoy the thrill of the new. The chefs we bow down to don't get stale, because many of them don't stay put in one place long enough to gather moss.

And the champion is Greg Couillard. If Joseph Wechsberg were to write that book today, his epicurean peregrinations might be a way of describing a gourmand's relationship with Couillard. One would hardly bother keeping track of the man (let alone genuflecting) were he not an *original*. He was the first chef in these parts to apply western techniques and ingredients to Thai flavours, and for a long time he did it better than anybody else.

I follow Greg Couillard to every damn restaurant he opens because *nobody* makes Jamaican jump-up soup like he does. The compendium of sweet, sour, hot and sassy is a fireburst of flavour, uniquely Couillard. Nobody can paint tandoori marinade on a fat hunk of salmon and barbecue it to such succulent spicy perfection. And so we have followed Couillard to his various restaurants: Stelle, The Blue Room, Oceans, China Blues, Notorious, Avec, The New Avec and now Sanona. Couillard has, in a sense, come home. Sanona occupies his first restaurant space: he cooked first at Beggar's Banquet (later The Parrot) at 325 Queen Street West. Today that restaurant is Sanona.

Any resemblance between the cosy old Parrot and Sanona is purely geographic. Above Sanona hangs a huge sign: "SO HIP IT HURTS." Does that refer to the restaurant? The patrons? The Queen Street locale? Is anybody's tongue in their cheek? We're too unhip to know, but we begin to suspect the joke is on us one day at lunch when the maître d' (unshaven) saunters to the door to greet us (if you can call it that). We tell him we might like the window table, but wonder aloud if it will be draughty. He snorts with contempt and tells us haughtily that it's *never* draughty.

OK....

Funny then, 20 minutes later, when the front door sticks open for a while, producing arctic air. The maître d' doesn't notice. The diners two tables down finally get fed up and close the door. The service at Sanona is like that. So hip it hurts.

The food is Couillard, but sometimes he seems, well, tired. Is the spicemeister fed up with opening

Sanona

restaurants that don't last? Is he forlorn from too much loving and leaving? His food seems to speak that message. Some items are vintage Couillard: the jump-up soup is as vibrant as ever, the chicken 911 (rather like chieng mai chicken, in Thai spicy sauce) will still wake up tired taste buds. When he grills vegetables it's still a stellar event, and his potsticker dumplings would put any Chinese chef to shame.

But nonetheless the maestro is not at his best. We regret the pallid flavour of pho noodle soup Vietnamese style. We want the spicy steak to be more delicate, and why isn't the banzai tuna red in the middle? One day the tandoori salmon has marinade slapped on too thick, producing a spice 'n' slurp effect. And the osso buco with sage-scented ravioli is a pleasant item we'd be happy with in any normal restaurant. But Greg Couillard isn't just any normal good chef. He is the spicemeister, he is the artiste who can make East meet West the way angels meet dewdrops in the dawn. We want it, Greg. We want your best. We know it's there. And please... hold the Attitude.

Grande Luxe

Roof Restaurant
Park Plaza Hotel

Park Plaza Hotel, 4 Avenue Road (At Bloor)

416 924-5471

Expensive. All major cards.

HOURS: Dinner daily 6 p.m.-10:30 p.m.

Open major holidays.

Wheelchair accessible. Licensed. Allergy aware.

Reservations recommended.

Romance is a strange thing. Having been around the block once or twice, I have come to believe the romantic grand gesture to be oxymoronic. The only romance that's really romantic (as opposed to the Hallmark Card variety) comes in smallish doses, delivered daily, with love. By definition that sort of romance is not a grand gesture. Any cad can come up with a dozen long-stemmed red roses—it just takes a phone call to the florist. My valentine seldom bothers with the Hallmark form of romance. Instead he cherishes me daily, delivering yearlong valentines in the form of affection, kindness, fun and good cooking.

So we don't plan candlelight dinners in romantic restaurants. But those who do should reserve a table in the Roof Restaurant at the Park Plaza Hotel. This sweet little dining room overlooking downtown rises far above the Park Plaza's ground level record of pathetically bad food and service.

We're still mystified how the food downstairs in the Prince Arthur Room can be so ordinary while up on the 18th floor it's a heyday for both taste buds and sensibilities. The only clue is that the Roof has its own kitchen, physically isolated from the ground floor hotel kitchen and thus has its own "boutique" mentality that gives its chefs the freedom to strive for excellence.

Service is smooth as silk on the roof. Coats are whisked away, aperitifs brought, luxe wrapped around you like eiderdown by waiters wearing starched white shirts with taupe bow ties and suspenders, in quiet counterpoint to the dusty rose watered silk balloon blinds on those splendid huge windows. The room is lovely—small, elegant and blessed with that special, 18th-floor view.

The menu was at first very nervous-making: what usually happens when a dowager hotel plays with pesto and goat cheese and newfangled unpronounceable vegetables? Bad things happen. Rubber chicken kitchens don't understand wild mushroom risotto and Thai purple rice.

What a wonderful surprise then to dine at the Roof, where chances are being taken with mouth-watering results. Asparagus and wild mushroom tart is a superb combination of sautéed oyster and shiitake mushrooms

Roof Restaurant Park Plaza

with asparagus in a fine and buttery crust. Marinated shrimp in Asian pesto is splendid, perfectly cooked shrimp with piquant sesame-flavoured mayonnaise-style sauce. Lobster and truffle ravioli is chewy fresh pasta with chunks of the real thing inside, on a pool of limpid beurre blanc.

Grilled eggplant soup is a big risk with a big payoff. Eggplant is the vegetable that separates the cooks from the mere pretenders. When its unique needs are unmet, eggplant has the flavour of a wet bath sponge. It contains so much water that in order to have taste it first must be salted for an hour or so to bring out its water and then squeezed to dry. After that, eggplant needs either smoky grilling or high-temparature frying to bring out flavour. Can the Roof chef cut it? Like a hot knife through butter. His grilled eggplant soup is slightly smoky, full of flavour and low in fat to boot.

The main courses are equally entrancing. The chef's only false move is overcooking the steamed salmon, which is otherwise charming in a low-fat ginger and orange glaze. The chicken breast is perfectly cooked, stuffed with beautifully spicy goat cheese and sitting on pretty terrific wild mushroom risotto. Sea bass is properly cooked (another low-fat item) and garnished with charred sweet potato (good tasting, seasonally appropriate) and ancho chili ketchup. (Close your eyes and think of HP Sauce.) Carnivores will perhaps be happier with deeply garlicky rack of lamb that comes with spoonbread flavoured with Romano cheese and a fine translucent brown sauce.

The desserts at the Roof have definite aphrodisiac qualities. Serious chocolate fiends will need some of the dark chocolate cake as foreplay, and lovers of eggs and cream will swoon over the crème brûlée. The bread pudding, served warm, is not exactly unerotic either. Skip the cheeses. They are fridge cold and will thus do nothing for the gonads.

Truffles

Four Seasons Hotel

21 Avenue Road (North of Bloor)

416 964-0411

Expensive. All major cards.

HOURS: Dinner Mon.-Sat. 6 p.m.-11 p.m.

Closed Sun. Closed Boxing Day,

but open most other major holidays.

Wheelchair accessible. Licensed. Reservations

recommended Mon.-Thurs., necessary Fri.-Sat.

There is magic in a grand hotel. It contains mystery, and a delicious, almost dizzying freedom from the real world. There is the doorman, all tricked up in his footman-to-the-rich costume, and there is the door, magically opened for you. Here begins the fiction: we are even too pampered to open the door!

A drab or mediocre hotel would never support the drama, but an elegant one escalates it as soon as you enter the lobby. How? With carefully trained people and beautiful things that invite you to imagine yourself at home here amongst the grandeur. Giant bouquets of expensive flowers, custom carpets, every surface polished till it glitters, helpful smiling staff behind the desk. Eureka—luxe belongs to us.

Roof Restaurant Park Plaza

Then there is the anonymity factor. Sweep into the lobby and you can be anybody. Queen for a day. President of IBM. A foreign dignitary. You are who you pretend to be and no one's the wiser. The job of the staff in a great hotel is to ignore reality, support your chosen fantasy and pamper you accordingly.

This is the fresh context they create, which is why hotel dining rooms—the good ones—have a completely different feel from free-standing restaurants. In a free-standing restaurant, reality walks in the door with you. In fine hotel dining rooms, you jettison reality somewhere between the lobby and the entrance to the restaurant.

On a lot of days this is heaven. It surely goes a long way towards compensating for the often less-than-stellar cuisine of the hotel dining room. Even the best hotels have trouble producing food that's really fun to eat. Bureaucracy is the problem. Large organizations are the enemy of creativity and anathema to the sensuality that underpins great food.

The food and beverage manager might be great at managing a department, but when the yokel who's serving asks my (male) dining companion how *we're* doing, and then forgets to bring the mineral water, nobody gives a damn about the department. The executive chef may be a great cook but you can bet your copper bowl he didn't make the crème brûlée himself. And with many hundreds of dinners being served in the hotel daily, likely he didn't even *see* the nasty thing, with its soggy topping and overcooked custard.

But still and all, the Four Seasons is a great hotel. And its main dining room, Truffles, was renovated to the tune of a million dollars in 1993. It left the baroque behind and joined the twentieth century. There is no substitute for windows, and Truffles doesn't have them, but the space is light, and filled with the lovely output of local artists, in the usual Four Seasons manner.

The Four Seasons has also done its usual splendid job of menu planning, including its Alternative Cuisine choices, which are low in calories, cholesterol, sodium and fat. The buying power of the large hotel is felt in the superb collection of ingredients on the menu: here are the most pristine and varied designer greens in the city, many kinds of perfectly fresh fish, fresh morels, fresh fattened duck liver from Quebec and fresh Dungeness crab from BC. Fresh herbs galore adorn the plates. Money talks.

And it cooks too. Truffles serves dinner only, the recession having put paid to the expense account lunch trade. It's no trouble at all for two people to run up a $150 tab for dinner. The appetizers are the most elaborate in town, made with the best ingredients, and executed with great care.

There is snail and vegetable ravioli, exactly as it sounds with a perfection of small cut al dente vegetables freshening the earthiness of the snails. A little stew of asparagus and wild mushrooms (oyster, morel, portobello and shiitake), essence of a woodland spring. And for razzmatazz, a combo plate: three raw oysters with a crispy crunchy lobster and coriander spring roll.

Main courses are also big production numbers, the greatest ingredients mixed and matched with infinite variety, garnished with splendour. Sautéed lobster out of its shell, with basil green whipped potatoes, taro root chips and tomato lobster oil. Juicy veal tenderloin with sweetbreads glazed in lime and port. Rack of lamb, pink and pretty, with eggplant, zucchini and tomato, and a lacy little deep-fried potato cup cradling creamed garlic purée.

Truffles

Everything is very good, nothing startles. This is the product of the very best intentions, and the very best staff and facilities and ingredients that money can buy. What's missing are the high peaks and the low valleys that come from small artisans. The team will never have a really bad day, nor will it attain the artistic heights of the passionate chef/patron in his own kitchen.

It is in the desserts that the weakness of the corporate approach shows its hand most openly. There is that soggy crème brûlée, the unchocolatey chocolate pyramids, the banal apple cake and the cotton wool tarte tatin, the caramel mousse with no flavour and the personality of gelatin, and the scooby doo cookies, made much of by the waiter, that have the texture of cardboard.

In an owner-operated restaurant, the boss would not let those desserts leave the kitchen. Here at the Four Seasons we are surprised. This is the hotel where the french fries in the coffee shop come wrapped in damask. This is the hotel that never stops surprising us with its mastery of the pleasure principle. This is the hotel that breaks the rules about hotels. It needs to break a few more rules in the dining room.

Greek

Pan

516 Danforth Avenue (Between Logan and Carlaw)
416 466-8158
Moderate. All major cards.
HOURS: Lunch daily 12 noon-3:30 p.m.
Dinner daily 5 p.m.-1 a.m.
Closed major holidays.
Wheelchair accessible, except to washrooms.
Licensed. Allergy aware. Reservations necessary
for parties of more than six.

Pan opened in 1994 in a *grand mal* spasm of Hellenic hipness. My mother taught me early in life that a lady never wears black patent after Labour Day. That rule has gone the way of quiche and kiwi, but certain of Mom's strong principles stick with me. One trembles at the thought of Mom's response to the fashion choices of some of the waiters at Pan. The black leather vest is charming, hardware and all, but does he have to wear it with nothing underneath? Armpits are grand, but

GREEK

they don't go all that well with soup du jour.

The people who run Pan are likely too hip to care how I and my mom feel about issues like armpits. And indeed they don't need to, if the current state of business is an indicator. The Danforth is so starved for Greek food of quality that people line up to eat at Pan, which serves the best Greek food Toronto has ever known. And at Danforth prices. Praise be the kitchen gods.

The area around Danforth and Logan, where Pan is located, is a carnival of casual restaurants, all Greek, all festive and fun, with tables spilling onto the sidewalk in the manner of tavernas on a cobbled street in Crete. And like their forebears in Greece, the restaurants on the Danforth tend to specialize in overcooked meat. No extra charge for grease.

Pan breaks the mould.

The executive chef is Laura Prentice. (No, she isn't Greek.) Ms. Prentice divides her time between The New Avec (former perch of Greg Couillard) and Pan. She cooks four nights a week at Pan. What Pan and The New Avec have in common is their owner: John Katsuras (a.k.a. Johhny K.) has owned a succession of restaurants and nightclubs in Toronto for almost two decades. He first owned Johnny K in the Beach, later The Liberty on Church Street and then a series of clubs. Mr. Katsuras has not until now opened a restaurant that expressed his Greek heritage.

Pan is Johnny K.'s culinary homecoming, done with heart and soul. Between his knowledge of the delights of the authentic Greek kitchen, and Laura Prentice's respect for the nature of ingredients, they make a delicious team.

Other chefs are content to buy their phyllo dough. Laura Prentice rolls out her own phyllo dough (plain

Pan

for the spanakopita, chocolate-flavoured for the baklava). It's unorthodox, thicker than it should be, but so tender and buttery that all we want is more. Her salad of artichokes and potatoes is sublime: fresh artichoke hearts and new potatoes are cooked to order and served warm, dressed in lemon sauce.

Ms. Prentice stuffs squid with olives, feta and tomato salsa, to superb affect (without overcooking the squid). She poaches mussels in broth scented with lemon and spinach. Her tzatziki (pressed yogurt and cucumber dip) is a 10-megaton bomb of creamy garlic.

The Pan main courses begin with a bow to tradition. Say goodbye to tired, old, overcooked lamb and greasy roast potatoes. Pan's braised lamb with dandelion and avgolemono (egg lemon sauce), with roasted potatoes and vegetables is a superb re-make. The lamb is pink and pretty, the avgolemeno is light and the roasted vegetables are a late summer rainbow, *sans* grease. The shrimp with garlic, lemon, feta and spinach orso (rice-shaped pasta) are slightly overcooked but in such a delicate sauce that all is forgiven.

Swordfish is wrapped in grape leaves and grilled. Rainbow trout is made fragrant with a stuffing of onions and raisins, and it comes with splendid mashed potatoes flecked with black olives.

For dessert there is the aforementioned chocolate baklava (unorthodox and not entirely successful but rich) and hearty *galactobouriko,* the classic Greek confection made from phyllo pastry rolled around cream of wheat custard. Dinner at Pan will cost less than $60 for two, including pleasant Greek wine. That and its kitchen make it both at home on the Danforth and out of this world.

Indian

Cuisine of India

5222 Yonge Street (North York City Centre)
416 229-0377
Moderate. All major cards.
HOURS: Lunch 11:30 a.m.-2:30 p.m. Dinner
5:30 p.m.-10:30 p.m. Closed Christmas Day.
Wheelchair accessible. Licensed. Allergy aware.
Reservations recommended.

The other day I was eating greasy dim sum on Dundas
Street with my friend Margie (she thought it was good),
and the subject of Indian food came up. Margie hates
Indian food. But being a generous person, she didn't
leave it at that. She said: "If I didn't have to eat curry, I
could go to an Indian restaurant."

Now there's an open mind. And I have found the
perfect Indian restaurant for the woman who hates
Indian food; Cuisine of India, in the nether reaches of
North York, can convert the staunchest curry-hater.

A lot of the time, Margie is right about Indian food. I
wouldn't give a pinch of stale curry powder for most of

INDIAN

Toronto's Indian restaurants, and I am a curry lover. Most are purveyors of look-alike curries that have been sitting on the stove all day under a roof of grease. Appetizing. Some profess to offer traditional Indian tandoori dishes, which have been petrified via assiduous overcooking. Was this the food of the maharajahs?

Not bloody likely.

For a rare taste of Indian food as it was cooked in the times (and places) when there were people paid to do nothing but grind fresh spices all day, go to Cuisine of India. It's a strange restaurant, possessed of some elegance, but usually crowded and not blessed with good service. But while you wait—for water, for wine, for bread—it's wonderful watching the tandoori chef practise his craft behind glass walls.

The tandoor is a barrel-shaped oven made of clay and fired with charcoal. The tandoori chef pats balls of bread dough into small circles and then slaps them onto the sides of the tandoor for cooking. Once taken from the oven, each bread, called a nan, is brushed with melted butter and served hot and flaky.

The superb nan goes rather well with tandoori mahi, a whole fish also cooked in the tandoor. A fresh salmon trout is threaded on a long skewer and cooked so fast (in the tandoor) that it arrives sizzling, with completely blackened skin. Our hearts sink. Has this fish been cooked or incinerated? But breach the creature's flesh with a fork, lo and behold, it's pink and moist, cooked until barely done. On the tandoori platter with it is a colourful tangle of raw julienne of onion, beets, carrot and red cabbage.

Also from the tandoor and its precise chef come the classic tandoori chicken, marinated in yogurt and spices, other fine meat items and an unfortunate tandoori shrimp that is both overcooked and covered in spicy white goop.

Other than the strange shrimp, Cuisine of India's kitchen is almost flawless. There are the standard Indian deep fried appetizers (samosas and pakoras) but additionally an edible artifice called chaat papri: supercrisp flaky pastry rounds about the size of a quarter are smothered in lightly minted yogurt mixed with a sweet/tart tamarind chutney. The mulligatawny soup has its customary rough edges smoothed with coconut and cream. The curries, each an individual response to the food it's built on, are a splendour of fresh ginger, onion, cardamom and, often, tomato.

To cool the palate there is raita (yogurt with cucumber) and divine kachumber, a salad made from small chunks of tomato, cucumber and onion lightly spiked with fresh coriander and ginger. A large dinner for two will cost $50. If it was good enough for the maharajahs, it's good enough for me.

Kebab House Restaurant

1409 Gerrard Street East (At Coxwell)

416 466-8242

Cheap. Visa and Mastercard.

HOURS: Open daily 11:30 a.m.-11 p.m..

Open major holidays.

No wheelchair access. Not licensed.

Not allergy aware. Reservations not necessary.

Are you tired of designer water? Is the ubiquitous presence of goat cheese and roasted red peppers on fashionable menus beginning to seem repetitive? Would you like a break from the halogen and high ceiling school of decor?

Try the Kebab House, on Gerrard Street East in Little India. This is the antidote to creeping epicureanism. This is the restaurant with four tables (gray formica) and a counter, where the water comes from the tap to you in plastic juice jugs. Some days the waiter remembers to put plates on the table. Some days you have to remind him. If he's not too busy, you'll get most of your food at the same time. Kebab House is not the home of serious pampering. But when dinner for two is costing $30, one doesn't complain.

On busy days the progression of dinner is unpredictable. You can count on the (always delicous) soup coming first. If they have soup that day. Then the chef behind the counter reaches into the charcoal-fired tandoor and pulls out a long skewer of spiced minced beef *(seekh kebab),* whose aroma is surpassed only by its complex flavour.

More delights cometh from the tandoor—in no particular order. You might get your raita and your rice 15 minutes after the rest of the meal. From the tandoor: *boti tikka,* chunks of very tender beef. Chicken tandoor, a classic commonly cooked so far ahead that it attains an advanced state of mummification. At Kebab House the tandoori chicken comes to you directly from the tandoor, only slightly overcooked and reeking of the most wondrous spices.

At some point in your dinner, (according to no apparent scheme) they bring your nan. Nan is to the Indian subcontinent what the baguette is to France. Both are farinaceous national anthems; both have been degraded by modern technology in aid of mass production. There are few pleasures more sensuous than the consumption of a proper baguette or nan, with simple accompaniments. And there are few proper baguettes and nans.

Like baguettes, traditional nans require a specific sort of oven little used today. Nan, a flatbread whose home is the Punjab, must be cooked immediately before consumption in a tandoor, an earthenware or clay oven preferably heated by charcoal. At Kebab House they do it in the traditional manner: a traditional nan is still a lump of dough sitting on a tray when you order it. The cook then pats the dough into a flat sphere and bakes it briefly over very hot coals in the tandoor. While it bakes the dough puffs, browns and crisps. It arrives at the table hot from the tandoor, alternately crisp and soft in all the right places, one of the great breads of the world.

INDIAN

In addition to the tandoor, which sends forth enough smoke to make Kebab House resemble an eastern bazaar with street food in full swing, foods emanate from the kitchen where a woman in an ornate sari and a man in a Sikh turban work over a small stove in a kitchen that most of us would call cramped. From thence come splendid curries of chicken and goat. The curries, and indeed all the stewed foods at Kebab House, are at the same time greasy and wonderful—full of complex and carefully balanced flavours.

Channa (chick-peas in curry-like sauce) is sprinkled with fresh coriander. Okra is stewed with tomato and onion and spices to great greasy effect. The lentils in dahl stay whole and are sauced with distinction.

The emphasis on meat and the total avoidance of pork are part of the dietary laws of Muslims. The Kebab House chef is a Muslim from Pakistan, and the restaurant's owners are Sikhs from India. Their collective culinary tradition is Punjabi, from the region of northern India and eastern Pakistan known as the granary of the Indian subcontinent. Hence the perfect nan.

Punjab cooking also relies heavily on milk, for which fact we are grateful at dessert time at Kebab House. To make *ras malai,* the careful cook must cook and stir a great deal of milk with sugar and a little bit of cardamom for a long time, until the milk boils down into a light eggless custard. Punjabi rice pudding involves the same laborious technique, minus the cardamom, with rice and almonds in the milk. It's the dessert that makes tiramisu look like child's play.

Italian

Acqua Ristorante & Bar

BCE Place, 10 Front Street West (At Yonge)
416 368-7171
Expensive. All major cards.
HOURS: Lunch, dinner Mon.-Fri. 12 noon-1 a.m.
Dinner Sat. 5 p.m.-1 a.m. (Kitchen open
until 11:30 p.m.)
Closed Sun. and all statutory holidays.
Wheelchair accessible. Licensed.
Allergy aware (dishes customized on request).
Reservations recommended.

Acqua opened in the spring of 1994 in BCE Place, under the soaring atrium and since the end of its very first week of life, the kitchen has experienced a revolving door of chefs. And that's not the half of it.

ITALIAN

The very week that Franco Prevedello opened the restaurant, Gatserelia Design sent out a very nervous press release announcing that they had taken over Acqua's design from Yabu Pushelberg at the eleventh hour, and at that point undertaken "a major redesign."

Perhaps the fact that not one but two Very Important Design Firms created Acqua goes a certain distance to explaining why it verges on overkill. All is, as usual for Franco, in the best possible taste. Oxblood leather chairs (designer style), pale yellow damask table linens with a fat white stripe, fine tableware, much marble.

The theme, Acqua, is all around. Water, water, everywhere. Portholes peek into the kitchen. Water cascades from brushed aluminum porpoises down a marble wall. Over the bar is an arched blue ceiling with wavelets of recessed lighting cut into it. All the lines—walls, ceilings, bar—undulate like oceans. The entrance is a glass wall with see-through bottles (almost all Grappa—*firewater*)—on glass shelves. Wrought iron sculptures are waves and sea fronds.

Above the dining room, brightly coloured jibsails flutter in the air-conditioned breeze. Around it, protecting it from the BCE Place concourse, Venetian lagoon pilings stand guard, multi-coloured and speaking of canals. But the air-conditioned breeze on those jibsails is too fierce and sitting under it is windy. The fact that the dining room juts into the BCE Place concourse makes it very like an open trattoria in a Venetian piazza, but we aren't comfy cosy.

The effect is startling and entertaining; Acqua is the most sophisticated theme restaurant outside California. It will never be comfy cosy, but then, neither are the 90s.

When Franco opened Centro, he said that trying to

get it up and running smoothly was like riding a wild horse. Acqua is 10 wild horses. One evening they seat us at this table under the sails where it's so windy that we are instantly shivering. Even the tablecloth is blowin' in the wind. We ask to move. They move us. Five minutes later they seat another couple at that table. The woman shivers. The man beckons the waitperson. They move. Three minutes after that, another hapless couple is ushered to the windy table. (We have an excellent vantage point.) Couple number three moves. I make a joke to our waitperson about the windy table. She pretends not to hear me. Less than five minutes after that, they seat couple number four at the unfortunate table. But things are different this time. Both members of couple number four are wearing quite heavy sweaters. They stay put.

And the moral of the story is that Franco's not always there. When he is, all the tastes perk up, and Acqua's Italian trattoria flavours are lively and fresh. The gnocchi are little clouds, the pizza has an impeccable cracker-crisp crust, the veal is tender, the mashed potatoes properly lumpy and rich. They make a wickedly creamy risotto, with changing daily flavours. They make magic with fish, searing fat filets of sea bass till it barely flakes and sitting them on sweet red pepper purée, with sautéed yellow and red peppers like gems in it.

Franco's menus do not set the world on fire. He is a classic nouvelle Italian, which is a relief. His heart is in the trattoria, not the Thai travelogue that too many chefs mistake for quality cooking and his feet are on the ground, walking the floor, working late to make it better. Acqua is the most interesting work in progress in town.

Bar Italia

584 College Street (Near Bathurst)

416 535-3621

Cheap. Visa.

HOURS: All-day menu daily 8 a.m.-1 a.m.

Closed Christmas Day, New Year's Day

and Easter Sunday.

Wheelchair accessible. Licensed. Allergy aware.

Reservations not necessary.

Italian Renaissance, Take Two: before the uptown fast-track appropriated Italian food, the strip of College Street near Clinton was Little Italy. Epicures under 40 (and those not reared in Hogtown) probably think that roasted red peppers were invented at Centro. But north Toronto is the johnny-come-lately. Toronto learned to eat Italian on College Street, and it all began at Capriccio.

Amidst the grey torpor that was 50s Toronto, Capriccio shone. It was a beacon of sensuality, a second floor exploratorium of the ethnic. Remember now: prior to the sexual revolution (circa 1967), candles in Chianti bottles, red wine and spaghetti were one of the very few ways to get laid. Capriccio had it all—the dark mystery, the ethnicity and pretty good tomato sauce besides.

As Capriccio went, so went College Street. Young Italians on the way up deserted Little Italy, trading their roots for monster homes in Woodbridge. As Italian money moved north, newer immigrants took over

College Street. It became a polyglot: Italian, Portuguese, Vietnamese and Filipino. Capriccio lost its lustre as its clientele left the neighbourhood. The food became mediocre, the furniture gathered dust.

Little Italy lost its taste buds, except from 1984 to 1989 when Andrew Milne-Allan (ex-Beggars Banquet) was doing his customarily superb cooking at Trattoria Giancarlo. Milne-Allan's partner there was Giancarlo Carnevale (more on him follows). The silent partner in that venture was a small man named Eugene Barone, who ran Milk, Nuts & Things, the variety store on College at Clinton. Milk, Nuts was no ordinary variety store: it was beloved for the Sunday New York Times and good coffee beans.

And Eugene Barone never gave it all up for Woodbridge. He used the money from Milk, Nuts to buy Bar Italia in 1988, the down-at-heels pool hall a few doors away. In 1990 he hired Andrew Milne-Allan to make a kitchen and a menu at Bar Italia. The result is a *non-pareil* hangout. Where else can you play pool and munch on a crunchy sandwich of prosciutto, bocconcini, tomato, basil, roasted peppers and arugula? Or sip lemon lentil soup while ogling some very artsy folks shoot pool?

Caro

1404 Yonge Street (At St. Clair)

416 969-8571

Moderate. All major cards.

HOURS: Lunch Tues.-Thurs. 12 noon-2:30 p.m.

Dinner Tues.-Thurs. 6 p.m.-10 p.m.,

Fri.-Sat. 6 p.m.-10:30 p.m.

Closed Sun.-Mon. and major holidays.

Wheelchair accessible, except to washrooms.

Licensed. Allergy aware. Reservations

recommended for Fridays and Saturdays.

There is a theory (held by some, including myself) that you can tell a lot about a restaurant by who's eating there. Call it Urban Sociology 101. This theory sounds like unbridled snobbery, but its only defence is its accuracy. Poor folks can't afford expensive haircuts, clothes or restaurants. Money eats well. The people with the good taste are, in general, the people with the good bank accounts, the good haircuts and the good wardrobes.

It's easy to figure out where the upper crust dines when it's on display. See them strut their feathers at Centro, Splendido, North 44 and Scaramouche. But when a bird of bright plumage isn't either mating or deal-making, where does it go to eat? Surely not chez le Big Mac? And (perhaps even more interesting) what does it wear?

Caro

For the answer to both these questions, check out Caro on a Saturday night. Caro, on Yonge Street south of St. Clair, is the scion of Il Monello and apparently the place where Rosedale unbuttons its stuffed shirt. Plenty of baggy jeans and not-too-trendy wardrobe items are there. Clearly, Saturday night is the time when power lunchers rebel against the rules of dress-for-success. Why, it's kind of sweet to see all these upscale folks looking so downright dowdy. Kind of like the Queen walking her corgis at Balmoral.

And what do the other .01 percent eat when they're not power dining? North 44 this ain't. Caro is upmarket Italo-Yuppie comfort food. It is never less than pleasant and rarely much more than that. But reliable. Competent. No surprises.

Pizzas and pastas are soothing in their pleasantness. One can hardly go wrong with the likes of shrimp, basil and tomato, or spinach with ricotta. The chef understands cream soups (another ultimate comfort food): his are glowing with flavour and based on good chicken stock with lots of fine vegetables. His goat cheese soufflé, flecked with fresh greens and encircled with oak leaves in a vaguely curry-scented vinaigrette, is the star of the Caro menu. It is cheesy and yet light and strong with flavour.

Given Caro's close relationship with Il Monello (where perfectly grilled fish is the raison d'être), we can't understand why the fish is overcooked at Caro. Grilled either Cajun or Italian style (in herbed olive oil), its flesh cries out for less time on the fire.

We are also upset by Caro's veal meatloaf. Meatloaf is dangerous. Too many chefs are shipwrecked on the shoals of "mom food." Mom food may be trendy, but it is not easy. Food writers eulogize mom food like crazy, but the truth is that most moms' meat loaf (and shepherd's pie and rice pudding and apple pie) was awful. Mom doesn't make it any more because she hated it too. Mom likely wouldn't like Caro's brown, overcooked, flavourless meatloaf any better than her own. Even the spicy mushroom sauce on top can't save it.

Given its proclivity for comfort foods, Caro needs a meatloaf recipe. The 72 Market Street Meatloaf, from the *New Basics Cookbook,* is probably the best meatloaf in the world. That meatloaf, served with mashed potatoes and a Cookstown Greens salad, would perhaps bring all of Rosedale to the door on a Saturday night. Perhaps they would even bring their moms.

Centro Grill and Wine Bar

2472 Yonge Street (Near Eglinton)

416 483-2211

Expensive. All major cards.

HOURS: Dinner Mon.-Sat. 5 p.m.-11:30 p.m.

Open most major holidays.

Wheelchair accessible. Licensed. Allergy aware.

Reservations recommended.

Franco Prevedello did not become the godfather of half a dozen important Toronto restaurants by accident. Men of grand vision are not common in the restaurant business. His vision for Centro was a piazza in the Italian Veneto, the region where he grew up. And there it is: fluted granite in grey and salmon outside; 18-foot ceilings in the dining room; with fat white columns, oxblood leather armchairs and Rosenthal china; on walls the colour of a raspberry milkshake, magnificent colour blowups of Franco's hometown, Asolo: a grandeur of vision.

The physical space is the creation of an artist. Other people camouflage their waiter stations with formica. Franco used a slab of marble. Other restaurateurs buy glasses. Franco's tumblers are squared off crystal gems. Other restaurateurs do not spend a year in work boots and jeans sweating on their renovations. Franco did. He spent blood, sweat and $2 million on dreamlike art deco indirect lighting, on etched glass—the profile of an Italian hill town—for the mezzanine, on the most exciting Italian wine cellar in Toronto, on huge skylights recessed in midnight blue wells, on bevelled mirrors and a wood-fired pizza oven.

Chef Marc Thuet and maître d' Tony Longo each own a piece of the action at Centro, but Franco is in the driver's seat, and the knife-edge service reflects his vigilance. There is no such thing as a bad dinner at Centro. It is not the finest food in the city, but few mistakes are made. The kitchen maintains an even keel, serving the classics of the new Italian cooking—meat, fowl and fish in simple and robust sauces, flavours painted with broad strokes, good pasta.

Centro is larger than life and it is one of Toronto's most important bistros. The man who built Biffi and Pronto and was godfather (i.e., landlord, father-figure and consultant) to Le Gourmet, Trappers and Grano is probably the only man in Toronto who could pull off a splendid stunt like Centro. He smoothes out the corners and rounds off the rough edges. How? By not being too important to stand by the dishwasher.

College Street Bar

574 College Street (Near Bathurst)

416 533-2417

Moderate. Visa and Mastercard.

HOURS: Brunch Sat.-Sun. 11 a.m.-3 p.m.

Dinner daily 4:30 p.m.-1:30 a.m.

Closed Christmas Day.

No wheelchair access. Licensed. Allergy aware.

Reservations not necessary.

While Eugene Barone was working on Bar Italia, his partner Giancarlo from Trattoria Giancarlo was opening the College Street Bar just down the street. Giancarlo has a former souschef of Milne-Allan's working for him and a menu in the Milne-Allan mould. This is the new College Street: a minimalist bar/café. Over the bar hangs sculptural black wire with halogen spots. On the menu is the PoMo Italian lexicon.

Grilled fresh sardines drizzled with extra virgin. Chick-pea and pasta in classy chicken broth. Polenta with porcini. Olives sautéed (!) with celery, onions, thyme and chilies. Swell. Linguini with mussels and white wine. Credible risotto with roasted red pepper purée, for a mere $8.50. And of course tiramisu for dessert. The College Street Bar is made for penniless but epicurean Italophiles who can tolerate cigarette smoke and service so laid back it almost disappears.

College Street Bar

Commisso Fine Foods

28 Roytec Road (Near Weston Road, north of
Highway 7, south of Langstaff Road), Woodbridge
905 856-3663
Moderate. Visa.
HOURS: All-day menu Sun.-Thurs.
11 a.m.-12 midnight, Fri.-Sat. 11 a.m.-1 a.m.
Closed Chirstmas Day and New Year's Day.
Wheelchair accessible. Licensed. Allergy aware.
Reservations not necessary.

I have been upbraided—in the epistolary sense—by an irate gastronome in the suburbs. This gentleman (for I presume he is such) writes to say that contrary to my oft-stated opinion, the 'burbs are more—not less—civilized than downtown. He is almost convincing. For example, the parking: he says that in the boonies you can always find a parking spot in front of the restaurant, and it's free. He further refers to traffic jams downtown, unsafe streets, bad air and bad attitude. Of course none of those plague the suburbs.

My correspondent goes on to strew superlatives on the epicurean efforts of the 'burbs. He says it's not just the parking that's better north of the 401. That's where he and I part company. There isn't much out there that can give Centro a run for its money.

ITALIAN

But I have seen the light and it is called Commisso Fine Foods. In Woodbridge. A foreign land. This is where Italian-Canadians go when they feel cramped downtown and can afford 5,000 square feet of marble and mirror. And where do they stop in for a pizza or some gelato and a cappuccino after dinner? Commisso Fine Foods.

Commisso is a food hall. Downtown you'd go broke in a hurry dreaming food in technicolour like this. A huge room is broken up into different spaces: there is the bakery corner, where they sell olive bread and crusty baguettes and wonderful chewy cornbread. The pasta freezer, with things farinaceous, both stuffed and otherwise. The gelato counter, full of frozen sweets, adjacent to the bakery. The giftware area ($150 chrome espresso pots, a design statement for the 90s).

And the two sweet little sitdown restaurant areas, which feel *exactly* like something you'd find in a back street of Florence or Rome. The tables are of dark wood, and a dark young waiter saunters over to place stiff white damask placemats on them. There are huge glasses of slightly tannic house red, the cheap fun stuff you'd get in Italy.

But this is no back street *boîte*. Here we have Italian Design, PoMo style. Welcome to Splendido north: from the high ceiling dangle giant triangles, squares and circles in red, green, yellow and blue. A harlequin pattern in green, burnt sienna and peach runs like a frieze high on the walls. The ceilings are burnt sienna and peach, lit by the light from tall windows.

This is a restaurant for everyone who would rather be in Italy. Pre-kids, pre-killer mortgage, pre-middle age, we used to travel to Venice. Now we travel to Woodbridge. Like most of the good restaurants in Italy, Commisso is completely informal. The waiters move at some unrevealed inner pace and all matters are taken casually. Save for one: cooking.

At lunch there are antipasti available that bring back the takeaway food shops of old Bologna: fresh artichokes barely braised, roasted spring fennel, fresh salmon and swordfish cooked in lemon juice and sliced thin, huge oyster mushrooms marinated with yellow peppers, multi-layered eggplant parmigiana, perfectly grilled eggplant in olive oil, fresh crabmeat, piquant squid salad, divine "torta di patate" (a potato loaf), purée of chicken *en gelée,* and more. I have also enjoyed very light gnocchi in tomato cream sauce, creamy broccoli soup, your classic veal sandwiches and credible osso buco. Finish with a double espresso to fortify yourself for the afternoon's labours.

In the evening, there is table service that marches to that special Italian beat and, in addition to the antipasto splendours, a full menu is available. Skip the high ticket items. Keep to the basics: Commisso bakes some of the best pizza west of the Mediterranean Sea. The absolute is Number 31, pizza trifolata, a pristine white affair, unsullied by both tomato sauce and cheese, a simple statement of thin and crisp (but never cracker-like) crust topped with olive oil, marinated mushrooms, onions and garlic.

The kitchen's third strength lies in the pasta department: feathery gnocchi, thin spaghetti with toasted whole garlic cloves and fresh basil leaves, spirals with fresh porcini. These are the noodles of my dreams, the darlings of every Italophile.

Da Dante

3353 Yonge Street (North of Lawrence)

416 486-2288

Moderate. All major cards.

HOURS: Lunch Mon.-Sat. 12 noon-2:30 p.m.

Dinner Mon.-Sat. 5:30 p.m.-10:30 p.m.

Closed Sun. and major holidays.

Wheelchair accessible, except to washrooms.

Licensed. Allergy aware. Reservations

recommended.

Breeding tells. Not only in the sense of one's own social position being determined by one's parents, but also in the sense that by the time your hair has turned to grey, you are to a certain extent the creature you have bred. The face in the mirror tells more stories of who you are than of what you were given. This is good news for people inclined to hard work and perseverance.

It's easy to find people who work hard in the restaurant business, but most of them are young. Restaurants burn people out. The long hours, the night work, the alcohol and the illusions play hell with marriages and families. The result is a lack of stability that produces lower standards: relative beginners don't do things as well as seasoned veterans. Long service has not bred cooking into their bones.

Da Dante

How often do we eat a meal cooked by a chef who's been wearing the white toque for 50 years? Dante Rota is that man.

His father was a *sommelier* (wine steward) in London, England, where Dante was born in 1930. When war broke out, his mother, who was Italian, took young Dante home to her parents' village, Subine, near Turin in northern Italy. After the war, in 1946, when Dante was 16, he went back to London and took up a trade: cooking. He began in the kitchen of a men's club.

The day he turned 18 he was called up to fulfill his military obligation as a British subject. Dante Rota served his king for two years as a cook in the Royal Air Force. Having been honourably discharged, whisk in hand and toque on head, he set out to conquer the culinary world. And did.

Dante cooked successfully in London for 19 years, during which time he and his wife, Rina (whom he had met while she and her parents were living in Subine), raised two boys, Marco and Carlo. In 1980 the Rotas came to Toronto and Dante became executive chef of the then-august Windsor Arms Hotel. When Dante left the Windsor Arms in 1985, he bought Noodles restaurant from the hotel and began to run it himself. A combination of factors (the beginning of the recession, an out-moded concept), brought Noodles to the brink of bankruptcy, and Dante bailed out in December 1990.

When Dante and Rina opened their own little restaurant, Da Dante, all those years of finding out what works and what doesn't, and all that hard work that is Dante's history, went into one small room. Da Dante is the repository of the Rota family's dreams. You can smell their commitment. It smells like the sharp sweetness of balsamic vinegar smoothed by the velvet of extra virgin olive oil, the bite of garlic tamed by the absorptive charms of rice and pasta.

There's only one way for a family to survive 50 years in the restaurant business: they're all in it together. Dante and Rina are the chefs. He's 66 and she's 61. Their work day begins at 10 a.m. and ends around midnight, six days a week. On Sundays they imitate vegetables. Son Carlo waits tables at Orso two nights a week, and spends the rest of his time working the room at Da Dante. Son Marco helps sometimes. His wife Leslie waits tables at Da Dante two or three nights a week. Leslie's cousin makes the apple flan and the amaretto pound cake for the restaurant.

It's hard to imagine that a restaurant with this pedigree could be anything but wonderful. Small touches reveal and recall Dante Rota's past as the head honcho of what was then one of Toronto's finest kitchens, the Windsor Arms: his fried calamari crackle like glass, so crisp and ungreasy. His thin pizza is a triumph of the bread baker's craft, in its flavour and crunch.

The menu is small—as it should be if you want to eat food that has been cooked, not thawed. There are strong soups and superb grilled vegetable antipasti, splendid cooked-to-order risotto and robust pasta dishes. For dessert, there are the aforementioned daughter-in-law's cousin's excellent patisserie, but nothing equals Rina Rota's gossamer tiramisu. Inhale it.

Da Dante

Gio's Italian Food

2070 Yonge Street (South of Eglinton)

416 932-2306

Moderate. All major cards.

HOURS: Dinner Mon.-Sat. 5 p.m.-11 p.m.

Closed Sun. and major holidays.

Wheelchair accessible, except to washrooms.

Beer and wine only. Allergy aware.

Reservations not accepted.

In another life (before the small children and the big mortgage) we were travellers. We frequented the museums and streetscapes of Europe, but I was in it for the restaurants. Travel is broadening: I took that literally. If food is love, then every museum was intensely aphrodisiac, inducing prodigious hunger. Consuming culture was good, because one had to do something between meals. And I always managed to squeeze one museum or gallery into a hectic day's schedule of cafés and restaurants.

Some travellers read the guidebooks to Great Sights or Important Art. Some don't read at all. I read up on where to eat. Anyone who thinks that reading gastro-guides is for lightweights ought to try cross-referencing three different guidebooks on the subject of the same city, with the goal of finding a perfect place to dine tonight. Whom to believe? *Gault Millau* oozes praise for

ITALIAN

Restaurant X, the *Michelin Red Guide* dismisses it with one curt phrase and *Fodor's* likes it.

The farther south you go in Europe, the easier the task becomes, simply because there are fewer of everything. The tourist in Florence is faced with the challenge of choosing from overwhelming options. The tourist in Bari (in southern Italy) faces the challenge (so the hotel concièrge told us) of getting to and from the only two interesting restaurants in town *sans* rendezvous with a purse-snatcher.

Travelling in southern Italy is like that. At first blush this is not an appetizing prospect. But once we had the method figured out (all jewellery off, eliminate purses, off city streets after dark), southern Italy became home to dazzling gastro-adventures.

Critics are gaga over northern Italian food, but I have eaten much better in the south. From Rome north, Italian food is fraught with dissembling. Too many temporarily brain-dead tourists (This is costing a fortune so it must be fun.) have schooled northern Italian restaurateurs in the art of the quick buck. From factory-made tortellini to frozen tiramisu, they do it all for you— in the mass market manner. This is not to say that *all* northern Italian restaurants have renounced their roots. There is still great food, but you have to know where to find it and you pay megabucks once you get there.

In southern Italy, the people retain their connection to the land. Neither industry not tourism has arrived to rescue them from their roots. Every time a southern Italian makes a meal, that connection is reaffirmed. If this is November, they're eating wild mushrooms and the very last of this year's fresh figs. The fishermen are still netting baby squid, the farm women make their fresh cheeses every day and they're still picking rapini

Gio's

in their gardens. These are the foods they eat at home and these are the foods they sell in restaurants.

Truck-ripened tomatoes and kiwis like cardboard would never appear on a southern Italian menu, because of the people's religious fervour about their local products. People from one village enjoy shouting matches with people from neighbouring villages over the relative quality of each other's sausages. Or olives. Or farmhouse cheeses. By definition, local means seasonal means fresh. Means uncomplicated and full of flavour.

And in Toronto, means Gio's, a southern Italian restaurant on Yonge Street south of Eglinton.

Gio and Marilena Rana are both from southern Italy, she from Abruzzi and he from Bari. They sometimes have shouting matches about which place is better, even though both came to Canada as small children. Their first restaurant was Gio's in The Beaches, where they hung up a four-foot pink plaster and wire nose in lieu of a sign, and then spent the next two years (early 1989 till late 1990) fighting all the way to the Supreme Court for the giant schnozz's right to protrude a few millimetres on public property.

The Supreme Court ruled in Gio's favor, but he and Marilena were tired of fighting by then. They took the nose down, closed the restaurant and went off to southern Italy. But they realized, said Gio, that "Canada is my country now," and came home, dusted off the nose and put it up in front of a tiny room on Yonge Street. No sign. Just the nose.

Gio's is an authentically southern Italian restaurant: grungy, unadorned, informal, with shoot-from-the-hip flavour. The nondecor of Gio's includes 30 seats (all different), tables covered in various cheap plastic tablecloths, and a kitsch chandelier garnished with plastic fruit. On the walls is low culture bric-à-brac: pasta packages, espresso machines, old black and white film photos, Brio bottles. There's no marble here.

At the front of the restaurant, behind a chest-high plywood barrier, Gio's cousin Rosa Caporusso presides over the stoves—two ancient domestic four-burner models. She and Gio make everything there, except for the restaurant's sole dessert (torta de la casa), which is made by Marilena's mother-in-law (when she's in the mood).

The menu is southern Italian, offering four small courses, ridiculously priced at $3.95 to $5.95 each. You begin with antipasto: mixed antipasto, sweet little calamari sifted with flour and pan-fried or spicy sausage fried in bread dough with tomato sauce. There are superb fresh artichokes breaded and fried, with tomato sauce. Then you have a *primi:* pasta with robust tomato sauce or maybe rapini and anchovy. The portions are small. You go on. To *secondi* of meat or fish. Gio does a splendid chicken with lentils, an honest stew of shark, shrimp, mussel and clam in tomato sauce, and credible veal with sun-dried tomatoes. Then there is *contorni,* a simple salad. And after than comes *dolci:* Mama's torta, sponge cake layered with proper pastry cream and then soaked in anisette and rum.

Dinner for two costs $40 if you eat a lot. Gio and Marilena are yelling down the length of the room: *un espresso per la signora.* All is well in Toronto's very own outpost of Abruzzi. Or is it Bari?

Gio's

Giovanna Trattoria

637 College Street (Near Bathurst)

416 538-2098

Moderate. All major cards.

HOURS: All-day menu Mon.-Fri. 11:30 a.m.-11 p.m.

Dinner Sat.-Sun. 5 p.m.-12 midnight.

Closed major holidays.

Wheelchair accessible. Licensed. Allergy aware.

Reservations necessary on weekends.

Across the street from the College Street Bar, Bar Italia and Capriccio is Giovanna Trattoria. Giovanna owned (and controlled the kitchen of) Masaniello when it opened. Her sensibilities are Italian traditional, robust and honest. Giovanna is the most comfortable and the least artistic of the new College Street restaurants. She eschews minimalism for white tablecloths, great bunches of both fresh and dried flowers and an Italian menu that reads ordinary but eats extraordinary.

The mixed appetizer platter is a gargantuan bouquet of superlative vegetables: eggplant marinated, eggplant roasted with cheese, grilled marinated zucchini, mushrooms, red peppers and much more. Giovanna does great credit to every pasta she attempts (Fettucine Natasha is a high point, with barely cooked smoked salmon and just enough cream to be sinful), but her specialty is the divine chicken panzanella. She stuffs fresh rosemary under the chicken's skin, roasts it briefly, and serves it on a bed of Tuscan bread salad (bread, red onion, tomato, extra virgin, wine vinegar).

Mediterraneo

2075 Yonge Street (South of Eglinton)

416 322-0161

Moderate. All major cards.

HOURS: All-day menu Mon.-Fri. 12 noon-11 p.m.

Dinner Sat.-Sun. 5 p.m.-11 p.m.

Closed major holidays.

Wheelchair accessible, except to washrooms.

Licensed. Allergy aware.

Reservations recommended.

Italian restaurants in Toronto have changed substantively over the past five years. Even as late as 1990, the available Italian restaurants broke down into two clear types: the neighbourhood spaghetti parlour that had added tortellini alla panna to its repertoire, but was still a spaghetti parlour, and the upmarket anglicized Italian restaurant like Centro. Neighbourhood Italian restaurants were either pathetically narrow in range (a.k.a. spaghetti parlours) or they charged too much money and tried to serve 16-ounce veal chops, à la Centro.

But thanks to the recession (which rendered the 16-ounce veal chop all but obsolete, thank goodness) people are turning to their neighbourhood restaurants for a quality dining experience, and good Italian

Giovanna

cooking is appearing in neighbourhoods that are about as Italian as my Boba's borscht.

Vide Mediterraneo, in the Eglinton/Yonge/Mount Pleasant area. Mediterraneo is big and airy, with glass garage doors that open to let in Yonge Street (which is not, just below Eglinton, kissin' cousin to Piazzo San Marco). But indoors, Mediterraneo pays fitting homage to its namesake, with terra cotta tile floor and sponge-painted burnt umber walls.

After one ghastly lunch at Mediterraneo (gummy gnocchi and jawbreaker pizza with a hard crust and much too much gooey cheese) I was ready to write it off. But that must have been chef's afternoon off, for subsequent dinners at Mediterraneo have been fraught with flavour. Grilled calamari are tender and just slightly smoky. Orechiette con broccoli are a southern Italian specialty—little pasta ears bathed in emerald purée of broccoli and sprinkled with aged provolone. Risotto is made with crispy little asparagus tips and wild mushrooms and needs only three more minutes of cooking to be perfect.

Our only edible complaint is the house antipasto, which is a greasy collection of not-very-interesting items. And the waitpeople: the service at Mediterraneo is appalling; they deliver the food, but no cutlery. Wild gesticulating is the only way to get a fork. One could always use fingers, but this ain't Medieval Times. Heaven forbid you should need something during the course of eating: nobody visits the table to inquire. And on departure, should you have to squeeze past two waitpeople who are happily chatting at the bar (and blocking your way), that doesn't seem to bother anybody. If I were the chef at Mediterraneo, I'd be throwing pots—at the waiters.

Pazzo's Restaurant and Café

505 College Street (At Palmerston)

416 921-9909

Moderate. Visa and American Express.

HOURS: All-day menu daily 11 a.m.-12 midnight.

Open major holidays.

No wheelchair access. Licensed. Allergy aware

(options on menu). Reservations not accepted.

Although technically east of Little Italy (on College Street at Palmerston), Pazzo's is a contributor to the Italian Renaissance of College Street. This is a tiny room, defiantly plain save for a blown-up fragment of Michelangelo's Sistine Chapel ceiling on one wall. The menu is your usual yuppified Italian (from bruschetta to tiramisu).

I have found Pazzo's pasta pallid, the antipasti good-looking but carelessly cooked and, as for the daily soup, they passed the chicken over the pot but not for too long. The exception to all this fashionable mediocrity is the pizza, which is of astonishing quality. Pizza rustica, with perfectly roasted vegetables (tomato, garlic and peppers) might by the best pizza money can buy in Toronto, with its yeasty crisp crust. The most sophisticated item on the menu is quattro formaggi—pizza with four cheeses (goat, parmesan, bocconcini and fontina). The combination of the diverse melted cheeses with fresh rosemary on hot crust is too wonderful for words.

In spite of its imperfections, Pazzo's shares significant qualities with its College Street *confrères:* like the others, it is a re-make of the Italian idiom, with new and lighter approaches to Italian cooking. It is an unpretentious place where fancy people are tolerated but not preferred. The majority of main courses cost less than $10. And this is the heart of the College Street Italian renaissance: it's accessible. You don't need a Gold Card to join.

Positano Restaurant

633 Mt. Pleasant Road (South of Eglinton)
416 932-3982
Moderate. All major cards.
HOURS: Dinner Tues.-Sun. 5:30 p.m.-10:30 p.m.
Closed Mon. Closed Christmas Day and
New Year's Eve.
Wheelchair accessible. Licensed. Allergy aware.
Reservations recommended.

The lira is up, the mortgage is a ball and chain and, besides, even if one did have the spare bucks for a couple of round trip tickets to Rome, who would mind the kids? The solution is simple: we tell ourselves we don't need jet lag, that Toronto still has more Italians than any city outside of Italy, and that the Italian food is thus plenty good here. And guess what, it's true—even in neighbourhoods not celebrated for their cultural Italiana.

Positano is splendidly authentic, expect for its price tag, which is much lower than anything of similar quality in the mother country. Positano troubles to keep the dinner tab below $60 for two, which they do by concentrating on plainspun pizza and pasta, with only a few more expensive daily specials.

Positano is cramped and cosy, with polished service and fine food. The pizza crust is properly crispy, the pasta full of flavour. We swoon at the house antipasto, which is peeled peppers (yellow and red), baked garlic oozing with sweet balsamic vinegar, grilled eggplant, home-made mozzarella, stuffed peppers and a rainbow of other vegetable treats. So who needs jet lag?

Primi Ristorante

425 Spadina Road (At Lonsdale)

416 483-9312

Expensive. All major cards.

HOURS: Lunch Mon.-Fri. 11:45 a.m.-2:30 p.m.

Dinner Mon.-Sat. 5:45 p.m.-10:45 p.m.,

Sun. 5:45 p.m.-10 p.m.

Wheelchair accessible, except to washrooms.

Licensed. Allergy aware. Reservations recommended.

Are the rich different from you and me? Is this an inappropriate question for a restaurant columnist to be asking? Does it matter who the folks at the next table

Positano

are, and whether they got to the restaurant in a Toyota or a BMW? To some people, it probably doesn't. There are people who are so *good* that they don't look over their shoulders at the next guy. These are people who don't notice what you're driving, wearing or (by deduction) earning. We all know somebody that good.

For the rest of us, mired as we are in our hopelessly low consciousness, noticing who's around and how they dress and how expensive their haircuts are is one of life's unavoidable entertainments—or tortures, depending on how you experience these differences.

Let's say the woman at the next table has matching $300 shoes, handbag and gloves, a serious rock on her hand, and she's with a guy in a high ticket suit. They have that *expensive* look. And you're wearing baggy trousers from the three-years-ago winter sale, a shirt that can charitably be called ordinary and serviceable shoes. Your dining partner has attained a similar level of elegance. Your mother always said the most important thing about clothes was comfort. She lied.

If you're part of the .01 percent of the population who don't notice these things, you're fine. God bless and have a good life.

For the rest of us, it is not fun to be the only schlepper in a crowd of high rollers. A restaurant is a theatre piece, and fitting in with the scene as it's set *matters*. It doesn't matter in the way that bombs on Dubrovnik matter, but when you're spending $100 on dinner and using it as your major (and certainly most costly) form of entertainment, you want to feel comfortable. You want to fit in. In a better world, the socioeconomic stratification wouldn't matter. Maybe that day will come. Until then, folks, know thine environment and dress accordingly.

ITALIAN

Primi Ristorante is a case in point. Here we are in the centre of Forest Hill. Rich people live here. And Primi is the neighbourhood diner. The difference between rich people and you and me is that at their neighbourhood diner the clams in the spaghetti alla vongole aren't canned. Instead of burgers, there's carpaccio, and, instead of frozen fish, there's fresh salmon. The walls are a genteel shade of salmon, the ceiling recalls gothic arches, over the front door two cherubs cavort, and the waiters in their natty striped aprons make you feel very, very important. I love Primi. Is this why? Or do I love it because of its comforting consistency, the fact that it hasn't changed in five years: one can *count* on the same splendidly simple Italian food, day in and day out. In 1995, that comfort is no small potatoes.

Restaurants in less rarified neighbourhoods sell pizza too. Some of them even have wood-fired ovens like Primi's. But the others do not tend to put the likes of home-made sausage on top. Nor do they give away mountains of wood-fired focaccia with rosemary when you sit down.

This is an impeccable restaurant. Few restaurateurs have the smarts to set such simple goals, and then bring such dedication to attaining them. Primi's menu is a study in attainable gastronomical goals. Cooking schools should study it.

The appetizers are few and careful. The classic antipasto plate is made with quality ingredients. A superb minestrone soup is full of all good things from the garden. There is a sweet little seafood salad and the best Caesar salad I have eaten in a Toronto restaurant since Three Small Rooms, pre-1985. One is aware of the anchovies and garlic in the dressing. This is unusual

Primi

for Toronto. Don't think we aren't grateful for some garlic in our lives.

Then there is the pasta, upon which great attention and equally great restraint are lavished. The tendency among Toronto yuppie chefs is to throw everything in the culinary lexicon at pasta. Sun-dried tomatoes, mushrooms, eight different vegetables, three or four diverse but not necessarily harmonious cheeses, smoked salmon, vodka, some leftover meat and don't forget the heavy cream. At Primi, they respect Italy's favourite food too much to drown it under encyclopedic sauces. Matters farinaceous are in the main restricted to fresh zingy tomato sauces with appropriately quiet embellishments—fresh basil, fresh clams, mixed seafood. One night the kitchen sends out great terra cotta crocks of linguine with spicy tomato sauce and huge melt-in-the-mouth chunks of fresh lobster.

Meat and fish entrées are treated with the same cleverness as pasta: meat and fish are grilled in the open kitchen and not interfered with. Pink pieces of liver, small sweet squids, juicy steaks all come off the grill in peak condition, never petrified, never overwhelmed with sauce. This is simple food, without artifice. Only real professionals can do simple. Any idiot can complicate. Cooking without covering up takes courage, because you have to expose the nature of things and, with that, your own abilities.

ITALIAN

Ristorante Grappa

797 College Street (Near Ossington)

416 535-3337

Moderate. All major cards.

HOURS: Dinner Tues.-Sun. 5 p.m.-11 p.m.

Closed Mon. and all major holidays.

Wheelchair accessible, except to washrooms.

Licensed. Allergy aware.

Reservations recommended.

Grappa occupies the premises vacated by the former Regina, whose idea of decor ran to the dark and dour. The baronial kitsch of Regina remains at Grappa. Dark wooden beams lurk overhead. Fake arches and dark tavern chairs speak of gallons of cheap chianti downed with the soggy lasagna. But that was then and this is now. Now is nouvelle Italian.

The permanent printed menu is competent, but it's clear this chef puts his body English into the daily specials, the ever-changing products of the market and the imagination. One evening he bakes mussels with julienne of leeks and carrots. He makes a vichysoisse that rescues that old tired classic from oblivion, rewriting history with more pepper and less cream. His warm salads, which change daily, are homage to the rainbow of vegetables that turn June into the month of the pleasure principle for the orally fixated.

Grappa

The warm salads are the anthem of Grappa: a warm salad is a humble thing, made from vegetables, maybe a little fish or meat, a simple dressing. The keynote is freshness and à la minute preparation. You cannot make a warm salad in advance, hold it in the fridge and then warm it up. Or rather, you can, but you would be instantly recognized for a cretin. Grappa's warm salads have that homey honesty one wants.

Pasta dishes follow that same well-trodden path of careful combinations and fresh cooking. Two people could dine happily on salads and pastas, with wine, for $50. The more ambitious main courses (veal, shrimp and the other commonplaces of the modern Italian kitchen) are less exciting because on these the kitchen uses less restraint and more stuff on the plates.

Wash all this down with flaming sambuca (complete with the requisite three coffee beans) and rejoice in delicious baronial kitsch.

Sotto Sotto Ristorante

116-A Avenue Road (Near Bloor)

416 962-0011

Expensive. All major cards.

HOURS: Dinner daily 5 p.m.-12 midnight.

Closed Christmas Eve, New Year's Day

and Easter Sunday.

Not wheelchair accessible. Licensed. Allergy aware.

Reservations recommended.

The people at the next table are eating a very attractive dish: it came on a big platter, and appears to be an assortment of pastas. We break rules, lean over and ask them what it is. Pasta mista. But that wasn't on the menu. No, they say, looking important.

Is it because she is skinny and gorgeous and is wearing perfect plum lipstick, and he is just the other side of angry young man beauty, and we are two unchic middle-aged women? Is that why the glamour couple got bread and we didn't? Is that why they appear to have a full complement of cutlery, whereas we are reduced to sharing one knife between us? Is this, dare I say it, the issue that is not an issue in the 90s? G-g-g-g-gender?

Not a chance. How do I know? Because when I went to Sotto Sotto with a man, they didn't give us bread either, nor did they manage to put sufficient cutlery on the table.

Are we having fun yet? The draught whipping through

the restaurant is invigorating. Sotto Sotto occupies the premises that used to be Sisi Trattoria. It is a cramped, low-ceilinged basement with minimal attention to aesthetics. Ask the waiter what he has in wines by the glass. They're both dry, he says. Oh boy, that's exciting news. For white, he offers Soave, and for red, he mumbles the name of a sorry wine that shmecks like pig swill. Wake up and smell the chardonnay, fellas.

Why flog a dead horse, you ask? First off, Sotto Sotto is alive and kicking, doing business like gangbusters. And second, they serve some great food to all those masochists. The culinary roots are planted in high-yield ground: Osteria Romana, which was on the south side of Cumberland near Bellair (until the development there took its place) was owned and run by a man who had been trained in the kitchen at Joso's, where they have an acute understanding of fish, olive oil, pasta and other matters basic to southern Italy.

One of the owners and chefs from Osteria Romana opened Sotto Sotto, and that same understanding is present again. The act of grilling is deceptively simple: any idiot can do it. You don't have to be an Escoffier to throw a piece of fish on a grill. But you need hair-trigger timing and fine instincts for the post-grill dressing. Sotto Sotto's siren song is in the same acts of seduction that made Osteria Romana delicious and that keep them coming back to Joso's: perfectly grilled fish and pasta.

One would do well to start with grilled radicchio, in which the piquant bitterness of radicchio is balanced by a benediction of sweet balsamic vinegar. Or a shared pizza from the wood oven. The best of these is so-called vegetable pizza—spicy tomato and cheese sauce topped with paper-thin slices of grilled zucchini, sweet red peppers and mushrooms, all very happily mingling on a crispy thin crust.

For main course there is a variety of fresh fish daily, always grilled and always wonderful. Most special is the grilled squid, sweetly chewy in balsamic vinegar and olive oil. Pasta dishes are equally felicitious, especially the robust and simple affirs, like *puttanesca* (with anchovies, olives, capers, garlic, chilies and tomato).

But *caveat emptor:* give complexity a wide berth at Sotto Sotto. Maybe risotto is like getting enough cutlery on the table or ensuring that everybody gets bread: too complicated for a restaurateur with a slapdash attitude. For that is how Sotto Sotto feels: slapdash. It's great that they grill like champions and make perfect pizza and pasta, but that doesn't help when you paid $30 for a platter of seafood risotto for two and the shrimps are like leather (ditto the squid rings) and the sauce is the flavour equivalent of oat bran. Although not as good for you.

Then we ask the waiter what's for dessert. "Tiramisu," he shrugs. That's all? That's all. It's superb tiramisu, but we would have liked at least the illusion of choice. Does the waiter care? Not so it shows.

Maybe we're old fashioned. Maybe it's unchic to kvetch about details like cutlery and draughts and house wine, when obviously everyone in the restaurant (except us) is pretty cool. Maybe they all know the code—that you don't order risotto or anything with a sauce. But if you have to know the code, or be a regular, or look a certain way, then I'm not playing. I'm taking my marbles and my $80 for two and I'm going to play in somebody else's backyard, where hospitality means that the waiters care about everybody's good time. So there.

Sotto Sotto

Spiaggia Trattoria

2318 Queen Street East (Near Victoria Park)
416 699-4656
Moderate. All major cards.
HOURS: Dinner Mon.-Sat. 5 p.m.-11 p.m.,
Sun. 5 p.m.-10 p.m. Closed Christmas Day.
No wheelchair access. Licensed. Allergy aware.
Reservations necessary.

Chris opens the fridge beside my table. It is a round-edged 50s model, painted blue on the bottom and red on the top, and the red paint has been allowed to drip into the blue. When he opens the fridge you can see the freezer. It's lost its door and appears not to have been defrosted since relations froze between Chuck and Di. The guys at the next table ask for the light to be turned down. Chris reaches up and turns off one set of spots. We are plunged into darkness. He turns to the room and announces: "It's that table's fault."

The woman at the next table calls: "Christian, can I have some water?"

"Sure Bonnie," says Chris.

Chris is the waiter. He has long blond hair in a pony tail, a t-shirt, jeans and dirty white sneakers, and when he comes by our table to see about seconds on the white wine, it's "Can I get you a refill of the chard?"

The restaurant has 10 tables, each with red and white checked tablecloths covered in glass. It is the home of amiable clutter and always filled with thirtysomething Birkenstock yuppies, many of whom seem to know the waiter. If too much P.C. (politically correct) natural fibre doesn't get you down, then get thyself to the Beaches for dinner at Spiaggia. The big surprise is that the chef in that funky little *boîte* can cook circles around a lot of straighter arrows.

There are tender spinach gnocchi in a cream sauce with wild mushrooms, equally correct green agnolotti with goat cheese on the inside and a superbly spicy tomato sauce with basil on the outside. They make their own sausage, and lavish fresh herbs, julienne of leek, wild mushrooms and good cheeses on the pasta dishes. This is a kitchen that demonstrates the cosy connection between the counterculture and cuisine.

Perhaps Spiaggia's finest hour is its lamb shank. This heretofore unsung part of the lamb (the lower part of the leg) requires long slow cooking to be tender, whence its flesh turns to toothsome shreds. Lamb shank has become popular thanks to the resurgent interest in comfort foods, and this particular lamb shank takes comfort into the erogenous zone: its flesh falls sweetly from the bone and it sits in a pond of shiny brown lamb juice that has been reduced to an essence and flavoured with enough fresh rosemary to recall a Mediterranean hillside in May.

Fifty dollars buys dinner for two at Spiaggio. At the end Chris falls by your table: "Any coffees, caps, espresso?" Be cool. Lay back.

Spiaggia Trattoria

Splendido Bar and Grill

88 Harbord Street (Near Spadina)
416 929-7788
Expensive. All major cards.
HOURS: Dinner daily 5 p.m.-1 a.m.
(Kitchen open until 11 p.m.)
Wheelchair accessible. Licensed. Private
room for parties up to 40 people available.
Allergy aware. Reservations recommended.

If looks were everything, it would be fair to say that Splendido is Franco Prevedello, from the inlaid wood floor to the 14-foot ceiling. Splendido is what happened when Centro got whimsy, thanks to walls happily painted in the colours of squash purée, carroty orange and royal blue. Thanks to mirrors cut with wavy tops, lighting as fun sculpture, glorious huge painted flowers from artist Helen Lucas and a kitchen full of chefs in painters' hats, all behind a glass wall splashed with colours. Splendido is the result of a sophisticated aesthetic that cherishes fun.

But the food is Arpy Magyar's triumph, his own marriage of California and Italy, inspired by the high priests of arugula and radicchio, garlic and oil, with a wood-fired oven and sourdough starter for the house-made bread.

ITALIAN

Franco Prevedello's system involves getting what the corporate world terms "buy-in" by installing an owner-manager at the helm of each restaurant. His preferred method is the Splendido model: chef Arpi Magyar owns 37 1/2 percent of the restaurant. Paolo Paolini, the front-of-the-house manager, owns 37 1/2 percent. Franco owns 25 percent and, as well, he is part of a group that owns the building.

Franco provided initial financing, the administrative setup, the design, and a hand on the helm at the beginning. Then Arpi and Paolo, each on his own turf and always driven by their vested and mutual interest, took over the daily operations. It's a sweet formula, and the results are in the tasting.

This is the new Italian cooking at its best, wherein the old foods—polenta, rabbit, pasta, sausage, fennel, roasted meats, rapini, gnocchi—are executed with a lighter touch and a shorter cooking time. *Vide* the wood-roasted chicken with Tuscan bread salad: the chicken is perfect, succulent and moist, the bread salad a well-dressed triumph of Italian bread, currants and pine nuts.

We eat that Cal/Ital favourite, home-made lamb sausage with silken polenta and a fresh rosemary sauce. Perfectly cooked juicy quails with wonderful pasta in tomato sauce. Arpy roasts rabbit nicely and serves it in classic Italian style, with creamy porcini fettucine, kale and rapini. He even dares—and succeeds—at Mediterranean seafood stew. This is a hard one to get right: it requires hair-trigger timing on the fish cooking and a strong heart for building the tomato/fish broth. He does competent pizzas with the usual new age toppings. Nice light gnocchi. Rich strong soups with nary a hint of powdered base. These are the classics of the new Italian kitchen.

Splendido

Japanese

Ema-Tei

30 St. Patrick Street (University and Queen West)
416 340-0472
Moderate. All major cards.
HOURS: Lunch Mon.-Fri. 11:45 a.m.-2:30 p.m.,
Dinner Mon.-Sat. 5:30 p.m.-10:30 p.m.,
Sun. 5:30 p.m.-10 p.m. Closed major holidays.
Wheelchair accessible, except to washrooms.
Licensed. Allergy aware. Reservations recommended.

It has not been easy to be a lover of Japanese food in Toronto. We endure day-old sushi, fishy fish, too much sugar in the sauce and fake crab on the sashimi platter. Life is hard.

But take heart, o ye food freaks: solace is at hand. Ema-Tei is where the Japanese eating ideal meets reality, in an irresistible (but never cheap) marriage. The first clue is the menu: one side is in English, the other in Japanese. The same dishes are offered in both languages, but the presence of the Japanese characters is soothing to epicures in search of authenticity. Then we see the clientele: many Japanese people, few Caucasians. More cause for optimism.

Businessmen in from Tokyo bow to each other, remove shoes and step into the tatami room at the back. Whoopee. This is the beginning of something good. For once the world is unfolding as it should: to begin, the server brings a small bowl of shredded giant clam with ginger, soy and carrot.

One could survive quite nicely on a parade of appetizers at Ema-Tei, with sushi for dessert. There is *ohitashi,* a small salad of emerald spinach topped with a great flurry of dried shaved *bonito* fish. Beef *yanagawa* is a miniature flat earthenware casserole holding tender steamed beef (or eel) mixed with burdock root, an untranslatable but fragrant Japanese herb and slightly scrambled barely cooked egg. The *nasu dengaku* here makes the nasu dengakus of yesteryear seem like gooey mistakes. They have been fat slices of ordinary eggplant covered with a thick roof of sugary *miso* (fermented soybean paste). This nasu dengaku is small thin Chinese eggplant smeared with quieter miso.

Plump fresh shiitake mushrooms are steamed with soy sauce and a little butter. Tiny clams are steamed with sake and served in the resulting broth, which is at once subtle and strong. To those who order the special chef's dinner, he presents an appetizer of a hollowed persimmon (Japan's traditional signal that autumn has arrrived) filled with squid and melon salad.

This dinner is a waltz through Japan's most important cooking techniques, or variations on a fish theme. It begins with sashimi, a pretty plate of impeccable raw fish, including sweet abalone cut into a cornflower shape to tenderize it. Then comes steamed fresh grouper in a broth made from seaweed and dried fish (delicate and vaguely smoky) and cooked with sliced chestnuts.

Next is deep-fried food—a barely fried fresh splendid okra, and the only false note of the meal—an apparently reconstituted crab claw covered in flavourless shrimp paste. After that comes grilled food: fresh tilefish barely grilled, plump, juicy, wonderful. Then sushi, perfect raw fish to cleanse the palate. And, lest there be an empty spot somewhere in the gluttonous gut of the hungry gourmet, a bowl of fat fresh Japanese noodles, soba (buckwheat) or udon (wheat) with crunchy little tempura batter bits afloat in a fine chicken broth. The set dinner ends with a crisp Japanese pear as fragrant as perfume.

Katsura Japanese Restaurant

The Prince Hotel, 900 York Mills Road

416 444-2511

Expensive. All major cards.

HOURS: Lunch Mon.-Fri. 12 noon-2:30 p.m.

Dinner Mon.-Sat. 6 p.m.-10 p.m.,

Sun. 5:30 p.m.-9 p.m. Open on major holidays.

Wheelchair accessible. Licensed. Allergy aware.

Reservations recommended.

The cherry blossoms are not blooming at Katsura. We feel sad. The room is dark and feels old-fashioned. It could be a hotel dining room anywhere, more North American than Japanese.

JAPANESE

Hotel dining rooms are not our habitual locus of grand gastro-discovery, but we made an exception for Katsura, for several reasons: first, the hotel is owned by a Japanese company; they ought to have good sense about Japanese food. Second, the problem with Japanese food in Toronto has much to do with dollars and yen: Japanese ingredients cost a fortune and come from far away: hotels have more buying power than small, independent restaurants. Third, business people from Japan frequent the hotel and one would expect their custom to affect Katsura's standards.

One would be wrong, by and large.

Katsura makes a terrific first impression: do they take your coats? Not a chance. Go to the coat check and pay $1.50 per coat. It's not the $1.50 that irks; it's the thought that counts. One would have hoped for a more gracious attitude when dropping a hundred bucks for dinner.

Then you enter the dining room: dark, vaguely floral and bland. The menu goes from tempura to sushi with many stops in between, but little to awaken the jaded Japanophile. Sure, the *chawanmushi* is properly limpid and the beef sashimi is melt-in-the-mouth, the udon noodles are fat and friendly and the tempura is properly crisp. But ho hum.

But it is the sushi that saddens: assorted sushi are workmanlike, but hardly meriting a drive to Don Mills. We thought the Prince Hotel would have been flying raw Japanese exotica our way daily!

Having plumbed the skin-deep pleasures of the dining room, we venture into stranger territory: Katsura's sushi bar is a bit of a hike from the restaurant, in its own spartan little room. But if one were wanting a locus to begin a discrete extramarital dalliance, this would be the place. Sit at the bar and ply him or her with the suggestions of the friendly sushi man. All will be yours.

Katsura's sushi bar makes up for the shortcomings of the dining room. Here is the personal touch and the effort that sushi needs. There is sweetly gooey sea urchin, pink moist raw shrimp, fresh surf clam and red clam both, salt/sweet and firm. But most of all, there is the sense that somebody is home here: the sushi man offers what is fresh that day. We are not stuck with the dining room's set menu.

It is also thus at the *robata* bar, a separate counter seating area inside the Katsura dining room. Here presides a seafood grill cook who tells us proudly that he will make barbecued eel from his father's recipe, which has been used for three generations in the family restaurant in Japan. Hallelujah! The eel is soft, sweet, food to be inhaled smiling. He proffers raw tuna chopped up fine with chives and soy sauce, charcoal grilled mackerel at its most delicate, perfectly grilled sea bass.

The moral of the story is that old tired restarant truism: skip the big production dining room and go to either the sushi or robata bars, where individual cooks practise their craft, with reverence for their history.

Kuraya Restaurant

322 Adelaide Street West (Between Peter and John)

416 408-3406

Moderate. All major cards.

HOURS: Lunch Tues.-Fri. 11:45 a.m.-2:30 p.m.

Dinner Tues.-Fri. 5:30 p.m.-12 midnight.

Closed Mon. Open most major holidays.

No wheelchair access. Wine and beer only.

Allergy aware. Reservations recommended.

Kuraya is a restaurant so small and physically pinched that to walk in the front door necessitates negotiation with the people at the sushi bar. But Kuraya is large in spirit (and menu too). It serves some of the most delicate Japanese food in Toronto.

Many grand foods are briefly grilled, for example barely cooked very fresh oyster mushroms with a wonderful soy vinegar dipping sauce. Or pork with ginger sauce.

Fresh clams come in a great deal of sake and butter broth, of the sort that demands drinking. *Chawanmushi* is the ineffable Japanese custard made from chicken stock and egg and full of hidden treasures: green leaves, julienne of shiitake mushrooms, lemon zest. Seafood salad is a huge bowl topped with crisp shredded *nori* (dried seaweed). The sushi is fine, and tempura comes with lightly pickled bok choy and a vegetable stew of potato and carrot awakened with sugar, vinegar and soy. We bow to the East.

Kuraya

Rikishi Japanese Restaurant

833 Bloor Street West (Near Shaw)

416 538-0760

Moderate. All major cards.

HOURS: Lunch Tues.-Fri. 12 noon-2 p.m.

Dinner Tues.-Sun. 5:30 p.m.-10:30 p.m.

Closed Mon. Open most major holidays.

Wheelchair accessible, except to washrooms.

Licensed. Allergy aware. Reservations recommended.

Rikishi, on Bloor Street West, is a small cramped restaurant, warmly hued with knotty pine and made further attractive by sweet, friendly service. The menu is astonishing for such a small and unassuming restaurant: a full page of vegetarian specialties, diverse sushi and many fine hot foods.

The beef *tataki* (raw steak is sliced very thin) is properly eroticized with sesame, soy, rice vinegar and green onion. *Negi-hamachi* is a dream coupling of chopped raw yellowtail mixed with green onion. Beef roll is thin sliced beef rolled up around crunchy, barely cooked green beans. Oshi-sushi is "press sushi," which means they press the rice with the fish under weights until it assumes a somewhat cake-like (and very entertaining) personality. Pressed broiled eel is particularly interesting. *Saba-shioyaki* is salted char-broiled mackerel, a pleasantly unctuous fish whose flesh is sweetened by the salt.

Kids & Tourists

Masquerade Caffé Bar

BCE Place (Front and Yonge)

416 363-8971

Moderate. All major cards.

HOURS: All-day menu Mon.-Wed. 7 a.m.-midnight,

Thurs.-Sat. 7 a.m.-1 a.m. Closed Sun.

Open major holidays.

Wheelchair accessible. Licensed. Allergy aware.

Reservations not accepted.

Life is a cabaret. Should you have trouble with that notion, hustle down to BCE Place and eat at Mövenpick's Masquerade Caffé Bar. Life may not be a carnival, but dinner at Masquerade sure is. Imagine the European model, where the face of the café faces streetward (not inward, Canajun style), and indeed spills out onto the street, blurring the line between streetlife and café life. Cafés are built for speed, not for comfort. They provide social interaction, life in technicolour and quick food. This is Masquerade.

Finally Mövenpick has done something right. Mövenpick is the chain that likes to think of itself as a purveyor of haute cuisine. But chains don't make haute cuisine. Mövenpick is Howard Johnson's in Centro clothing. Their Toronto restaurants (Mövenpick Yorkville, York Street, Palavrion and the Marché in BCE Place) all share that split personality problem.

Some people (me included) get irritable when a place is "positioned" as one thing but the foods tastes like something else. When I go to HoJo's, I know what to expect. Fair enough: order clam chowder and fried clams. Expect pleasantly flavoured mucilage and gobs of grease. And that's what you get. Not cognitive dissonance. But when somebody decorates HoJo's to look like Centro, and they offer a Cal/Ital upmarket menu that comes out tasting lousy, I get irritable. Hence my short fuse with Mövenpick.

In designing Masquerade, the Mövenpick folks have finally decided to telegraph the essence more accurately: Masquerade is a riot of colour and shape, no two tables the same, the chairs, the glasses and the plates a carnivalesque mishmash, a coat of many colours. The café spills out into the huge atrium of BCE Place, proclaiming its casualness by the very permeability of its borders: Masquerade is separated from the atrium only by a curlicue of wrought iron. We are here to ogle and be ogled.

All made from splendid Murano glass (from Venice), the glassware, the multi-coloured lights, the variegated plates are only part of the fun. Masquerade is a party for the eyes. The open kitchen features chefs in tall red toques behind polished enamel cookstoves in many

Masquerade

colours. Strung from the ceiling are oversized Christmas lights from Murano. So your table is tiny and purple, with green and pink napkins; the table beside you is huge and it's green, with blue and red napkins.

The chairs are uncomfortable, many of the tables are tiny and tippy, but that's okay because we are not here to linger long. We are not here for a langorous gourmet meal. This is fast food for the hungry 90s, cheap and cheerful—very cheerful. Very, very cheerful. So cheerful you may need sunglasses.

The menu is simple. It changes daily. There is a daily soup, a daily ravioli, a daily risotto, a couple of salads, antipasto, one hot main course and a collection of sandwiches on wonderful Italian bread. Which of course is made by Mövenpick.

Which is easy to do because they already have an industrial bakery across the atrium at Marché. This is vertical integration that allows Masquerade to produce its own desserts, breads, ice cream, etc. They are not of the first quality, but nor are they expensive.

A small portion of ravioli, which is what Masquerade does best, is $4.25. The filling changes daily (one day veal and herbs, one day mushrooms, one day mascarpone, ricotta and spinach) but the constant is very good pasta and usually a fine butter sauce. The other food that Masquerade does well is the Italian sandwich, 12 of them to choose from and all edible fun: zingara is salami, mozzarella and artichoke; boscaiola is Italian ham, mushrooms and brie; pazzo is Parma ham with creamy goat cheese; vegetariano is eggplant, zucchini, tomato and mushrooms. Every combination comes on a slightly different crusty breads some with little gems such as sun-dried tomatoes embedded in the crust. And none costs more than $6.75.

KIDS & TOURISTS

We can live without the low-flavour risotto and the no-flavour seafood antipasto. We don't enjoy the service, which is haphazard. Some days you get bread. Some days you don't. Sometimes you order small ravioli and get a big one. Sometimes the reverse happens. The cappuccino is weak. But for once, we don't care. Masquerade is a lesson in not taking anything seriously, including dinner.

Mövenpick Marché

BCE Place (Front and Yonge)
416 366-8986
Moderate. All major cards.
HOURS: Daily 7:30 a.m.-2 a.m.
Wheelchair accessible. Licensed. Allergy aware.
No reservations.

Blown-dry stockbroker type to small, tired Oriental woman working the bread station at Mövenpick Marché: "I bet you're having a lot of fun here. Aren't you?"

She (trying for the delicate balance between truth, hers, and fantasy, his: "Well, not always."

At the grand Mövenpick Marché, hers is not the only struggle between reality and fiction. Mövenpick Marché is 18,000 square feet of food fun in BCE Place at Yonge and Wellington. It is the multinational corporate version of a medieval street market. It's Fauchon on a McDonald's budget; it's the collision between the good taste of the 80s and the slimmed down pocketbooks of the 90s.

The reality problem is this: Mövenpick Marché cost $6 million to build. Well spent dollars. It is beautiful, interesting and mind-boggling in its scope. Foodies on a budget will think they've died and gone to heaven: migawd it's all here, from oysters to Champagne, from quails to rössti, all made fresh as you watch. Dining becomes adventure. But take a closer look, and underneath the splendour of the design there lurks an upscale cafeteria serving less than scintillating food.

The Marché concept, untangled from the overstimulation and the carefully planned jumble, is simple: on entry you are given a "guestcheck" and a "Hey, This Is My Table" tent card. Every time you step up to a station and order food or drink, they stamp your guestcheck with a code. You don't pay till you leave, when all the stamped codes are totted up to create your total bill. Before starting to accumulate food, you are supposed to find a table and reserve it via your tent card.

Even the apparently simple act of finding a table is a voyage of discovery. Do you want to sit on the busy terrace, under the soaring glass atrium roof? Or in the quiet of La Poterie, with its stone doorframe, stone-framed window and medieval fountain? How about the deco sweetness of Place de L'Étoile? Or perhaps you'd prefer a table beside the flower market, in the bakery? Or a stool by the bustle of the oyster bar? A bamboo armchair at the counter offering today's paper? Themed seating, they call it. Mövenpick Marché has 480 seats, broken up into almost a dozen different areas.

Having "reserved" a table, guestcheck in hand, you start grazing. Yes, the Marché is a self-serve restaurant. You want it, you choose it from the appropriate station and you carry it to your table. You pick up wooden trays and cutlery at the food stations. There is the fresh orange and grapefruit station (squeezed before your very eyes), the pizza station, the daily pasta station, the rössti potato station, the spit-roasting station (quails, cornish hens, sausages, steaks, leg of lamb), the seafood station (daily fish meal, steamed mussels, smoked salmon), the oyster bar, the omelet station, the soup and sandwich station, the salad station, the stir-fried veg station, the bakery station, the pastry station, the wine-by-the-glass station, the cappuccino and café au lait station.

Every station is its own expression of gastro-porn, pretty as a picture, decorated with overflowing baskets of fruit and vegetables, bottles of olive oil, pots of fresh herbs, cotton awnings, hand-painted tiles, all the insignia of the good life.

At the pasta station the pasta machine is extruding fresh pasta. At the omelet station they make each one to order. At every station stands a cook (or two or three) to make your food, fresh, instantly, with few exceptions. You see your mussels steam, your smoked salmon carved, your rössti potatoes fried.

To increase the feeling of freshness and immediacy, they're peeling real potatoes at the rössti station, they're slicing up scallops and shrimps at the pasta station, real bakers are baking croissants and bread at the bakery station, whole fish are on display on a mountain of ice at the seafood station. Cinéma verité comes to the world of food!

We're happy. We're sold. Having been trained by gourmania, this is what we want to see. The buzzwords are fresh and natural, and here it is at Mövenpick Marché. We know for sure they're not popping frozen factory foods in the microwave, because we can *see* what's cooking. This is the smartest formula since the Golden Arches began.

That's the upside of Mövenpick Marché. The downside is that unlike normal cafeterias that run in straight lines with nothing to knock over, this one is all higgeldy piggeldy, with enough designer bric-à-brac at every station to make tray-carrying perilous. There is the additional stress of figuring out what to eat, finding it, standing in line for it (worst between noon and 1 p.m., and 6 and 7 p.m.) and then remembering where your little tent card is, and finding that table again. Did you wish bread and butter with the meal? Whoops, on your feet again. Relaxing this isn't.

Almost 4,000 people a day eat at the Mövenpick Marché. (It's open from 7:30 a.m. till 2 a.m., seven days a week.) Can 4,000 people be wrong? Their average check is just over $10—for the highest possible form of mass food. The many stations with their fresh 'n' natural decor make it all look epicurean. (Mövenpick, a Swiss company, operates 160 restaurants and 10 hotels worldwide.)

The flavours at the Marché are bland, the spit-roasted hens and quails overcooked, the rössti potato dishes greasy. The french fries are frozen. The soups taste like powdered base and the pastries are beautiful to behold, but in the mouth the puff pastry is soggy, the custards lack that real eggy richness and the cakes taste, well, mass-produced.

It's not *bad* food. Compared to most of the schlock that crosses counters at those prices, it's superb. Just don't be fooled by the marvellous market formula and the glorious visuals: Mövenpick Marché looks like *Gourmet* magazine, but it eats like a very upscale shopping mall food court. Which, after all, it is.

225

Palavrion

270 Front Street West (Near John)

416 979-0060

Moderate. All major cards.

HOURS: Wed.-Thurs. 11a.m.-midnight,

Fri. 11 a.m.-1 a.m., Sun. 9 a.m.-midnight,

Mon. and Tues. summer only.

Open some major holidays.

Wheelchair accessible. Licensed. Allergy aware.

Reservations recommended.

Park Your Cloud at the Door.... Total Customer Freedom.... It was fun for us having you....

Is this an ad for a disco? A sex shop? A night club? A game show? A Club Med clone? No, it's Mövenpick's new (in late 1994) Palavrion restaurant in the CBC Broadcast Centre at Front and John streets. Palavrion (which comes from the Latin root for "idle chatter," is a 380-seat extravaganza that cost $6.2 million and took a year to build.

Palavrion has the same menu as Mövenpick's Marché in BCE Place, and the same concept, but more so: at Palavrion the goal, according to Mövenpick's Canadian boss Jorg Reichert, is "food preparation with total transparency...our food is the show, our staff are the entertainers and you are the star!"

Wow! Zap! Gee whiz! Holy cow! A restaurant that

Palavrion

sells freedom and levity. How absolutely marvellous to be able to *buy* fun. Not that it's a new concept, but it is one that hasn't been floated much lately, for these 90s are not the gay 90s, except at Church and Maitland. It seems to me that the metaphysics of fun resist intentional methodology, but maybe Mövenpick knows something we don't know.

It would seem that they do. Can 3,000 people a day be wrong? Folks line up for an hour and a half on Saturday night to get into Mövenpick Marché in BCE Place. They crowd to Mövenpick's Masquerade, also in BCE Place. It is a truism among epicures that Mövenpick is Howard Johnson's in European clothing, but the people love it. If Marché is extravagantly, exuberantly decorated, then Palavrion is what happened, in restaurant terms, when Daniel Day Lewis and Meryl Streep mated.

Palavrion is the most astonishingly beautiful restaurant to open in Toronto this decade. The specialty painters who covered the seductive Matisse restaurant walls with French *faux* have done Palavrion. The floor tiles were designed by a French tile designer. Even in a 380 seat restaurant, $6.2 million goes far. Very far.

Everywhere you look there is another item of beauty, another splendiferous vantage point, all in the honey mustard tones so chic today. The chairs are designer diverse, some wood, some upholstered. There is wrought iron, ceramic, sisal, brass leaf, marbleizing, stenciling and more. Much more. the restaurant is on two tall levels, and the broad stairway between the two offers a look at four TV monitors showing the restaurant in action. Can we see ourselves walking down the stairs? Life doesn't just imitate art. It *is* art.

And perhaps there's the sex appeal of Palavrion

('cause it sure ain't the taste of the food): all the kitchens are open. As Jorg Reichert promised, the process is transparent. Distinctions between kitchen and dining room are purposefully lost. When you arrive at Palavrion the maître d' checks the computer monitor that shows which tables are vacant. You are led to a table and each diner is given a ticket with a bar code.

You then walk around to the various food and drink stations, and ask for and receive your food. When the cooks at their stations give you something, they scan your bar code with a light pen that automatically records your "purchase." You put your food on a wooden tray, cruise another station or two and then go sit down to eat. The computer is your friend. When you leave, of course, the computer tallies your total instantly. And it then sends a message to the maître d's monitor to show that "your" table is now vacant again.

The upside of all this is that what you see is what you get. Total transparency is true. All the ingredients are on display at the various open kitchen stations. Your wish is their command. Most things are cooked to order, and you get to see them doing it, which makes obfuscation difficult and requires Mövenpick to use only good ingredients. Which they do. The upside is also choice. You have the opportunity to see things being cooked for the people in front of you in the lineup before you order.

The downside is twofold: first off, who wants to pay for dinner and work so damn hard? They add an obligatory 10 percent service fee to each bill. For what? Better they should pay us 10 percent service for doing the schlepping and the waiting for food at the stations. And schlepping it is. Every single item of food that gets to your table gets there only one way: self service.

Palavrion

Gussy it up with fancy words, it's still work. And heaven help the klutz if this process involves the 23 stairs between the two levels or if it's a crowded day.

The second downside is the taste of things: while there isn't anything bad at Palavrion (nor at HoJo's), there is a general numbing blandness. At the seafood station all is glistening and fresh, but the seafood pot-au-feu and the mussels are both blah. The famed Mövenpick rössti (fried potato cakes) are pleasant, but neither crispy enough nor flavourful enough. The soups are bland, the salads are bland, the quail is overcooked and the desserts are bland. Are we having fun yet?

Lunch

Art Gallery of Ontario Restaurant

317 Dundas Street West (Near University)

416 979-6612

Expensive. All major cards.

HOURS: In winter, lunch Wed.-Sun. 12 noon-5 p.m.
Dinner Wed. 5:30 p.m.-8 p.m. Closed Mon. and
Tues. In summer, lunch Tues.-Sun. 12 noon-5:30
p.m. Dinner Wed. 5 p.m.-9 p.m.

Wheelchair accessible. Licensed. Allergy aware.

Reservations recommended.

My significant other and I were discussing the mode of
transit that both of us favour above all others: the
canoe. The question on the table was the relative merit
(for hard canoe-tripping use) of the Grumman aluminum
canoe versus the kevlar canoe, kevlar being a postmodern

plastic-like compound that is lighter than fibreglass but similarly durable. Significant other argued that we should favour the Grumman because it was virtually indestructible, cheap to buy and had a decent shape.

I spoke for kevlar's aesthetic qualities. Significant other smirked haughtily and drew his verbal six-guns: "You have to think about doing a *serious* canoe trip to the Arctic and then you would understand why the Grumman makes more sense." There went aesthetics, knocked into a cocked hat by macho logic. I sputtered about various different ways to define "serious." He, having easily taken the athletic high ground, made a daring but fraudulent attempt to occupy the aesthetic high ground as well and then left the table.

Aesthetics are strange, for the reason of relativity. Significant other had every right to speak of the beauty he ascribed to the Grumman's shape. Just because he was wrong doesn't mean I don't grant him the right to his opinion. He accuses me of being a snob, which of course is true.

If they were having arguments like that over the aesthetics of the restaurant in the newly renovated Art Gallery of Ontario, I would be delighted. At least that would show someone cared. But everything about the restaurant seems to scream indifference, as if there were High Art and then everything else, and everything else, which of course includes food, is not as important as High Art.

The AGO restaurant is the Grumman choice: it's functional, it was clearly inexpensive and it is an insult to aesthetes. To get to the restaurant, you walk through some of the most beautiful rooms in this country. The restaurant itself encompasses the splendidly airy Tanenbaum Sculpture Atrium and then a more "indoor" space, which has no discernible decor. Had we been parachuted directly into that area of the restaurant, we might think an inferior aesthetic was at work here, but having walked there from the gallery's front door, we can hardly use that excuse.

It is undecorated, save for a very few glass sculpture pieces, which are concentrated in the dim corridor leading to the coatcheck. It's nice that they're there because you'll probably be retrieving your own coat. Inside the dining room the walls are covered with burled pale wood and very little else. It is an oasis of bland in a sea of stimulation. Was that by design? Are our eyes being given a purposeful rest from art? Pity, when there is so much at hand to put on these walls. A visually boring restaurant just isn't on inside an art gallery.

At dinner, which is served only on Wednesdays and Fridays, the place more resembles a morgue than an art gallery. But lunchtime is a veritable traffic jam of blue hair and dark suits (the former outnumbering the latter by about four to one). Given the gallery's location and its beauty, the restaurant ought to be a wonderful place for lunch and Sunday brunch. If some taste were injected. Since the people who put the restaurant together seem to be fond of glass sculpture, perhaps they might ask for help from Rosalee Sharpe, the designer who did the Studio Café in the Four Seasons, which is a splendour in the glass and much more.

Lunch ain't cheap at the AGO. Two people would have to mind their p's and q's and skip both wine and dessert to get out of there for under $40. The menu veers wildly from Bubby food (vol-au-vent of chicken in a cream sauce? eggs florentine?) to thoroughly modern upscale: mango and blackberry chutney with the phyllo triangles, balsamic salsa on the chicken, crab cakes and polenta.

But the flavours are banal, the textures flaccid. There's too much cream and not enough pizazz. Roasted chicken breast (overcooked) with no skin! Crab cakes with the texture of old oatmeal that was left in the pot all day and then re-heated in the microwave. Even the items without cream seem to come from a 50s flavour-free zone. That seems inappropriate in Toronto's highest temple to aesthetics.

It's time for the AGO to throw in the towel, gastronomically speaking. They can save face by saying out loud what we know they're thinking: eating is trivial compared to Art. The restaurant is not a priority. It would make a nice cash cow to support Important Culture, but not if it takes a lot of effort. Ergo they ought to contract out the running of the restaurant to somebody who a) knows how to do it well and b) has a passion for food and does not believe dining rooms to be poor cousins of picture galleries. Wake up and smell the espresso, AGO.

Lox, Stock & Bagel

Hazelton Lanes, 55 Avenue Road (North of Bloor)

416 968-8850

Moderate. All major cards.

HOURS: All-day menu Sun.-Wed. 8:30 a.m.-7 p.m., Thurs.-Sat. 8 a.m.-10 p.m. Closed Yom Kippur.

Wheelchair accessible. Licensed. Allergy aware.

Reservations recommended for dinner.

Having failed utterly in my search for an edible potato latke in the delis of suburbia, I thought, if the uptown Jews can't make a latke, it's time to go downtown

Art Gallery of Ontario Restaurant

234

where the gourmets are. To the fancy Lox, Stock & Bagel in Hazelton Lanes. Better they should have called it Lox, Stock & Shmatta, because on the walls, what does this restaurant have? Ads for clothes from Alan Cherry's fancy shmancy women's clothing store, because he owns the restaurant too.

Maybe Alan Cherry's Boba had a problem. Maybe she golfed instead of cooked. Maybe she was a convert. But let me tell you, if my Boba (may she rest in peace, although this news is probably disturbing her eternal rest) could taste what Alan Cherry calls on his menu "home made chicken soup with Bubby's matzo ball," she would surely *plotz* (untranslatable between genteel covers, but it's not pretty). Did the chicken pass over the pot? If so, perhaps the relationship was fleeting. This so-called chicken soup ought perhaps to be re-named chicken powder soup, a.k.a. Bubby's revenge.

To commit an offence of that magnitude against the very cornerstone of Jewish cooking takes nerve. But it's only the beginning. There is borscht so pallid even Manishewitz would be ashamed to bottle it. Are the latkes worse than at a suburban deli? It's hard to tell. There is that same warmed-over porridge-like texture, with lots of oozing grease.

I grew up on the best chicken soup in the world and overcooked roast chicken. It was almost a religion with my Boba. Think of the microbes! I thought I knew from overcooked. But compared to the chicken at Lox, Stock & Bagel, my Boba was serving sushi.

The barbecue chicken is so dried out it's on the road to pet rock status. There is a pot-style chicken (in my family it's called boiled dinner) wherein the chicken and vegetables are boiled together in enough water to produce a soup dinner (Jewish pot-au-feu). We are delighted that the soup is real, but the chicken has petrified flesh from deeply serious overcooking. Extreme overcooking also attacks the chicken burger and the char-grilled red snapper.

The desserts cannot be ordered. One must walk to the display case and await service from not-very-friendly folks behind the counter. The desserts seem mass-produced, in the manner of cheap hotel mousses and cakes: dry and rather tasteless. The service too has that uncared-for feeling: the low point is a dinner when our waiter has left our table piled with dirty dishes for 15 minutes. He appears at the other side of the room several times and appears not to notice my increasingly desperate gestures of supplication. Finally there seems to be no other choice. I stand up and yell: "Fire." He comes.

My Boba would have been upset by the vegetables, which have the flavour and scent of something you'd buy pre-cut in a bag, and by the salad dressings, which have that sugary, un-fresh, bottled flavour.

But she would have been most upset, in a more personal way, by the scandal of a fellow Jew serving bad Jewish food. It seems almost a betrayal of our heritage that is so intensely bound up with cooking. When Jews are sick, we eat chicken soup. Our holidays are food-centred: Hannukah is latkes. Passover is the foods on the seder plate, plus matzoh ball soup. We atone on Yom Kippur by refraining from eating. On Rosh Hashanah we ask for a sweet new year with apples and honey. The feast of Purim is marked by the eating of hamentaschen, three-cornered cookies that recollect the tricorn hat worn by Hamen, the villain.

Our food reminds us who we are. If Alan Cherry wants to serve bad food, let him switch to Italian. Or

French. But please, let the food of our grandmothers (whether you spell them Boba or Bubby) be honoured by excellence. It is a peasant cuisine, demanding neither expensive ingredients nor back-breaking labour. It wouldn't be so hard to do it well. All you need is love.

Scaccia Restaurant

55 Bloor Street West (Near Bay)
416 963-9864
Moderate to expensive. All major cards.
HOURS: All-day menu Mon.-Sat. a.m.-8 p.m.
Closed Sun. and major holidays.
Wheelchair accessible. Licensed. Allergy aware.
Reservations recommended for lunch.

Here we go: another success story from the recession. These tales are intoxicating by virtue of their very rarity. To hear, in a period of despair, that a business can open and thrive, is like seeing a crocus in the snow. It engenders hope.

Scaccia is that crocus and, while everybody else is crying in their Chianti, Joe Saturnino, Scaccia's owner, is going to the bank with a wheelbarrow.

Scaccia is 1,800 square feet small. It is generating sales of well over $1 million a year. Per square restaurant foot, that is a prodigious volume. They sell a few dinners and a great many lunches and takeout meals. The secret: Saturnino plays to good taste. He sells Champagne on a beer budget.

Here we are in a mall, for God's sake, in the basement

LUNCH

yet. (They call it the Lower Concourse but it's still the basement.) The first thing you see is the glass case filled with pretty pasta salads and big blousy desserts. In the small dining room (88 seats) at lunchtime the cheerful bustle is nonstop: they line up for tables every day. Secretaries, company presidents, salesgirls and millionaires crowd in.

At dinner the essential reality of the mall basement asserts itself. There are grey-haired men from upstairs in the ManuLife apartments, eating alone, men with a permanent look of surprise on their faces. They never thought they would have to fend for themselves at dinnertime. They don't bring a book, their hands are restless, they're fretful. There is the pre-movie crowd, a quick hot veal sandwich and a beer. There are mall people, aimless, lingering too long over Scaccia's delicious straciatella soup. There are a few yuppie parents who've figured out that Scaccia's spaghetti and meatballs are an epicure's answer to McDonald's.

A fine and delicate sensiblity dreamed this room. There are gilded sconces on one wall and a rococo gilded mirror, botanical prints in gilt fames and two cherubim wearing wreathes of dried red roses. The tables are marble, each supported by its own fluted column and each holding bottles of extra virgin olive oil and balsamic vinegar. Wine glasses are in an antique wooden hutch; the walls are stencilled with urns of grapes and leaves marching in lines. They don't make mall restaurants like this. Yet.

When the server brings bruschetta and you inhale the garlic and the extra virgin, it's clear you're in the hands of an aesthete. And just how did Mr. Saturnino get that way? He grew up in suburban Toronto (not a hotbed of gourmania) but his parents are from Sicily.

Scaccia

238

When he was 20, he and his dad went home to Sicily for two months. There Joe Saturnino found his metier. The food called to him: "It turned me on, because it was so simple and so fresh. If you had seafood in a restaurant, it was caught that day. The fruit and vegetables were grown locally and they were so fresh too."

This is not to say that Scaccia's standards are up to southern Italy's. For $18 a person in Toronto you don't serve just-caught seafood or impeccable produce. But Joe Saturnino learned an *approach* in Sicily, a culinary philosophy, and to this he is true: "I'm just cooking what I like. What I'm doing right now is very very basic." It's basic and simple and, by and large, honest. No-frills southern Italian cooking, which is one of the sweetest pleasures on Earth.

My favourite thing at Scaccia is the scaccia itself. This is a hot Sicilian sandwich that Joe has modified slightly: in Sicily they make a scaccia by rolling up various fillings in pizza dough and then baking it. Joe uses bread dough (for its greater crispiness) and between two pieces of raw dough he puts your chosen filling, usually bound with mozzarella cheese. Then he bakes it until crunchy brown. Sausage scaccia, with sweet peppers, onions and mozzarella, is for Italophiles who have outgrown pizza, with regret. Scaccia of spinach with veal and mozzarella has the strong scent of fresh spinach and the pink delicacy of veal. This is finger food. Put it with a bowl of stracciatella and a glass of wine.

Scaccia concentrates on simple foods and does not stray into the land of high-ticket Italiana. The large menu majors in respectable salads (both pasta and vegetable), scaccia and other hot sandwiches, and a great many pasta dishes, with the emphasis on tomato sauce and other inexpensive ingredients. But be not misled by the less than lofty ambitions of this menu. There's a zing in the air at Scaccia, and you can eat it.

Studio Café

Four Seasons Hotel, 21 Avenue Road

(North of Bloor)

416 964-0411

Expensive. All major cards.

HOURS: All-day menu Mon.-Fri. 6:30 a.m.-11 p.m.,

Sat.-Sun. and holidays, 7 a.m.-11 p.m.

Open all holidays.

Wheelchair accessible. Licensed. Allergy aware.

Reservations recommended.

The Four Seasons second string dining room (a coffee shop by any other name...) is the Studio Café, a superbly light room with huge windows and a splendour of local glass art on heavy glass shelves. Everywhere you look there are works of glass art, in breathtaking colours that sparkle from sun and halogen. This is a room for the 90s, whose decor is all about light.

Its location requires the Café to be all things to all people—from club sandwich and french fries to roast quails and mussels with ginger. But the Café doesn't dish up frozen fries on a plate: these are fresh fries, well enough bred to nestle in white damask. And when there's artichoke on a pizza, it's fresh, not bottled or

Scaccia

canned. This isn't the most exciting cooking in Toronto, but there are no bad dishes.

In late 1994, the Four Seasons made a credible but short-lived effort to take the Studio cooking up a notch. They lured Danny Griesdorf (one of Toronto's best cooks), away from Messis on Harbord Street. But it turned out that the artist and the organization could not a marriage make. The issue of course was creative control. Griesdorf's tenure as Studio chef was brief. His legacy was a new menu, full of the iconography of the PoMo chef—lentils, smoked duck, warm salads, etc.

Sic transit gloria. (He went, by the way, to the Senator Diner.) Post-Griesdorf the food is still, well, *hotel food.* It's good hotel food, but that isn't saying a lot. It all looks so pretty, and nothing is awful: The Studio is a restaurant where the lights are on but nobody's home.

Mexican

Iguana

2050 Avenue Road (South of Wilson)

416 488-5947

Moderate. All major cards.

HOURS: Dinner Mon.-Sat. 6 p.m.-10 p.m.

Closed Sun. and major holidays.

Wheelchair accessible, except to washrooms.

Licensed. Allergy aware.

Reservations recommended.

Iguana's owner Ivan Garcia Rojas is the classic small entrepreneur who understands the pointed relationship between costs and survival. He doesn't need to pay a fancy waiter because he *is* the fancy waiter. He doesn't need a big name chef: the cooks are hired hands. They're good, but the culinary sensibility is his. This is a hands-on restaurateur with a finger in every pot.

To stay alive today, a restaurateur either has to be McDonald's, a giant with the ability to pare costs to the bone and still churn out something that can (charitably) be called food. Or follow the road taken by

MEXICAN

Ivan Garcia Rojas: be small enough and sharp enough that the overhead is laughably low and the word "supervision" takes on new meaning: You don't watch the floor, you're *on* it. You control the quality by creating it. The costs stay low and the people notice how good everything is.

If Mr. Rojas doesn't like it, he doesn't serve it. The Iguana kitchen is straight talking and full of vigour, serving Mexican food that combines the force of chilies and coriander with the delicacy of fish and seafood. The necessary exotica come to Iguana's kitchen every Tuesday by air from Mexico, via Detroit. Here are fresh chilies, red and green, big and small, hot and sweet. Boxes arrive full of fresh *nopalitos,* flat cactus leaves that turn to slightly citric ambrosia when grilled.

Iguana is a physical environment that says come on in and stay a while. It feels sufficiently home-made to be unintimidating and beautiful enough to uplift the spirit: splendid Mexican tiles border the open kitchen and Mexican fine art posters, many by Diego Rivera, turn the almost-adobe walls into more than just decor.

Before he opened Iguana, Mr. Rojas served seven years as a waiter in Toronto, mostly in high-end Italian restaurants where he absorbed certain important lessons about creating a welcoming restaurant environment. He seats you and little treats arrive automatically—small fried tortilla triangles with jalapeno peppers, fresh coriander, onions and melted cheese.

The remainder of the meal is a more sophisticated event, with the emphasis on fish and seafood. Any resemblance between Iguana's cooking and the tacos 'n' nachos version of edible Mexicana is purely coincidental. A soup at Iguana begins with pure and

Iguana

proper chicken stock and might then be flavoured with tomatoes, garnished with tortilla strips, jazzed up with coriander. Mussels are steamed in a light tomato broth with the gentle punch of fresh pasilla chilies.

If they do a taco, it has a touch of class: for example a filling of moist minced pork with raisins and nuts, for sweetness and texture. This is on the tapas menu, a changing collection of small treats for under $5. One could make a handsome dinner of three or four tapas: the aforementioned taco, a mean ceviche of seafood "cooked" in lime juice and seasoned with coriander and serrano pepper and a postmodern tamal of corn dough stuffed with rabbit and steamed in banana leaves.

The main courses are equally sophisticated: swordfish is presented in a corn husk, bathed in a green sauce flavored with tomatillos (those little green things that look like unripe tomatoes but taste like a cross between a lemon and a sweet pepper). *Cazuela marinera,* the classic fish stew beloved of every culture with a seacoast, is a lusty rendition in a spicy (but not mouth-burning) fish and tomatillo broth.

Then there is the *mole,* which I normally think of as Mexico's national abomination, the dish that gave Mexican kitchens their bad name. This is the famous "chocolate chicken" that in careless hands tastes like a marriage between Nestlé's Quik and Colonel Sanders. Too chocolatey, too cooked. Mr. Rojas cleverly uses a chicken leg and thigh, which are resistant to the scourge of drying out from long simering. And his mole sauce is everything it should be but so rarely is—the barest whisper of cocoa, a stronger scent of roasted nuts, a blend of many chilies, all in a dark brown sauce that balances its many flavours in silken smoothness.

The desserts are moderately entertaining variations on

crêpes. One might prefer a gossamer flan or some tropical fruit garnished with Gelato Fresco and light custard. But nonetheless for my $60 a couple for a meal from tequila to tip, Iguana is one of the best deals in town.

Margarita's

14 Baldwin Street (Near McCaul)

416 977-5525

Cheap. All major cards.

HOURS: All-day menu

Tues.-Fri. 11:30 a.m.-10 p.m.,

Sat.-Sun. 11:30 a.m.-12 midnight.

Closed Sun. and major holidays.

Wheelchair accessible. Licensed. Allergy aware.

Reservations recommended.

I am no expert on margaritas. Regular readers have no doubt noticed my lack of both knowledge and interest in alcoholic beverages, and margaritas are no exception. Although I do confess to an occasional weakness for a margarita. Imagine a warm place. Imagine palm trees. Imagine hibiscus flowers and bougainvillea in full and riotous bloom. Tropical colours—lush greens and lurid sunsets. In this setting I imagine a margarita, in a tall martini glass frosted with salt.

The glass itself is delicate and the lime juice in the margarita is fresh. Little time bombs of salt, cool lime and hot tequila go off in your mouth, with an aftershock to the cerebral cortex. This is the margarita of my

Iguana

dreams, and I did not find it at Margarita's on Baldwin Street. The glass recalled a small swimming pool in both size and delicacy, the lime juice tasted bottled and where was the salt?

It seems ironic that the restaurant's namesake is rendered so poorly, but everything else at Margarita's is splendid. It's a funky little cantina with the TV on (soundless) over the bar and Mexicana cluttering the walls: sombreros, Mexican beer posters, sheepskin rugs and a cactus mural. Ceiling fans turning slowly, Mexican music playing accompaniment to the (silent) Canadian TV news. This is business as usual on Baldwin Street: edible ethnofunk.

The food is your basic downmarket Mexican, not the stuff of *Gourmet* magazine but the fun food of the people, executed with sensitivity and verve. Soups tend to be chicken stock afloat with hominy, which is a special form of corn that puffs like tough popcorn when cooked. Guacamole comes in a black pottery pedestal crock. *Totope* is honest-to-goodness nachos as opposed to the packaged pap that masquerades under that name in most restaurants. These nachos are fresh, fried tortilla chips with real cheese, and they come either that way or topped with chili con carne with pickled jalapeno chilies just to keep your taste buds on their toes.

Most of the main courses are variations on Mexico's eternal triangle: the burrito, the enchilada and the taco. These of course are merely different versions of dough that in turn hold different fillings. The combinations are many: you can fill soft (corn) tacos with chicken. You can fill crispy deep-fried tacos with beef. You can fill a soft flour tortilla and it's a burrito. That tortilla can be deep fried and filled. And the beat goes on. Margarita's tortilla-type main courses are distinguished by pleasing ingredients (lots of green tomatillos, light on the jalapeno peppers).

They also offer seafood main courses, for the exalted price of $5.95 for the most expensive, which is scrumptious shrimp with very lightly pickled Mexican cactus, odiferous with much garlic. For dessert there is the ubiquitous Mexican flan, well rendered, or the ever-thrilling Gelato Fresco ices and ice creams. This is happy food.

Middle Eastern

Boujadi Moroccan Restaurant

220 Eglinton Avenue East (West of Mount Pleasant)

416 440-0258

Moderate. Visa and Mastercard.

HOURS: Dinner Tues.-Sun. 5 p.m.-11 p.m.

Closed Mon. and some holidays.

Wheelchair accessible, some assistance required.

Licensed. Allergy aware (patrons must inform

them). Reservations not necessary.

I have a friend (who shall remain nameless, for reasons that are about to become obvious) who has the palate of a 1950s Don Mills resident. (Could that be because she's from Ottawa?) She likes chicken—if it's plain. Sauces are scary. Eggplant is dangerous. Chinese food is problematic because you don't always know what's in it.

Going out to review a restaurant with my friend is really fun, because she's so willing to try the interesting dishes I need to test. I put up with that for lots of other good reasons, but it's no secret between us that she is a not exactly a fellow traveller on the road to epicurean adventures.

So I was surprised when she mentioned—several times—a restaurant she adored and that clearly was not a purveyor of meat-and-two-veg. Migawd, I thought, there's got to be lots of that *verboten* heavily ethnic food at any place that calls itself Boujadi.

"What if you hate it?" she said nervously, before we ordered.

How odd. How indicative of the hegemony of the gourmet craze that even a self-avowed contented gastro-lout was quaking at the thought that I, The Expert, might not like her favourite restaurant. She may not know much about food, but she knows what she likes— until The Expert tells her it's no good, and then the veracity of her very own taste buds is in question.

Her anxiety continues. It turns out that before leaving work that day, she had sought advice from an ethnic food expert in her department, and was assured that Boujadi was a fine restaurant and not to worry. But she couldn't help it. My august critical presence was enough to strike terror. Heretofore simple questions—What to order?—turned into a minefield of potential disasters.

She talked about the beets. Normally (of course) she hates beets. But please could we have some of Boujadi's unusual beets and she did hope I wouldn't hate them. Hate them? The beets, once arrived proved to be (in the opinion of The Expert, and therefore it must be true) supernal. These are no ordinary beets. (How did the gastro-lout know?) They are sweet little baby beets dressed in oil, lemon and great scads of garlic.

Harira, Boujadi's special soup, was found by The Expert to be equally entrancing. Made with lentils, split peas and kidney beans in good chicken stock and scented with fresh coriander, it is splendidly full-bodied, with nary a hint of the nasty bought powders that usually substitute for stock in inexpensive restaurants.

After the triumph of beets, soup, spicy Moroccan sausage and crispy phyllo triangles, she breathed a sigh of relief. Perhaps her gastronomic proclivities were not going to be slaughtered after all.

The main courses are either less dazzling or more unfamiliar, or both. The Moroccan kitchen uses much sweet with the savoury, for example cinnamon, prunes and raisins with phyllo-wrapped chicken for the national dish called *pastilla*. The chicken is only somewhat overcooked, but being neophytes at eating Moroccan, we keep thinking that phyllo and cinnamon equals apple strudel.

The dish that made Morocco famous is couscous. Boujadi uses only kosher chicken, and they cook the actual couscous (a form of pasta) not with water but with vegetable stock for more flavour. It is probably correct in Morocco to overcook the chicken and thus we ought to forgive. Served with summer and winter squash and chickpeas, in a light and lovely sauce with onions, prunes and raisins, it is a completely credible couscous.

Morocco's other national dish is the *tajine,* meaning a deep dish with conical lid, both made from glazed clay. A tajine is also the name for the meal cooked inside the tajine, in this case chicken with onions, sweet spices and broth. Here too we are on such unfamiliar ground that even The Expert is in the dark.

The combination of sweet (cinnamon, raisins) with braised chicken is sufficiently unfamiliar that we don't know exactly how it's supposed to taste. It's pleasant enough, the clay casserole is very beautiful and we only wish they had cooked the chicken a little less.

Boujadi is a tiny room with an open kitchen, open only for dinner. Behind the counter, never ceasing his labours, is chef/owner Charles Obadia in his red fez. Given that the majority of Boujadi's main courses cost less than $10, one is hardly surprised that the little room is much cherished. Whatever you do, don't forget the beets.

Byzantium

499 Church Street (Near Wellesley)

416 922-3859

Moderate. All major cards.

HOURS: Dinner daily 5 p.m.-11 p.m.

Bar open until 1 a.m. Closed major holidays.

Wheelchair accessible, except to washrooms.

Licensed. Allergy aware. Reservations necessary.

"...such a form as Grecian goldsmiths make
Of hammered gold and gold enamelling
To keep a drowsy Emperor awake;
Or set upon a golden bough to sing
To lords and ladies of Byzantium..."

from "Sailing to Byzantium," by W.B. Yeats

They called the city of Istanbul by the name Byzantium until the fifteenth century. As the poet wrote,

Boujadi

it was a city of golden excesses. The Byzantines seized every opportunity to decorate. No space was too small for an an intricate mosaic, no building too insignificant for the benediction of gold. Food received the same treatment: cardamom, cumin, coriander, cinnamon, raisins and honey and nutmeats were lavished. Adornment was the gift the Byzantines gave to food.

The "drowsy Emperor" is Michael Carlevale, a restaurateur who enjoyed chic success with his Prego and Enoteca at the corner of Bloor and Avenue Road (not exactly an outpost of hope, faith and charity). The time came for Carlevale to branch out.

Not that he was bored with Italian food, but a next step was in order, and nothing but the food of the Byzantine empire would do. Why middle eastern food? "Middle eastern was a logical response to the plethora of Italian restaurants. It would have been like falling downstairs to cook pasta and pizza in this neighbourhood (Church and Wellesley). I got drunk one night with Joey Bersani, who was selling this space (the defunct Soul Makossa on Church Street) and I said 'I like this location. It's like New York. It's got a high ceiling. It's a lousy 10 feet wide. I'll take it.'"

Which he did. Thus began Byzantium, a lousy 10 feet wide but designed by Richard Eppstadt who did Enoteca, and who understands the glitter of ages past. The restaurant was instantly successful, and Carlevale took over the space next door. *Faux* Byzantine mosaics adorn *faux* brushed copper walls, with a splendid long granite bar separating the smokers from the non-smokers (Hallelujah!). The service plates are Byzantine jewels from Villeroy and Boche. One is *not* on the Danforth.

Which is as Mr. Carlevale intended it: "In the mid 80s I would go out every night to the Danforth, and I was maddened by the quality of the food—that you couldn't get a decent piece of fish. Around that time I picked up a book on middle eastern food.

"In terms of having another idea in me (after Italian), it's middle eastern because I love it. I like the small dish aspect of the first course. I love beans and rice and vegetables. The whole knack of the damn thing is to blend the spices with restraint and proportion. The other important thing is that we've got good ingredients and technique. The kebabs on the Danforth stink because they're not that careful, but also because their lamb pieces are too small. We make ours with inch and a half pieces cut from fresh Ontario leg of lamb, so I can burn the shit out of it on the outside and keep some moisture inside."

Amen. Ingredients plus technique equals middle eastern food the likes of which Toronto has never seen. The little dishes that begin a typical middle eastern dinner are indeed better than elsewhere: All is careful and delicious, from the humble pleasures of baba ghanoush (puréed grilled eggplant) and hummus (chick-pea purée with sesame) to more sophisticated events like olive paste and *gibna bayda* (feta puréed with yogurt and dill) the hand is light and the touch deft.

There is an Italianate salad of roasted onions, peppers and eggplant, and wake-up-and-smell-the-coffee seasoning on just about everything: chick-pea soup is alive with cumin and coriander. Grilled spicy lamb chops are both correctly cooked and much blessed by a complex spicy sauce. Tangine of fish is alive with honey and raisins—and not overcooked! A good cut of lamb is stewed with chick-peas and raisins, to very good effect. Byzantium is the restaurant to keep a drowsy Emperor awake.

Byzantium

Cedars of Lebanon

394 Bloor Street West (Near Brunswick)

416 923-3277

Moderate. All major cards.

HOURS: Lunch (including buffet)

Mon.-Fri. 12 noon-3 p.m.

Dinner Mon.-Fri. 5 p.m.-11 p.m.,

Sat.-Sun. 5 p.m.-11 p.m.

Closed major holidays.

Wheelchair accessible. Licensed. Allergy aware.

Reservations recommended.

Cedars of Lebanon (the current Bloor Street West incarnation having descended from the original one on Avenue Road) serves an encyclopedic middle eastern menu. Main courses are somewhat indelicate; best bets are the traditional dips (hummus, baba ghanoush, labne), stuffed vine leaves, and awesome fried tomatoes topped with spicy garlic sauce.

Mandaloon

113 Yorkville Avenue

(Between Avenue Road and Bellair)

416 324-9814

Moderate. All major cards.

HOURS: In winter, dinner Tues.-Sun. 5 p.m.-10 p.m.

Closed some holidays.

In spring and summer, lunch daily 12 noon-5 p.m.

Dinner daily 5 p.m.- 11 p.m. or 12 midnight.

Closed some holidays.

No wheelchair access. Licensed. Allergy aware.

Reservations recommended.

Mandaloon is so user-friendly that Yorkville seems an inappropriate location. The small below stairs room is an indication of what the Gatserelia brothers design team (who also did Acrobat and Terra) can do on a budget. When Franco Prevedello gives these guys a million bucks to do a room, they go over the top and then some. But a shoestring reigns in their taste splendidly.

This is not to say that Mandaloon is a Superb Design Statement. It is, rather, both lovely and ethnic. The few Moroccan restaurants Toronto has seen have tended to be over-decorated and feel—to the untutored western eye—kitschy. But Mandaloon is beautiful and restrained. Tiny lights twinkle on the ceiling. *Faux* tiles are painted as accents. Midnight blue and terra cotta form the outlines of mosque roofs on the wall, there are

Oriental rugs on the floor and a fire burns in the fireplace. Cosiness reigns.

There are main courses, they are Moroccan and they are very good (lots of meat, liberally spiced, some fish, much rice) but the thrill at Mandaloon is in the *mezze,* which are plenteous small dishes. $14.25 buys one person a bountiful plate of *mezze,* which adds up to more than a meal.

Habitués of middle eastern cooking may sneer at the ordinariness of the items on the Mandaloon *mezze* plate, but each, even the humble hummus, is done so much better than one has been led to expect. After all the tired tabboulehs I have met in second-rate countercultural cafés, Mandaloon's tabbouleh (cracked wheat salad) is a triumph of fresh flavours made rich with great quantities of parsley.

Their baba ghanoush (puréed roasted eggplant with garlic and sesame) has the haunting—and requisite— fragrance of smoke with none of the unpleasant oiliness that so often creeps into baba ghanoush. The green beans with tomatoes, onion and garlic have been permeated with those flavours and yet not cooked unto geriatric mush. There is crispy-crunchy fallafel (deep-fried chick-pea balls) and ungreasy deep-fried sambousak turnovers filled with delicately flavoured ground beef. Even the olives are special, of good flavour and firm and they come with goat cheese marinated in olive oil with tomato and green onions. Who needs a main course?

Mezzetta Restaurant

681 St. Clair Avenue West

(West of Bathurst at Christie)

416 658-5687

Moderate. Visa and Mastercard.

HOURS: Lunch Tues.-Fri. 12 noon-2:30 p.m.

Dinner Tues.-Sat. 5 p.m.-11 p.m., Sun. 5 p.m.-10 p.m.

Closed Mon. and some holidays.

No wheelchair access. Licensed. Allergy aware.

Reservations recommended.

A darkly cute cherub ambles to the door. From the long black curls down past the jeans to the hiking boots, the chubby cherub projects warmth and comfort. It's in the walk and it's in the welcome. One feels, upon entering the man's restaurant, that one is a cherished friend arriving at a happy home. The feeling is casual without being careless. This is not a feeling to be taken lightly. Restaurateurs with more money that Yossi Omessi spend many thousands on training videos and big ticket consultants to try to convince their staff to create that feeling.

And mostly they fail, where Yossi Omessi succeeds with breathtaking simplicity: you walk into his restaurant, which is small and comfortable but not elegant, and you are made to feel instantly at home. The restaurant is Mezzetta and the man is an artist. Anybody who can make strangers feel like friends is possessed of a talent. By this I do not mean the artificial

Mezzetta

258

"friendship" practised by servers at places like The Keg, where it's "Hi, I'm Susie Q and I'm your..."

I mean, rather, the magician's art, which means the metamorphosis of a restaurant from commercial transaction to home-away-from-home. Few restaurateurs understand that if you can make the people feel truly welcome and at home *from the moment they arrive,* they are yours forever. The man who understands this best hereabouts is Franco Prevedello (*vide* Centro and Splendido); Yossi Omessi is a downscale Franco Prevedello.

Mezzetta is a café restaurant serving "eggplant and jazz." The eggplant etc. happens at lunch and dinner Tuesday through Sunday, and on Wednesday nights at 8:30 and 10:30 live musicians play jazz for a cover charge. They also do takeout. And catering. Yossi, an Israeli of Egyptian parentage, cooks and serves in addition to making his particular magic.

The Mezzetta of the restaurant's name refers to *mezze,* from the Greek, the Turkish and the old Persian, and meaning "a variety of small appetizers." This restaurant is for heavily addicted grazers. Food ambivalence (i.e., the inability to decide) finds a home at last. $23 buys 10 mezzetta, which adds up to a brutally piggish dinner for two. You can sample little plates ad nauseum and never have to choose.

And such lovely little plates they are. This is the food of the eastern Mediterranean, rich in olive oil, reliant on eggplant, centred on vegetables. The cuisine of the Mediterranean is somewhat coarse, often greasy and never bland. For example, Mezzetta's various efforts at eggplant: there is baba ghanoush, eggplant roasted and smoked over flames and puréed with sesame seed purée (tahini). There is the same purée with the addition of garlic (superb) and dill (insufficient and insufficiently fresh). There are eggplant chunks in vinaigrette with onions and garlic. Eggplant appears again in so-called Egyptian mush, which is ratatouille by any other name. Eggplant's only misfortune at Mezzetta occurs when they deep-fry it, resulting in overcooked and overgreased.

The same dreadful fate (overcooking and too much grease) befalls potato and beef moussaka, but save for these two lapses, the aesthete is safe at Mezzetta. The tabbouleh (salad of cracked wheat with cucumber, tomato, mint and green onion) is fresh, the hummus leguminous velvet, the roasted green peppers properly peeled and sweet, the green beans crisp in garlic vinaigrette and the steamed carrots scented with mint.

Yossi makes a mean fallafel (deep-fried balls of chick-pea flour) to be stuffed into pita with his wonderful spicy tomato and coriander sauce. His vine leaves stuffed with rice and minced beef are impeccably delicate. His daily soups, most often based on lentil or yellow pea, are alive with the scent of cumin and coriander. His little meat kebabs (chicken, lamb or veal) are delicately seasoned and properly cooked. And there are crispy little pastry nothings enclosing spinach or cheese.

From this prelude one would expect the usual impenetrable too-sweet Danforth-style baklava for dessert. Skip the apricots and almonds in cream; they are the essence of predictable. But what a surprise to find one's fork sliding through fresh phyllo married to just the right amount of sugar in the baklava, with a dollop of cream (half whipped, half sour) on the side for balance. Even more unusual is the house-made bavarian cream, an ambrosia made from cream, egg and gelatine. In France they call this *crème bavarois*. In Tuscany it's *crema cotta*. On St. Clair Avenue at Christie, it's a dream come true.

Mezzetta

Montreal

Primadonna

3479 boulevard St. Laurent (At Milton)

514 282-6644

Expensive. All major cards.

HOURS: Lunch Mon.-Fri. 11 a.m.-3 p.m.

Dinner Mon.-Wed. 5:30 p.m.-12 midnight,

Thurs.-Sat. 5:30 p.m.-1 a.m., Sun

5:30-12 midnight. Closed only on Christmas Day.

Wheelchair accessible, except to washrooms.

Licensed. Allergy aware. Reservations necessary.

Passiflore

872 avenue Querbes (North of avenue Van Horne)

514 272-0540

Moderate to expensive. All major cards.

HOURS: Lunch Tues.-Fri. 12 noon-2 p.m. Dinner

Tues.-Sat. 6 p.m.-10 p.m.

Closed Sun.-Mon. in summer.

No wheelchair access. Licensed. Allergy aware.

Reservations recommended.

Le Passe-Partout

3857, boulevard Decarie (Near avenue NDG)

514 487-7750

Expensive. All major cards.

HOURS: Lunch Tues.-Fri. 11:30 a.m.-2:30 p.m.

Dinner Thurs.-Sat. 6:30 p.m.-9:30 p.m.

Closed Sun. and major holidays.

Wheelchair accessible. Licensed. Allergy aware.

Reservations recommended.

Once in my youth, while I was in the throes of yet another romantic trauma, a wise older woman told me: "When you see the axe coming, start chopping first." I ignored this perfectly good advice at my peril time after time, but the 20/20 hindsight of middle age has taught me its wisdom. It seems to me now that English Canada is following my old friend's advice with respect to the province of Quebec. We are facing *La Belle Province* with some of that middle-aged ennui that has self-protection at its core. It's as if we're tired of hoping they'll stay, and with that resignation comes a resulting reduction in our general interest in Quebec.

Who do you know who goes to Montreal for fun? Five years ago Anglos complained that it wasn't fun anymore to go to Montreal, because we were treated contemptuously, damned if we did and damned if we didn't (try out our inadequate French, that is). But these days it isn't even a topic of conversation.

This sea change speaks not only about our loss of faith in Quebec, but also about the growing exoticism of the city that used to be famous for rolling up the sidewalks at 10 p.m. As Toronto has become more interesting, it has become less necessary to enjoy our racy sibling to the East.

Time was, Toronto restaurants were a joke compared to the exotic finesse of Montreal's. As recently as five years ago we were still struggling to outgrow the suit and tie dining mentality, while they had the superhip bistros of St. Denis, where perfect pot-au-feu met jeans and Gitanes. But how things change. The hottest of the hot in Montreal today is Primadonna, on St. Laurent. This place is so hip they don't even need to *decorate* it. Minimalist chic *avec* a 50s overlay (in the lighting) makes Primadonna seem very, uh, Queen Street.

Forgive us if we exhibit culture shock. The menu is Italian but there's sushi too. Are we in Toronto or Montreal? Is this a new Quebecois idiom or are they copying us? Not to say that the compulsory cultural expression of Quebec ought to be limited to Quebecois forms, but if they're going to abandon the indigenous and do Cal/Ital/Points East, then shouldn't they do it as well as bland boring Hogtown?

Primadonna is expensive (Dinner for two easily stays on the high side of $100.) and crowded with the chic, the ultra-chic and the suits that support them. The only thing that glitters more than the crowd is the fat gold-painted Primadonna pillars. The food, however, does not shine.

The menu is scary because there's too much on it. Three full pages of Italian items make me worry that the kitchen isn't paying close enough attention to either ingredients or technique and the eating bears it out. I see risotto with green peas, prosciutto and fennel. How strange for a fancy restaurant to offer this spring classic out of pea season. Does Primadonna know something we don't know? 'Fraid not. The peas seem both frozen and overcooked.

Other pastas are better, but we find various grilled sea creatures overcooked. This feels like Centro on a bad night. Pleasantly derivative. We thought Montrealers knew better.

Another current Montreal favourite is Passiflore with its plum walls and huge dining solarium. Here we suffer appalling service and the resulting tourists' dilemma: is it because they know we're Anglos and they're treating us accordingly or is the service really bad? Some of Passiflore's cooking is careless (tiny awful shrimp in the seafood salad, crème brûlée with pockmarks from overcooking) but there is a star of the French firmament in this kitchen: the meats are perfectly cooked and each comes with its own flavour of clear strong sauce.

If, however, it is French cooking you're after, there is only one place to dine in Montreal: Le Passe-Partout is fraught with paradox: it is located at the border of Westmount and Notre-Dame-de-Grâce, twin bastions of old Anglo Montreal. The chef/patron is James MacGuire, not exactly from *habitant* stock. And his culinary roots are strictly the French of France. The poster in the *pissoir* says it all: it is a wine poster, signed by Charles Barrier, one of France's beloved restaurateurs, who suggests to his friend James' clients that they drink wine copiously and urinate accordingly.

James MacGuire learned his trade from Charles Barrier in Tours, France. From Barrier he learned not only the arts of the kitchen but of the *boulangerie,* the bakery, as well. Le Passe-Partout is small, elegantly simple, always warm but never hip. It feels more like Montparnasse than Montreal.

MacGuire's small menu changes completely each day. Each dish is a jewel, each element a carefully chosen statement from the classic French repertoire. His pâtés and terrines are ungreasy and full of flavours, his soups strong and smooth. One evening he offers a fat hunk of awesomely fresh halibut, perfectly cooked, with mushroom purée and a citric beurre blanc underneath, with tiny emerald snippets of chive. And a pink moist loin of veal with poached cucumbers, house-made noodles and another limpid sauce.

One feels like a 90s Alice gone down the rabbit hole, when the server brings room temperature raw milk cheeses with house-made walnut bread. Where are we? Is this the Grand Tour, the France of Michelin and triple crème cheeses, from the days of yesteryear when you could gain five pounds in a day and not regret an ounce or a franc?

And then there's dessert. One evening MacGuire makes perfect *pithiviers,* a dessert so French that few outside the homeland even dare it: puff pastry filled with almond paste, deceptively simple and yet incredibly easy to screw up. Most bakers turn puff pastry into either cardboard or mud. In MacGuire's hands the pastry is crispy-light, the almond paste gossamer. His tarte tatin (a classic too often dared by amateurs) is a triumph of caramelized apple and buttery crust.

It was enough to genuflect at the man's feet, but he had to do more. He gave away the bread! On weekend evenings, when diners leave the restaurant, James MacGuire takes bread from the shelves of his adjacent bakery (which also sells his superb pâtés) and gives it to them! A loaf of sublime walnut bread, some pungent sourdough, the French stuff with the crust, or a few crackling croissants for breakfast. "Take it," he says, "it's a prezzie. Usually I give it to the poor, but it wouldn't be fair if only the poor got it, would it?"

Oriental Noodle Houses

Forkchops

1440 Yonge Street (South of St. Clair)

416 944-8410

Cheap. Visa and Mastercard.

HOURS: All-day menu daily 11:30 a.m.-9 p.m.

Closed major holidays.

No wheelchair access. Licensed.

Allergy aware (no MSG)

Reservations not necessary.

Cheap is wonderful. While it is true that I am not exactly an aficionado of hamburger chains, I adore and revere the world of cheap 'n' cheerful, as long as they keep the additives to a minimum.

There are two kinds of cheap restaurants: The fast food chain, and the small-mom-and-pop-style ethnic dive. Each has its own virtues and failings. The fast food chains thrive on our PoMo insecurities: on a crumbling toxic planet, we are comforted by the apparent cleanliness (all that shiny new plastic!). In a world fraught with breakneck change, we are soothed by the consistency. Every Arby's one visits, from Toronto to Mexico City, has the same food. And it hardly ever changes. And (perhaps most of all) the fast food chains create a kind of *Sensurround* comfort: from TV ad to table, they breed familiarity. The unknown is banished.

The good thing about the ethnic dives is simple: the food tastes good.

So by the millions we put up with high-fat low-flavour cooking at the chains and creative grunge in the little ethnic places. And then along comes Forkchops Noodle House, McDonald's without the additives, ready to blow fast food out of the water, or at least redefine it.

Cheap noodle houses provide sustenance for millions of people every day in the Orient. We have only to look at Spadina Avenue near Dundas for the model of this form of gastronomy: cheap Vietnamese restaurants serve splendiferous bowls of "noodle in soup" garnished with coriander, fresh mint, bean sprouts, lime, shrimps, chicken and not quite the kitchen sink. Dinner will cost under $10.

Forkchops clearly looks to this model for its inspiration, but caters to a more upscale clientele, being located on Yonge Street just south of St. Clair. And being designed by Yabu Pushelberg (who did Oceans and other restaurant extravaganzas). Yabu Pushelberg on a budget looks like pine veneer tables, chipwood panelling, a curvaceous pine veneer eating counter facing the open kitchen, and some rice paper light fixtures. Cheap 'n' cheerful. *Très* clean.

Is Forkchops the perfect compromise between chain food and ethnic, for the low-cal grazing generation? As

Forkchops

clean as McDonald's, as ethnic as a Spadina noodle house.

In theory, yes. In practice....

With a few pleasant dim sum and a couple of salads for appetizers, the rest of the menu is composed of noodles. There is one noodle stir-fry. A collection of broth types (fish based, chicken, beef) form the base for one's chosen noodles (buckwheat, thick wheat or thin wheat) and a list of toppings are offered. Kind of like ordering pizza. You choose your broth, your noodle and your several toppings from the list that goes from mushrooms to toasted seaweed.

For the faint of culinary heart there are three pre-fab combinations. But whether you design it or they do, the problems are the same: the broth is weak-kneed and the garnishes too quiet. We long for the robust chicken broth of the Vietnamese soups. At Forkchops the flavours are in hiding. There's nothing *wrong* with the taste, but not enough that's right.

A similar plight afflicts the garnishes. They are all impeccably fresh and in generous proportions, but the vast majority are unadorned vegetables. Noodle soups need more action: mint, coriander, chilies, sesame oil, lime.... This is a flavour emergency. Dial GASTRO 911.

If the waitpeople were not so sweet and helpful, if the location were not so convenient, if the design were not so welcoming, one would be tempted to write off Forkchops. But instead, one makes the silly suggestion: get a chef! Fast food restaurants don't usually bother with chefs, but Forkchops needs one. An aesthete who will baby the broth and jazz up the garnishes. Then Forkchops will give the Golden Arches a run for their money.

Tiger Lily's

257 Queen Street West (West of University)

416 977-5499

Cheap. All major cards.

HOURS: In winter, all-day menu

Mon.-Sat. 12 noon-9 p.m. Closed Sun.

Open most holidays. In spring and summer,

all-day menu daily 12 noon-9 p.m.

Open most holidays.

No wheelchair access. Not licensed. Allergy aware.

Reservations not accepted.

To those who preach of the silver lining lurking in every single cloud, I say b.s. The recession has been remarkably ungenerous with silver linings, but here's one (depending on your perspective, of course): during the glamorous 80s, Dinah Koo was *the* society caterer. When big shrimps and snow peas circulated on fancy shmancy crackers in Rosedale or Forest Hill, it was courtesy of Dinah Koo's hired help in the kitchen. Her gourmet store on Cumberland Street was the flagship, where one could drop big bucks on delicacies from caviar to Belgian chocolates.

Dinah Koo lost most of it during the recession and was chastened by the experience. Her new venture is built lean for the post-recession 90s: it is a noodle house. Gone are the tiger shrimps, the snow peas and the caviar. Gone are the slick waiters and the extravagant displays of affluence. And we are the beneficiaries. Tiger Lily's Noodle House is the silver lining.

Tiger Lily's is cheap 'n' cheerful, plain and simple, but controlled by the legendary Dinah Koo tastebuds. Which are at their most interesting in the noodle house form. Oriental noodle houses proliferate in Toronto. You can eat udon in Japanese restaurants, great bowls of chicken broth filled with fat noodles (buckwheat, wheat or rice) and various meat or seafoods. There are splendid Chinese noodles in soups on Dundas Street near Spadina; there are oodles of noodles in the many Vietnamese pho houses on Spadina and on Dundas. Pho means noodles in broth with a variety of available garnishes.

But Tiger Lily's is uniquely Dinah Koo, the result of her many years catering to the rich and famous. It is prettier than the more traditionally ethnic noodle houses, with persimmon walls decorated with pale coral wooden cutouts and dried flowers. It is a plain room, but informed by a sophisticated aesthetic. And there is no smoking in the restaurant. Hallelujah!

The service system is homespun and interesting: you choose a table and then walk up to the small counter, beside which are hanging (on clothespins appended to strings) pieces of cardboard that announce which items in Tiger Lily's repertoire are available at that time. You order from the counter person, pay for the meal and then retire to your table to await delivery of your food.

The three constants at Tiger Lily's are egg rolls, steamed shrimp dumpling, and noodle in broth. This egg roll bears small resemblance to any other (and I, being a lifelong gastro-sinophile, have eaten a great many egg rolls). Only now, after eating at Tiger Lily's do I know why they call it *egg* roll! The casing, instead

ORIENTAL NOODLE HOUSES

of being the usual thin anonymous flour skin, is distinctly eggy. It is crispy on the inside, but in a puffy way (rather like good pastry) with a splendidly eggy inner layer. Very scrumptious and filled with all manner of interesting vegetable matter, instead of the more common bean sprout filler.

The shrimp dumpling (a happy familiar to dim sum aficionados) is also far better than usual, with big pieces of shrimp in a very fresh rice flour dough, and great scads of very fresh pickled ginger on top. Yum.

And noodle in broth is equally superb. One can order vegetable or meat broth, each being full of flavour, with hints of coriander, garlic, chilies and onion. Various garnishes are available (slightly spicy and very tender Shanghai chicken, black bean beef, very toothsome wontons). You build your own noodle meal in a bowl by choosing broth and garnish. The results are aglow with flavour and texture.

There is also a revolving collection of heavier main courses. The Cantonese fried noodle cakes are crispy on the outside and soft on the inside, and dressed in a fine collection of stir-fried vegetables in a perfect Chinese soy sauce, with a choice of tofu or meat for garnish. Thai sesame peanut stir-fry noodles has that same option and a creamy/nutty sauce. Two people can dine at Tiger Lily's for under $30. Welcome back Dinah Koo!

Tiger Lily's

272

Vietnamese Noodle Houses

Anh Dao Restaurant

383 Spadina Avenue (North of Dundas)

416 598-4514

Cheap to moderate. Mastercard.

HOURS: All-day menu daily 11 a.m.-12 midnight.

Closed holidays.

No wheelchair access. Beer only. Allergy aware.

Reservations not accepted.

Pho-Hoa

393 Dundas Street West (At Beverley)

416 597-8395

Cheap. No cards accepted.

HOURS: Daily 9 a.m.-9 p.m.

Closed Vietnamese holidays only.

No wheelchair access. Not licensed. Allergy aware.

Reservations not necessary.

South Vietnam

444 Spadina Avenue (Near College)

416 960-2032

Moderate. Mastercard and American Express.

HOURS: All-day menu daily 10 a.m.-10 p.m.

Open holidays.

Wheelchair accessible, except to washrooms.

Licensed. Allergy aware.

Reservations necessary on weekends.

Phee phie pho phum.

I smell the smell of a deal well done.

The absolutely, without-a-doubt best-tasting and most sweetly priced deal on restaurant food in this city today is pho. Pho is the meal in a bowl from Vietnam. It takes many forms, but the basics are always present: noodles in broth. It is usually sweet strong beef broth, although chicken is sometimes involved. The noodle choices are many and various: thin rice noodles, thick rice noodles, rice vermicelli, "normal" vermicelli, egg noodles.

Having chosen your noodle type, the next task is the other stuff that goes into the gargantuan bowl. These possibilities veer wildly from the mundane (beef noodle soup) to the bizarre (pig-leg noodle in soup). But what the heck—when an entire meal's adventure is costing five bucks a bowl, one can afford to make a mistake.

At my favourite pho restaurant, Anh Dao on Spadina

north of Dundas, there are 21 different kinds of pho. After the noodles, the second other constant that unites all phos is the garnish: every pho restaurant I know brings a platter of splendidly fresh bean sprouts, mint and basil leaves, along with a couple of fresh hot chili peppers and lime wedges, to throw in the soup.

And here lies the secret splendour of pho: imagine yourself in a grotty hole with formica panelling, a not very nice smell and the atmosphere of the bus terminal. In three of my five recent pho experiences, local fauna were in evidence: two places had mice, another some quite cute cockroaches. So you're in a downmarket dump paying $10 for lunch for two, and they bring this huge plate of sparkling fresh bean sprouts, herbs and chilies to put in the perfectly flavoured, all-natural beef/chicken broth. Go figure.

Most pho restaurants share an obsession with beef. The most popular pho restaurant in Toronto is Pho-Hoa, a franchise operation with more than 35 outlets in Canada and the U.S. Hereabouts Pho-Hoa is at 393 Dundas Street West, and in Mississauga and Scarborough. Pho-Hoa is the cleanest and the most crowded of the pho spots. It is also traditionally Vietnamese in its monomania. Every single soup but one features beef: steak, flank, brisket, rare, well done, this noodle, that noodle. But always beef, and always the splendiferous plate of vegetable garnish.

But for variety nothing beats Anh Dao. Here they throw pho caution to the winds: order the egg noodle pho with meat and seafood and vegetable, and your broth will be far lighter than usual, scented with vegetable and seafood. The garnish platter will include fresh coriander and lightly sugar- and vinegar-pickled carrot and white radish. There are bamboo shoots with the beef and a splendour of vegetables. Aesthetes rule!

A person with a thick enough skin to resist the lowering skies of South Vietnam restaurant on Spadina just south of College will appreciate their soups. The restaurant *is* depressing. Deserted and dirty, with holes in the tablecloths and a sad air, it is not explicitly a pho restaurant. But for $5.50 South Vietnam serves a wonderful big bowl of broth with thin rice noodles, shrimp, chicken, shrimp purée, squid and the usual vegetable garnish.

A bowl of pho is an edible history of one of the most historically complex countries in the world. Vietnam's history stretches back in time to long before the birth of Christ. Vietnam already had a strong culture when it was conquered by China in 111 BC. Ensuing imperialist cultures (India and France) made their salutary mark on Vietnamese kitchens too. It all comes together in pho: the vegetables are Chinese, the spicing and the chilies Indian and the broth is French. One can only thank the gods of gastronomy that the American chapter in Vietnamese history failed to turn pho into a Campbell's production.

Anh Dao, Pho-Hoa, South Vietnam

Seafood

The Fish House

144 Front Street West (At University)

416 595-5051

Moderate to Expensive. All major cards.

HOURS: Lunch Mon.-Fri. 11:30 a.m.-3 p.m.

Dinner Sun.-Thurs. 4 p.m.-12 midnight,

Fri.-Sat. 4 p.m.-1 a.m. Closed Christmas Day.

Not wheelchair accessible. Licensed. Allergy aware.

Reservations recommended.

Are all oyster-eaters upper crust? If this were the 80s, somebody would probably do a PhD thesis on the correlation between the number of raw oysters consumed annually and the eater's average annual income. My guess is that a high positive correlation would be the result. Meaning, in plain English, that it's mostly the well-off who eat fresh seafood, because it's usually expensive.

Usually.

But The Fish House has taken the snob appeal out of fresh fish. The dollar signs have been slashed by this

huge barn of a seafood emporium at the corner of Front
and University, where the ghastly Whaler's Wharf used
to preside. At first glance, The Fish House gives off
equally bad vibes. You have to hang up your own coat.
Good luck finding a hook. The servers have that
excessive bonhomie that you find in a Keg restaurant,
and the industrial hugeness of the place makes an
epicure nervous. (Lotus this ain't.)

Then there are the sea insignia on every wall:
stuffed fish of various sorts, lobster traps and floats,
oars, anchors and the usual sea stuff found in mediocre
seafood restaurants. But a lighter sensibility is at work
here: huge fake fish cavort on the walls, some painted,
some sculpted. Behind a big counter are major mounds
of bluepoint oysters, which a server is busily opening.
Bluepoints! In large quantity! We are mollified by
molluscs, optimistic even. Maybe these folks are
actually bringing *good* seafood to the masses. It would
be a first.

We get very nervous again when they bring the
soup. It comes with Saltine crackers in a cellophane
packet. Help! Have we stumbled into cafeteria-land? It
doesn't help that we have ordered both oysters and
soup, and they think it's proper to bring the soup before
the raw oysters. Hellacious! Things get worse: instead
of the correct bread and sweet butter, they bring white
rolls and little tin foil butter packets with the oysters.
And having been spoiled by Rodney's seven sauces and
five different kinds of oysters, we are not amused by
only bluepoints and only red seafood sauce.

But hey, they're oysters! And they're raw. And
they're fresh. And they cost $15.98 a dozen. That's
cheap (all things being relative). And the soups (despite
those scary Saltines) are scrumptious. New England

clam chowder has nary a hint of the mucilaginous character normally found in cheap restaurants and it's full of clams. Shrimp bisque has lots of small sweet shrimp in a strong smooth saffron and brandy stock.

Have we died and gone to discount seafood heaven?

It seems that way when they bring Thai bouillabaisse, a strong yet fine lemon-grass-scented broth full of barely steamed julienne of leeks, fresh oyster mushrooms, little flecks of fresh tomato and barely overcooked seafood. Or sizzling calamari sautéed with capers, tomatoes and roasted garlic. Or coconut tiger shrimp, which makes fine bedfellows of shredded coconut and deep-fried shrimp. Or teeny tiny Manila clams steamed in garlic sauce until they just open.

The Fish House offers 15 different kinds of fresh fish daily. They can be ordered blackened, jerked, steamed, grilled or broiled. They also use the traditional west-coast cedar-plank cooking method, wherein fish fillets are tied to aromatic cedar planks and then grilled. The Fish House uses this to great effect on fresh, wild arctic char, a pink-fleshed fish far sweeter-fleshed than most of our farmed fish (e.g., salmon and trout).

We wish they wouldn't overcook the fish, and with the exception of fruit pies as flaky as grandma's, we find the desserts industrial, but hey, there's free valet parking after 6 p.m., and every night in the bar at happy hour $12.99 buys all the raw oysters you can eat: one guy put away 84 of them recently. Can you beat that?

Joso's

202 Davenport Road (At Avenue Road)

416 925-1903

Expensive. All major cards.

HOURS: Mon.-Fri. 11:30 a.m.-3 p.m. and

5:30 p.m.-11 p.m. Sat. 5:30 p.m.-11 p.m.

Closed Sun. and major holidays.

Wheelchair accessible, except to washrooms.

Licensed. Allergy aware. Reservations necessary.

Joso's is a time warp. Enter its cramped confines in 1995, and you are instantly thrown back a decade. None of the excesses (both decorative and gastronomical) that have rocked the outside gastro-world have affected Joso's—not a wit. Joso's was making wonderful fresh fish in 1985 and they're making it still, with benedictions of the same olive oil.

Is Joso's version of decor more offensive now than it was then? Probably. The restaurant is festooned with breasts, big ones. In sculpture, painting, drawing, literally everywhere you look there are huge, bulbous mammaries staring you in the face. The restaurant's only saving grace, in the visual sense, is that it's all too ridiculous to take seriously.

The second saving grace is the thoroughly wonderful seafood. Nobody in Toronto makes a better octopus salad or crisper fried calamari. Their pasta with tiny fresh clams in light, white wine sauce is better than anything else this side of Venice. And nobody else even *tries* to make risotto *nero*—squid ink risotto, inky black and flavoured with the deep.

It is routine at Joso's for the waitresses (the waitstaff tend to be good-looking young women dressed for display) to bring you the fish of the day for inspection. You eyeball very fresh snapper, striped bass, trout, porgy and whatever else Joso found fresh that day, and then you choose your cooking method. Joso's excels at grilling fish. Just remember to tell them to use half the usual amount of salt, because their *bête noir* is horrendous oversalting of otherwise impeccable fish.

Rodney's Oyster House

209 Adelaide Street East (Near Jarvis)
416 363-8105
Moderate to expensive. All major cards.
HOURS: All-day menu Mon.-Sat. 11:30 a.m.-1 a.m.
Closed Sun. Open major holidays.
No wheelchair access. Beer and wine only. Allergy
aware. Reservations recommended for weekends
and for parties of more than two on weekdays.

If I were going to have an extramarital affair, I'd start it at Rodney's Oyster House. All good things begin with dinner, and there is nothing sexier than the slither of raw oyster down the throat. It's tough to be orgiastic nowadays: most of the ways we know to do that are either fattening, too high in cholesterol or otherwise dangerous to one's health.

But a person can eat an enormous amount of raw or barely steamed shellfish; this is safe sensuality. In France they do it all the time. The custom is called *dégustation de coquillages* (shellfish sampling): you fork over about $80 for two (that's without the wine) and they bring a wire stand about a foot tall on which sits a huge round platter with a bed of chopped ice cradling an astonishing collection of shellfish, all raw: oysters, clams, mussels, periwinkles, snails and sea urchins. My experience of this extravaganza of the sea is that there is never enough and it is always wonderful. The exchequer is the only limit.

Canadians are not generally in love with raw sea creatures. But go to Rodney's Oyster House, Toronto's only restaurant devoted exclusively to animals enclosed in shells, and you will find a large and happy coterie of oyster, clam and quahog aficionados. They go to the oyster bar after work and for more serious seafood dinners.

Even after a major expansion in 1994, Rodney's remains a funky basement, really a rendering of a Maritimes fish shanty, with a corrugated tin oyster bar, formica wood tables and rounded metal chairs that suggest ye olde washtub. Should your galvanized tin wine bucket be taking up too much room on the table, no problem, the waiter will hang it on a hook on the wall. That's if he's not busy showing you how to eat a steamed clam: pull off the slimy black scuzz on the foot, wash it in the broth to get rid of sand and then into your mouth.

Rodney keeps the clams not in the fridge, as most restaurants do, but swimming (if you can call the langorous opening and shutting of shells swimming) in a saltwater tank. Ditto his seductive scallops, lobsters and oysters. Thanks to this, these sea creatures are

Rodney's

fresher than any others in town. You can have Rodney's quahogs (large hard-shell clams) sweetly steamed with garlic and white wine, which is very very nice, but for a taste of pink fleshy paradise, order your quahogs raw. No, they don't scream when you bite.

The only trouble with the raw quahogs is that one doesn't know when to stop. Order half a dozen. Then four more for the table. Then a few more (at a dollar each). Intersperse it with a dozen Malpeque oysters, briny and rich. Rodney's cash register is ringing, I can't stop myself and we haven't even gotten to the lobster yet. Or the barely poached singing scallops. Or the many varieties of raw oysters with seven different dipping sauces.

Rodney cooks sea creatures as well as serving them raw, and when he restricts himself to the steamer, it's very good. As in live lobsters from the tank steamed unto perfection. Or the cute little steamed clams. But Rodney has a penchant for creativity that must be stopped. He steams mussels with too much garlic, his shrimp curry is pleasant but bland and he makes dreadfully mucilaginous flapjack soup (a.k.a. oyster chowder).

Sea creatures are so sweet and flavourful that they stand quite well on their own, and so fragile as to be easily overwhelmed. They don't need embellishments, and it takes an especially delicate hand to add to the statement a fresh scallop makes. In France, where they know their bivalves, the highest honour a cook can accord to a mussel is to steam and serve it naked, as if to say: there it is, isn't it perfect? Like a diamond, it needs no decoration.

Rodney gets that part of it right, in his relentless insistence on shellfish so fresh they're swimming. For a really great orgy, take $100 for two to Rodney's and eat it raw.

See and
Be Scene

Acrobat Bis

1221 Bay Street (Near Bloor)
416 920-2323
Expensive. All major cards.
HOURS: Dinner Tues.-Sat. 5 p.m.-1 a.m.
Closed Mon.-Sun. and major holidays.
Wheelchair accessible. Licensed. Allergy aware.
Reservations recommended.

Acrobat opened in 1992, scion of Franco Prevedello (Centro, Splendido, Terra) and Charles Khabouth. Franco recalls: "Acrobat took off like a rocket when we opened, and the attitude of the managers was 'Let's cater to the shooters.' Every second word was 'shooter.' A shooter is a guy who spends big, drinks Champagne. But the shooters come and go very fast. You open a new place, they're in and out. Acrobat was almost an 80s dream."

When the shooters left, and when Franco figured out that his partner Charles Khabouth (ex of Stilife,

SEE AND BE SCENE

Oceans and other nightclubs) was not going to do the daily babysitting of Acrobat, he did two things: Franco bought out Khabouth and in the summer of 1994 he closed Acrobat. He was closing the door on a $1.4 million investment.

Acrobat Bis, which is Acrobat's new name, re-opened in early 1995. Before the closure, butter wouldn't melt in the Acrobat staff's mouths. This time out, the waitpeople actually *care,* and deeply it seems, if we're happy. They hurry, they scurry, they smile and they curtsy (figuratively) to make us happy. Speaking of butter, they're figured who's buttering their bread and that even lumpy, unchic, middle-aged women can keep a restaurant (and hence their jobs) alive. This time out, they're downright *sweet.*

We like that.

But we still don't like the Acrobat decor. The Gasterelia brothers extravaganza is almost too beautiful. Every *objet* in the place is gorgeous, from the handblown decorative aquaria to the fabulous acrobat sculptures and the etched glass and the marbles embedded in walls and the inlay on the hardwood floor and, and, and, and....

We're in hyperstimulation—we don't know where to look. It gets worse. Above the bar are two huge screens on which movies and TV play incessantly. Do we like eating dinner while trying to ignore the real estate ads on TV? Not too much. The decor has been slightly altered, but not sigificantly: saffron and persimmon cloth undulates around pillars now. More cool chatchkas hang from the ceiling.

Then there is the matter of the food, which is in process. The menu is the standard Prevedello Cal/Ital/nouvelle (*vide* Centro, Splendido, Terra), with a casual spin. We are enchanted with the delicate sea

Acrobat Bis

scallop risotto enriched with mascarpone and with the tomato purée (with a dab of mascarpone in the middle) that comes instead of butter with the bread. Deep-fried calamari and Spanish onions are crispy-crackly tender and the seared scallops are perfectly cooked.

But the vegetable spring rolls are flavour-free, and the signature Acrobat potato galette, fried shredded potato cake (a.k.a. rössti, a.k.a. latke) with smoked salmon, is a bit heavy. Ditto the roast veal. Ditto the ambitious pizzas.

But hope exists. Franco will not rest until Acrobat Bis is as delicious as he knows how to make it. We have faith. He fixed the service: he can fix the food. Just watch him.

Alice Fazooli's Italian Crabshack Saloon

294 Adelaide Street West (West of John)
416 979-1910
Moderate. All major cards.
HOURS: Lunch Mon.-Fri. 11:30 a.m.-4 p.m.
Dinner daily 4 p.m.-1 a.m. Closed Christmas Day.
Wheelchair accessible. Licensed. Allergy aware.
Reservations recommended.

Imagine being a guy. Not just any guy. A tall, good-looking heterosexual guy with a good job, nice pecs, no wife, no kids and a healthy interest in sports. The world is your oyster.

SEE AND BE SCENE

And Alice Fazooli's Italian Crabshack is your hangout. This is the restaurant where real men don't eat quiche. This is the bar where the game is always on TV. But Alice Fazooli's is not for boys only. There are plenty of girls there too, especially on weekend evenings and most especially in the bar, where boy meets girl is the name of the game.

Anyone who leads a sheltered life, whether it's Swiss Chalet or Centro, owes themselves a visit to the bar at Alice Fazooli's on a Saturday night. It's another country, but you won't need a guidebook. First note the paintings on the walls of the bar: lots of women with naked breasts and frequent homage to our very own Blue Jays. Here it is, Alice Fazooli's subtext: what comes after T and A? T and B (B for baseball).

The bar is further adorned with the glory of the Game on TV. This season, Saturday night means hockey. Watch the boys in the bar when a fight breaks out on the ice. They leap to their feet, convulsively clutching their beers, clapping hands to fevered brows. The overcooked shrimps in the buckets are forgotten in the passion of the moment. Suddenly, man demonstrates his close connection to his primate cousins: the boys yell, they cheer, with grunts and groans they exhort the combatants to greater feats of gratuitous violence.

Then some girls walk by. The storm passes. Attention swiftly switches from aggression to mating. The photographer from *National Geographic* should be here any minute.

One may dine (if such be the word) in either the restaurant or the bar at Alice Fazooli's. The restaurant, taking advantage of the former warehouse's high ceilings, is possessed of a casual elegance. Reading the menu, only the most case-hardened cynic feels doom approaching. Normal people are excited by the Italian trattoria/seafood combo. Take everybody's two favourite foodstyles and put them together with reasonable prices: it's sweet seduction.

Who is Alice Fazooli anyway? Is she the Mamma stirring the pots in the kitchen, or the proprietor's Mamma, from whom he learned how to make tomato sauce back home in Calabria?

Dream on. Alice Fazooli's is a *concept* restaurant. A concept restaurant is a themed product, wherein the decor, the food and the general ambience are designed to elaborate the theme. The medium is the message and the package is the product. Ordinary restaurants sell food and decor and service. Concept restaurants sell *experiences*. Old fogeys who go to restaurants just for the food are hopelessly out of place in concept restaurants. They probably wouldn't like Disneyworld either.

Concept restaurants come from teams of high-powered entrepreneurs who dream 'em up, open 'em and then move on. To the next concept. The daily repetition of cooking and serving is not what interests them. *Vide* Peter Fowler, father of Alice Fazooli's Crabshack; Mr. Fowler was recently deified in a restaurant industry magazine as "the immaculate conceptualizer."

His career began in the mid 80s when, as a business student at University of Western Ontario, Fowler was delivering pizza for Mother's (which his father started). After graduating, Fowler the younger started inventing concept restaurants. His first was a roadhouse called McCabe's (outside Hamilton), of which there were three by 1988. Then he opened a wholesale tapas bar called Catalan's in downtown Toronto. It fizzled, but Fowler and his partners (Grey Sisson and Rick Montgomery)

SEE AND BE SCENE

followed it fast (in 1989) with The Loose Moose Tap and Grill, which has enjoyed enormous success.

Peter Fowler is also part of the CAFE Restaurant Group, which operates a number of concept restaurants. In a concept restaurant, theme is everything. The other crucial element is *bonhomie,* which is carefully created by trained-to-be-friendly waitpeople who are usually not too hard to look at either. The food has to sound spiffy on paper and look modern on the plate, but little more is demanded. When concept restaurateurs get really smart (like the folks at Disney), they make cooking easier by doing the real work (sauces, soups, desserts, complex entrées ready for re-heating) at a central commissary and then trucking it either fresh or frozen to their various restaurants to be heated and served. Concept cooking lends itself to the central commissary approach because the theme and the servers carry the restaurant, so nobody's looking too hard at the food.

Alice Fazooli's is the exemplar of that salutary (for the conceptualizer) reality. Look at the people lining up to eat Alice's food. And look at what they're eating. The simple foods: overcooked fried shrimp. Overcooked fried squid. Overcooked alligator even. Overcooked grilled salmon with red pepper coulis in a little plastic cup. Caesar salad with flavour-free dressing. Antipasto with the grand luxe of no-taste scallops. The complex foods: stuffed blue crab à la tapioca pudding. Pasta fazool, Italy's national bean soup, which has been turned into a travesty resembling Lipton's beef broth.

An Italianate chicken breast "cornmeal dusted, sautéed, then roasted with a rosemary fiorentina sauce, served with linguine pasta in a porcini mushroom cream sauce..." Here is a triumph of the hyperbolic

Alice Fazooli's

menu writer's craft, although even the sharpest conceptualizer cannot disguise badly overcooked chicken. But who cares anyway? Are we having fun yet?

The Left Bank

567 Queen Street West (Near Bathurst)

416 504-1626

Expensive. All major cards.

HOURS: Lunch Mon.-Fri. 12 noon-4 p.m.

Dinner Mon.-Wed. 6 p.m.-10 p.m.,

Thurs.-Sat. 6 p.m.-11 p.m., Sun. 6 p.m.-10 p.m.

Open holidays.

Partial wheelchair access. Licensed. Allergy aware. Reservations necessary.

Can you judge a book by its cover? See The Left Bank, the hottest new item on Queen Street. So hot there's no sign, just a facade that screams hip, à la française— shades of ochre and sienna, tall window/doors that open onto the street, ornamental plaster trim, art deco lights. And that's only the outside! Inside, the restaurant is a splendour of *faux*-Renaissance, with huge paintings, cherubs, gilded candelabra. Even the floor is *faux,* with Oriental rugs painted on it.

And speaking of *faux,* there is the food. The menu is a riot of politically correct 90s Cal/Ital/Yupstyle, with the usual references to the East. Other than splendid soups (e.g., cream of squash with ginger, topped with salsa and sour cream) there is *gaucherie* in the kitchen.

SEE AND BE SCENE

Is this related to the restaurant's name?

There are greasy spring rolls, badly overcooked burgers, uninspiring fancy salads, overcooked lukewarm fries (both ordinary and sweet potato), undercooked lentils and overcooked shrimps. But it's all packaged so smoothly, on the menu and in the room, that the people are flocking. Which proves (again) that Mr. Barnum was right on.

Milano Billiards Lounge and Bistro

325 King Street West (At Peter)

416 599-9909

Moderate. All major cards.

HOURS: Mon.-Fri. 11:30 a.m.-1:30 a.m.,

Sat. 6 p.m.-2 a.m., Sun. 6 p.m.-1 a.m.

Open major holidays.

Wheelchair accessible. Licensed. Allergy aware.

Reservations not accepted on weekends,

otherwise recommended.

Wake up and smell the Campari. Life is a fashion statement, and if yours isn't, well, get a life. Actually, a lifestyle will do. A life is the pages inside the book. A life*style* is the cover.

Milano is pure cover, through and through. It is food as fashion, with no apologies. The restaurant's full name is Milano Billiards Lounge and Bistro. But don't expect green baize. The pool tables here are purple (with the occasional red one), to match the purple walls, which complement the variously coloured banquettes and chairs, some of which have straight backs and others of which have backs that rise to a double point like a jester's hat.

Or do the pool tables go with the huge tangerine silk shades that hang from the ceiling lights? Or the patterns on the floor? Or the swirly trim on the fishtank sunk in the wall? Or the waitresses' cobalt blue dresses? Or the 14 television monitors that silently showcase both fashion TV and old movies? Or the rock 'n' roll blasting from the state of the art sound system? Or, or, or...

Are we just a tad overwhelmed by Milano?

Are we getting tedious when we say (again) that it must be an age thing? But it *isn't* an age thing. There is plenty of grey hair at Milano and lots of comfy late middle-aged paunches too, as well as the tourist trade. And they all seem to be having a really good time.

But we're not having fun yet. We must be dreadfully old-fashioned and completely uncool. It doesn't matter to us that Milano is the most happening place in town. We feel like the rats in the overcrowded cage, the ones who start chewing on each other's bodies when there isn't enough room to move. This is not to say that Milano is crowded, for it isn't. But it's hectic and noisy and overstimulating.

We must be boring. Here we are in the midst of a major Design Statement, and all we want is a quiet corner to eat dinner and have a conversation. So we leave the jangle of the main floor one evening and go downstairs. But the table where we eat is adjacent to a purple pool table where four guys from Bay Street are playing a

SEE AND BE SCENE

heavy game, *avec* second-hand smoke galore. We're glad they're having fun, but we're not having fun yet.

We know we're *supposed* to have fun at Milano. We know a lot of talented people have put their best efforts into making it fun, and no expense has been spared in the creation of its hectic beauty. But dammit we couldn't find a quiet corner and, when the food came, our curmudgeonly tendencies went ballistic.

Cozze Armani have the right label but the wrong cooking: they have been sufficiently overcooked to shrivel. Ditto the calamari, although overcooked squids tend more towards petrification than shrivelling. The so-called home-made sausage with "herbed egg" tastes more like spicy sausage one buys in any College Street butcher, with greasy scrambled eggs on the side. The salads are more pleasant: perhaps it's best not to ask this kitchen to *cook*.

Main courses kinda bear that out. They make some fine sounding sandwiches on Italian focaccia bread, but there's many a slip 'twixt the menu and the lip: the salmon on one sandwich is heinously overcooked, ditto the broiled minced lamb on another and the swordfish on yet a third. There are pasta and pizza entrées as well. Here too we have suffered disappointment by both overcooking and absence of finesse.

But the desserts say it all: they're by Dufflet. We adore Dufflet desserts, but a restaurant with 400 seats (!!!) and a design budget in the stratosphere is surely making a statement about how highly it values food when it refuses to hire a pastry chef and serves store-bought desserts instead. Dufflet desserts are great for the Ma and Pa operation that can't afford a pastry chef. But Milano is big enough, and wealthy enough, to make its own desserts. This is a question of

Milano

priorities. The eye eats first, but let us not neglect the belly. Purple pool tables and custom-made chairs are great, but you can't eat them.

Montana

145 John Street (At Richmond)
416 595-5949
Expensive. All major cards.
HOURS: All-day menu daily 11 a.m.-12 midnight.
Wheelchair accessible. Licensed. Allergy aware.
Reservations recommended.

Imagine yourself in another country. The inhabitants look pretty much the same as you, and they appear at first to be speaking your language. But it quickly becomes obvious that it's some other language they're talking (lots of common nouns and verbs, but both meaning and idiom differ). And they don't really look the same: their women wear more makeup and tighter clothes, and use more hair chemicals, and their men are pink-cheeked and smooth-faced.

The only difference between our country and theirs is 15 or 20 years, but it feels more like a couple of light years when we dine at Montana, the happening place on John Street just south of Queen. The first thing to separate middle age from youth is noise. We have a lot of it in our heads; they like it piped through speakers at maximum decibels. If you're under 30 (which seems to describe the Montana habitués), there's nothing strange about having to shout above the rock 'n' roll while you inhale your corn chowder. To those of us who have entered the state of grace known as middle age, it's nothing short of a nightmare.

The Rolling Stones are fine people. Their opus is terrific for those times when you're working up a sweat in order to shed pounds (i.e., exercise class). But when your goal is to *add* weight, as pleasurably as possible (i.e., at a restaurant), something a little more mellow might better suit the aging digestion. Not to mention the aging ears.

But it would be a bad idea for Montana to switch to Vivaldi. All the real customers (as opposed to the tourists like us) would leave in a snit. The real customers line up for half an hour on weekends, because Montana is a singles bar. In the second floor bar there is a movie showing on a huge screen (no sound). In the ground floor bar the show is the passing parade of pulchritudinous people.

And what's going on in the dining room? It's kind of hard to know because I'm so confused by the *scene.* If you were to remove the excess stimuli (open plan à la warehouse, noise, movie screen, two levels of bar traffic, huge open kitchen) and pay attention to the food alone, you would say that the menu is in the ambitious Thai/Ital/Cal bistro mode (L.A. via Rome and Bangkok), and that the execution is terrific on the appetizers and good enough on the main courses. For a singles bar, it's bloody wonderful. Full speed ahead and damn the lemon grass.

Certain of the appetizers are as good as anything you get in Toronto: the seafood risotto is a buttery rice medley, fraught with sea flavours and garnished with perfectly cooked shrimp and squid. Shrimp satay are fat shrimp barely grilled and served with a piquant

Montana

little scallion dip and a sexy multi-bean salad. The grilled calamari are sweetly tender and the corn chowder strong and rich. The pizzas come on impeccable crispy crust and their garnishes are splendid, especially the fresh vegetable rainbow that is the vegetarian pizza.

The rest of it is high-class ho hum. Toronto needs another soggy spring roll like a dog needs side pockets. The same goes for chili sadly low in garlic and cumin and steamed mussels with too much powdered ginger in the sauce. Although the chicken wings are pleasant and the hamburger in sourdough bread is certainly pedigreed, does the world need them? Although the ravioli (variously filled or garnished with cheese, sweet potato purée, spinach and quails) are decently done, can the world do without them? Likely.

But there are only three serious disappointments at Montana: one, the so-called hickory-smoked chicken has no smoked flavour. Two, the swordfish is overcooked and oversalted. And three, I'll never be 21 again.

Shark City Athletic Club Bar & Grill

117 Eglinton Avenue East (Near Yonge)

416 488-7899

Moderate to expensive. All major cards.

HOURS: All-day menu

Mon.-Fri. 12 noon-12 midnight or 1 a.m.

Dinner Sat. 6 p.m.-1 a.m.

Closed Sun. and major holidays.

Wheelchair accessible; however, access to

washrooms requires use of a freight elevator.

Licensed. Allergy aware. Reservations necessary,

especially on weekends.

Shark City Athletic Club is the hottest new joint in the Yonge and Eglinton area. The decor is fabulous, a cross between Milano and Acrobat, with a PoMo underwater motif: sea-green velour upholstery, fat columns undulating with sea-coloured glass mosaics, black iron waves and fishes in windows and instead of walls, TV sets tuned to undersea adventures; even the floors are inlaid with sea themes. The food is appalling. Save for credible pizza and calamari sautéed with a garlicky tomato sauce, Shark City is Lime Rickey's in drag.

Shark City

For the Show

Medieval Times

Exhibition Place

416 260-1234

Moderate to expensive. All major cards.

HOURS: Dinner Wed.-Sat. 7:30 p.m.,

Sun. 4 p.m. Closed Mon.-Tues.

Wheelchair accessible. Licensed. Allergy aware.

Reservations necessary.

I was the wrong person to send on this assignment. It is all a matter of perspective. (Any writer who denies her ownership of a unique and opinionated perspective is either too young to know better or lying.) So there are two (or more) possible perspectives on this one. The happy one belongs to my almost-nine-year-old, who was into it before we left the house.

She insisted on dressing in leggings and a long belted jerkin with a sword tucked into the belt. Her little brother (the junior knight) brought both sword and shield to Medieval Times Dinner & Tournament. They both brought their imaginations. When Milord and Milady (in medieval getup) greeted us at the door, the junior members entered an altered state of consciousness. At least it's healthier than hallucinogenics. When we paid ($39 per adult, $27.95 per kid) and were issued crowns, the children happily metamorphosed into royals. For the camera, of course (pics for sale later, we are told).

They saw a medieval hall with a knight in full armour on his horse atop the bar. "Mommy, is he real?" I saw a full hour of souvenir-buying time yawning before me, having been told by the Medieval Times ticket folks to arrive an hour early in order to "get a good seat." Small-fry saw swords on the walls, heraldic flags hanging from the high ceiling, suits of armour and real stallions behind glass ("Mommy, how come it's so long?"). I saw "serving wenches" in pink polyester.

During that interminable hour we bought the small-fry Shirley Temples at the bar, narrowly avoided purchasing a knighthood ($12 for the scroll and ceremony, plus $81 for a junior sword or $104 for a senior sword), resisted the Museum of Torture (adults $2, children $1), and cruised the many souvenir counters. No, we did not sink money into the fortune teller or the family crest scroll or a sword or a dagger.

At the end of the interminable hour, two courtiers blew a flourish on their trumpets, to announce his highness, the count, lord of the castle. The count then knighted a number of birthday boys. (Never before was a blue velvet cloak whipped on and off so fast, with photo ops.) After which we were ushered into the arena and seated in various sections depending on the colour of our cardboard crowns. The tables are counters arranged in graduated tiers around the arena.

Medieval Times

Each section was instructed to cheer for the horseman bearing its colour, and our serving folk came round to say hello. Polyester princess: "I am your cocktail wench." Waiter: "I am your slave for the evening. Please raise your hands in the air: see those? Don't lose them, because that's all you've got to eat with this evening." Thinking of the dry cleaning bill, our hearts sink. The children jump for joy. It's all a matter of perspective.

We were also introduced to the extras: a buck for the colour-correct banner to wave to inspire our champion. $7.95 for the commemorative program that *already* had mounted inside it the photo taken of small-fry with Milord and Milady when we arrived. That's $7.95 for each program, each being important because each child is in a separate photo and hence a separate program.

Shortly after we sit down, along comes another Nikon-bearing polyester princess to shoot yet another photo (this one of the whole family, to be offered later, also mounted, for $7). Meanwhile the real fun (?) begins: riders on Andalusian stallions demonstrate splendid dressage technique. The court chancellor, also on horseback, takes us back to the year 1093, when knights were brave and battle was to the death.

Meanwhile we munch on wizened celery and carrot sticks dipped in a plastic container of thousand island dressing. Before us unfolds a show of equestrian derring-do and medieval violence. There is a plot: knights on horseback are introduced, they troop their colours, they compete in jousting, throwing the lance at a target and other medieval games. They fight—on horseback and then off—with sword, lance, battleaxe, ball and chain.

Meanwhile we eat: cream of vegetable soup (*pace* Mrs. Campbell) slurped from fake pewter crocks.

FOR THE SHOW

Cornish game hen not badly cooked. Dragon's toes (a.k.a. ribs). Baked herbed potato. It's all quite greasy when eaten with the fingers. Again, perspective is everything. While my small-fry were approaching nirvana ("Look mommy, no hands!"), I craved vegetables and wished for a fork.

And the knights fought on, locked in combat to the (choreographed) death. "Mommy, is he really dead?" Subplots unfolded, peopled with Saracens brandishing scimitars, a smoke-enveloped wizard and an executioner in black hood brandishing his bullwhip. Small-fry were entranced, while I scowled at the deep-fried jam turnover (à la Harvey's), and the server's plea for a tip ("Not included, Milady.")

Knights in lurex chainmail throw carnations into the audience. Chivalry isn't dead. It's for sale. With extras. There are Medieval Times "castles" in Florida (at Disneyworld), California, New Jersey, Illinois, Texas and two (the originals) in Spain. But ours is the biggest one of them all, holding up to 1,355 people at a sitting. Now aren't you proud?

Officers 1893

Stanley Barracks, Marine Museum,
Exhibition Place 416 597-1893
Expensive. All major cards.
HOURS: Dinner Thurs.-Sat. 7:30 p.m.-10:30 p.m.
Closed Sun.-Wed.
No wheelchair access. Licensed. Allergy aware.
Reservations necessary.

At the door stands a soldier in full parade dress. As we pass, he salutes smartly and shoulders his musket, saying: "Good evening, madam." Ohmigawd. Is this to be an evening of theatrical and gastronomical embarrassment, wherein we suppress snickers while soldiering through inedible food? One fears it could hardly be otherwise.

The premise almost requires it: Stanley Barracks (housed in the CNE Marine Museum) has turned itself into an attraction: Pay $75 per person for "a historical re-enactment of the officers' mess gala dinner party as given in the year of our lord 1893." Having made it past several more saluting soldiers in regimental red and blue with gold braid, we are welcomed by young women in Victorian raw silk gowns (complete with décolletage and small bustles).

They send us into the Welcome Room, a small, dank gaslit parlour—likely historically correct. Yet another officer in regimental red serves rum punch that resembles Juicy Juice, one of my childrens' favourite supermarket products. Uh oh. Is this a cocktail party of the absurd?

FOR THE SHOW

Soon an officer appears at the door: "Lieutentant Crossley, please... Major Barnes, please." And so on, each of our names being announced (in newfound military roles), and each of us being led (by a lady in Victorian dress) into the officers' mess.

The tables are a splendour of Victoriana: silver candelabra with long white tapers, blue and white Spode china, cut glass and silver goblets, flowers and fruit bowls, battle paintings swathed in grosgrain ribbon and, of course, at the head of the room, a portrait of our sovereign. Whom we toast immediately (on the instructions of the captain of the mess): "To the queen, Victoria."

The year is 1893. The gentlemen, who have been seated on the inside of the horseshoe-shaped table arrangement, are instructed to remain standing while toasting the colonel, the regiment and, last but not least, the ladies. Aah, Victoriana.

But suddenly the door slams, the lights go out, thunder crashes, lightning flashes. In a mirror appears a white-faced apparition wearing soiled regimental colours—a ghostly apparition, à la Disney. The ghost relays his sad tale: in 1893 he was a gallant young officer living in the very barracks where we now sit.

One sad night he and his officer friends drank to excess (as was their wont) at their local, the Wheat Sheaf Tavern. Walking home to the barracks along the seawall, our ghost, busily declaiming Tennyson's "The Charge of the Light Brigade," gestured too wildly, lost his balance, fell into the cold lake and drowned. And thus has been haunting these very barracks for 100 years. "But sshh," sez he, "don't tell the officers and staff serving you. It'll be our secret."

With that, a magnificent theatrical conceit is born.

Officers 1893

Throughout the evening (a three-and-a-half hour performance cum dinner) our ghost reappears frequently to comment on history, to entertain and to preview each course. First comes perfectly respectable consommé princess, borne in china tureens by officers, served by the Victorian ladies. "Ladies serving in an officers' mess?" inquires the ghost.

These ladies take turns seating themselves at the baby grand piano and giving us Victorian songs between courses. Our lieutenant sings an Italian song, from Tosti, who has been, he tells us, resident in London since 1880 as music master to the royal family. The ghost interrupts to speak of the forthcoming salmon, fished from our own lovely Don River. It is indeed very good smoked salmon trout, far better than the ensuing small watery oysters in puff pastry with cream sauce, which are served with ribald ghostly jokes concerning the oyster-eating habits and resulting sexual potency of the officers of this fort.

We are then given a song by Miss Rose Tremaine, who is, the captain of the mess tells us, busy fund-raising for the new Massey Hall. She sings "After the Ball," a hit at the Chicago World Fair and drops a sweet litle curtsey afterwards. So sweet that we cannot fault the unloveable little chunks of lamb in creamed curry sauce with white rice, a thoroughly beige dish that would likely have delighted the officers in 1893.

Even though the venison is overcooked and the creamed turnips play hell with the fat count, the evening is a success as environmental theatre. The food is not bad enough to complain about, and both menu and recipes are historically accurate. From both ghost and officers come many references to the Toronto of their moment, from the genesis of the Stanley Cup to the current (for them) Sunday shopping debate. The military fantasy, while horribly out of fashion, has a poignance that is carefully rendered so as to be almost touching.

Toronto so rarely attends to its Anglo past that any telling of that story is of interest. This particular telling, packaged around dinner and full of history told with lightness and humour, is a Victorian treat, with buttons, bows, gold braid and lace.

Prelude Restaurant at the O'Keefe Centre

O'Keefe Centre (Front and Yonge)
416 393-7478
Expensive. All major cards.
HOURS: 5:30 p.m.-8:00 p.m. on performace nights only.
Wheelchair accessible. Licensed. Allergy aware.
Reservations recommended.

Putting on fine clothes and going out for an evening of dining and theatre is a very un-Torontonian thing to do. We have the fancy dinners and we have the theatre, but the two do not customarily inhabit the same corner of the planet. One would hardly expect the twain to meet at the stodgy old O'Keefe Centre, but wonders never cease: Ken Peace has been chef there since 1988,

Officers 1893

and in 1993 they renovated the lower lounge to give him a real restaurant.

Prelude's decor is in the soporific mode set by its home: the motif is theatrical insofar as there is a motif. It is expressed via painfully subtle pictures of theatre moments and some equally blah curtain effects on walls. The feel is 50s country club. At any moment I expect Mom to appear and chide me for failure to coordinate lipstick colour with my outfit.

So why are we here?

Because Ken Peace, whom one would have expected to be cooking in a *boîte* on Queen Street, can cook the pants off most of the chefs in Toronto. Peace is your classic *chef moderne*. He uses—and promotes—organic ingredients, avoids cream and butter and cherishes the gifts of the seasons. All of which adds up to a menu that is far more interesting than its surroundings suggest.

The choices are few and they rarely change, which hardly matters. After all, how often are you going to pay almost $100 a person for an evening at the O'Keefe? Dinner costs $27.95 each plus tax, tip and wine, but only theatre patrons are invited to dinner; add the price of a good theatre ticket to the meal, and it becomes a Big Night on the Town.

Dinner begins with three choices: Ken Peace's trademark wild mushroom and fresh tarragon soup, which is full of flavour, salad of organic greens with designer seedlings and petals, in an appealing blueberry ginger vinaigrette, or the appetizer of the day, which was sold out by the time we got there.

Sold out is a problem at Prelude. Our excellent waitperson warns us up front that we'd best order desserts at the beginning of dinner, so they won't be sold out. But the one we want is sold out anyway. One

FOR THE SHOW

would think that a professional kitchen might be better at these matters of inventory, but maybe one expects too much. That happens when the evening is costing $100 a person.

Still, Ken Peace's food is so wonderful that it's hard to stay angry. The poached salmon is perfectly cooked (i.e., barely) and its grain mustard beurre blanc (with a hint of saffron and lemon grass) is all grace. Roast leg of lamb is redolent of rosemary and garlic and decorated with crispy litle french fried shallots. The duck breast has a honey glaze, and with everything comes an al dente bouquet of organic vegetables.

Having inhaled the ultimate womb food for dessert— bread pudding with a very serious whiskey sauce—it won't matter much whether the rain in Spain stays mainly on the plain—or anywhere else, for that matter.

Takeout

Chopstix and Rice

1 Adelaide Street East (At Yonge)

416 363-7423

Moderate. All major cards.

HOURS: All-day menu daily 11 a.m.-10 p.m.

Closed major holidays.

Wheelchair accessible. Licensed. Allergy aware.

Reservations recommended for lunch.

In the heyday of Chinese food in Toronto, people in the know did not order in. That was for gastro-cretins who did not understand about wok frying and the necessity to eat Chinese food fresh from the blast furnace. Ordering in was for sweet and sour chicken and wonton soup people.

And that's what we've become. What else is there? We ordered from Chopstix and Rice, where the soups (hot and sour or wonton) are respectable, the spare ribs ungreasy and most of the main dishes are the pleasantries of the Cantonese kitchen, executed with competence. Mango chicken, shrimp vegetable stir-fry, Singapore noodles: this is as good as it gets for Chinese food downtown, so stay home, and let your fingers do the walking.

Thai

Sukhothai Restaurant

136 Yorkville Avenue (Near Avenue Road)
416 920-5811
Expensive. All major credit cards.
HOURS Lunch Mon.- Sat. 11:30 a.m.-3 p.m.
Dinner Sun.-Thurs. 5:30 p.m.-11:00 p.m.
All-day menu Fri.-Sat. 11:30 a.m.-12:00 midnight.
Open on holidays for dinner.
No wheelchair access. Licensed. Allergy aware.
Reservations recommended.

Hell hath no fury like a gastronome disappointed: witness epicurean Toronto's desertion—en masse—of our downtown Chinese restaurants. They are enjoying so little of our custom that it is actually possible to park a car on Spadina Avenue in the evening these days—should you not mind running the risk of getting caught in crossfire or being panhandled by someone on something stronger than Tylenol. Which brings me to another point: the demise of the downtown Toronto Chinese restaurant scene can only be partly blamed on soggy spring rolls and greasy Shanghai noodles. The added aversion factor comes from the social problems in the neighbourhood: Spadina from College Street south to Dundas is no longer a fun place to be after dark.

We have jilted Chinatown for Thaitown partly for this reason: the Thai restaurants are mostly in much more sanitized places. Take, for example, Sukhothai on Yorkville Avenue. The only assault likely to take place on this strip is the one on your credit card. Sukhothai is what our favourite Chinese restaurants never were: luxe. (Ah, the comforts of middle age.)

Bamboo poles decorate walls and ceiling. A huge bronze urn guards the door. Our chairs are stylishly slipcovered in cotton, with pointy tops that resemble the horns of oxen. In the front room, whose colour scheme is teakwood accents on dark persimmon walls, the slipcovers are olive green. In the equally splendid back room, with *faux* brushed aluminum walls, the slipcovers are the colour of a dusty peach. The decorator is working overtime here.

Too bad the chef isn't.

The flavours at Sukhothai (in contrast to the colours) are pallid. We were delighted by our first visit, but in retrospect that may have had something to do with who was doing the cooking. And to what: that first evening we ordered the Thai version of hot pot (Mongolian hot pot in Chinese, *shabu shabu* in Japanese), wherein you are given a small gas burner on the table and a platter of raw food, with several dipping sauces.

In the case of hot pot, if the cook knows enough to buy and set out fresh ingredients and can make a

Sukhothai

half-way decent dipping sauce, all is well. The distance between this and a clever curry is long (to our chagrin).

The Thai version of hot pot involves a subdivided pot with two compartments, one containing spicy lemon shrimp soup and the other containing not-spicy lemongrass soup. The server brings several lovely dipping sauces and a munificent platter of raw food: lobster, shrimp, salmon, various exotic mushrooms, mussels, beef, chicken, shrimp ball, meat ball, grouper, oysters, scallops, squid, fake crab, Thai noodles and yams and assorted greens.

Your job is to cook, dip and eat. Not too unpleasant a task.

But eating the foods that issue forth already cooked from the Sukhothai kitchen is another kettle of fish. Yucky fish. We have been burdened with pad Thai (the national Thai noodle dish) pale of both colour and taste, flat-tasting soups, deep-fried shrimp cakes with the texture of hardened glue, deep-fried chicken wings that mimic the Colonel's best efforts, basil chili quail with the same personality and curries with taste you have to hunt for.

You win some; you lose some.

Thai Magic Restaurant

1118 Yonge Street (Between Bloor and St. Clair)

416 968-7366

Moderate. All major cards.

HOURS: Dinner Mon.-Fri. 5:30 p.m.-11 p.m.,

Sat. 5 p.m.-11 p.m. Closed Sun. and Christmas

Day, Thanksgiving and New Year's Day.

Wheelchair accessible, except to washrooms.

Licensed. Allergy aware.

Reservations recommended.

Rosedale is gaga for Thai. Mink coats and men's cashmeres fall off coatracks insufficent to the task of supporting all the outerwear of the hungry locals with money—and mouths—to burn. Thai Magic doesn't serve the best Thai food on the planet, but it doesn't have to. It's very good, which is good enough for a neighbourhood restaurant. The price is right: two can gorge for $60. The ambience is easy-going and warm, with a noticeable absence of the attitude that plagues some Rosedale restaurants.

People are tired of over-priced Cal/Ital bistros serving precious compositions involving goat cheese and red peppers. They don't even want to hear about extra virgin any more. Ethnic is good. Cheaper is good. Thai is hot.

Sometimes too hot. In Thailand the food blows the

roof off your mouth, which raises the question of how to judge Thai food in Toronto. Should it be authentic, and so spicy that most of us can't take the heat, or ought transplanted Thai cooks to produce a tourist cuisine that caters to our inability to appreciate the real thing?

Some like it hot, but maybe the restaurant could let the diner choose the chili count of every dish ordered. Take, for example, Thai Magic's incredible Thai Magic mussels. They're steamed with curry sauce and unctuous coconut cream. The curry sauce is divine, but so hot that incredible can be inedible. Ditto for the otherwise lovely chicken coconut soup, Thailand's national soup, which is an amalgam of smooth (coconut) and sharp (*kha,* a ginger-like root).

The menu has a chili count (from one to three chilies to denote success levels of danger). As it stands, many of the most interesting dishes are two-chili events, which translates into a call to the fire department for all but the most tough-tongued.

Barbecued foods, a piece of Thai magic served with sweet/spicy peanut sauce, are short on chilies and long on charm. Even the satay is very good, as far as satay goes (which is not very far, considering the relative banality of meat on a stick).

There is an entertaining variety of classy deep-fried appetizers. For those who liked the Bo-Bo platters of 50s Polynesian restaurants, but then outgrew them (almost), Thai Magic's appetizers will be welcome. There are crispy spring rolls, little shrimp nuggets, lovely fried fishcake and wonderful deep-fried "golden baskets" of chicken and bamboo shoots with Thai basil.

This is not the best Thai food in Toronto. The beef salad at Thai Shan Inn is rarer and crisper. The coconut chicken soup at Bangkok Garden has more flavour. But all the others make more mistakes than Thai Magic. They use too much sugar, or the curries are overcooked and the meats greasy. Thai Magic is consistently very good and there are no lousy moments.

Vanipha Lanna

471 Eglinton Avenue West (Near Spadina Avenue)
416 484-0895
Moderate. Visa and Mastercard.
HOURS: All-day menu Mon.-Thurs. 12 noon-11 p.m.,
Fri.-Sat. 12 noon-12 midnight.
Closed Sun. and major holidays.
No wheelchair access. Licensed. Reservations
recommended.

Vanipha Southalack, former chef and owner at Vanipha's on Baldwin Street, left that estimable restaurant in the hands of family members, and opened another sweet, unchic little place. Vanipha's place is cramped, pleasant but inelegant, and delicious.

Vanipha could coax flavour from a roasted earthworm. Her soups (both Thai hot and sour and coconut ginger) are strong and smooth. Her chicken and seafood dumplings, which arrive in a bamboo steamer, are delicate. Her spicy salads have the spice of chili, the sweetness of red onion and the joy of coriander. Her pad Thai is a triumph of noodle and spice sorcery and her curries are the iron hand in the velvet glove.

Vanipha's move uptown glamourized her presentation:

sticky rice comes in a raffia cylinder. Plates and bowls are cradled in dainty wicker baskets. Dumplings come in bamboo steamers and even table napkins are prettily wrapped in slender floral ribbons. The only thing about Vanipha that didn't move uptown was the price.

Young Thailand
(Church Street)

81 Church Street (North of Adelaide)

416 368-1368

Moderate. All major cards.

HOURS: All-day menu Mon.-Sat. 11:30 a.m.-11 p.m.

Dinner Sun. 5 p.m.-11 p.m.

Open major holidays.

Wheelchair accessible. Licensed. Allergy aware.

Reservations recommended for weekends.

High Thai: Wandee Young's second branch of Young Thailand occupies the 81 Church Street premises of the former Abundance. Ms. Young's second location is everything that her Gerrard Street restaurant is not. Gerrard Street is downscale; it feels like a glorified cafeteria, and the food is good but not enthralling. The Church Street branch restaurant is big and beautiful, the closest Ms. Young has come to elegance.

At Church Street both food and decor take a commensurate leap in quality. The satays are tender, the peanut sauces jumping with flavour, the salads full of the vigour of fresh herbs. *Tom kha kai,* the Thai national soup of coconut milk and chicken with lemon grass, is almost erotic in its high-flavoured creaminess. The pad Thai (noodles with everything in them but the kitchen sink) is sweet and pungent. Basil curries are rich with oodles of very fresh basil. This is the food to banish the blahs.

Young Thailand Restaurant
(Gerrard Street)

111 Gerrard Street East (At Jarvis)

416 599-9099

Moderate. All major cards.

HOURS: All-day menu Mon.-Fri. 11:30 a.m.-11 p.m.

Dinner Sat.-Sun. 5 p.m.-11 p.m.

No wheelchair access. Licensed. Allergy aware.

Reservations recommended for weekends.

If every two-bit cook who reads a restaurant column has taken to trying Thai cooking, is that Wandee (pronounced Wendy) Young's fault? Yes, and she deserves some credit for it. The Canadian-born newly minted Thai basil mavens have every right to jazz up their repertoire with borrowings from the East, but they are followers. She is the leader.

In 1981, Wandee and her then-husband, Andy Young,

who owns a driving school, opened Young Thailand on Eglinton Avenue West near the Allan Expressway. As far as I know this was Toronto's first Thai restaurant.

It was strange. A decade ago who knew from coconut milk soup? We wondered if lemon grass was something you smoked, and we knew hot chilies were for other people. It was all decidedly *un-Torontonian*. It was also divine, and it widened our eating boundaries: people who never went near Young Thailand nonetheless enjoyed its effects, thanks to both amateurs and chefs who ate there and then spread the gospel according to Bangkok. Wandee Young's influence spread far beyond her own stoves. Wandee and Andy separated and sold the business in 1984. The restaurant, now called Thai Shan Inn, is still in business, but the current cook uses too much sugar (a common problem in Thai cooking).

After she sold Young Thailand, Wandee became chef at the BamBoo, culinary queen of Queen Street. Here she laboured for seven years, producing superb Thai curries and soups. In 1991 she opened her own restaurant, Young Thailand, on Gerrard Street East.

The Young Thailand on Gerrard Street has 85 seats and walls covered in raffia matting. During the day Young Thailand is a fast food counter selling Thai/Chinese steam-table food incredibly cheaply. $3.95 buys a plate of stir-fried vegetables and Thai noodles.

At five o'clock, the restaurant metamorphoses instantly. Tablecloths go on. The lights drop. Table service begins. And from the kitchen issue forth the classics that Wandee Young has been cooking for Torontonian Thai addicts for 15 years.

There is her silken *tom kha kai,* Thailand's national soup, based on coconut milk and chicken stock with the citric thrill of lemon grass and the whammy of hot chilies and *kha,* a ginger-like root. There is blazing hot seafood soup, and equally mouthburning salads—seafood, beef or green mango—all alive with fresh mint and basil leaves in great green profusion.

Chef Young's curries are full of fresh fine ingredients and strong with many flavours. Her grand finale is sticky rice: she boils Chinese sticky rice in coconut milk with sugar and serves it very hot, beside cold sliced fresh mango. The combination of hot and cold, sugary/rich and juicy/fruit, is the embodiment of Thai cuisine that speaks of the harmony created when the soprano and the bass sing together.

Young Thailand

Vancouver

Imperial Seafood Restaurant

355 Burrard Street (Near West Hasting)

604 688-8191

Expensive. All major cards, except for Mastercard.

HOURS: All-day menu daily 11 a.m.-10 p.m.

Open all holidays.

Wheelchair accessible. Licensed. Allergy aware.

Reservations necessary.

'Twas spring in Vancouver and the town was a riot of blossom. Daffodils, tulips and hyacinths turned the ground into a festival of reborn hopes. On every street the pink blooms on trees proclaimed the joyous news: the words "Spring has come" are writ so large by Vancouver's effusion of flowers that it's easy for a Torontonian to feel hard done by. Our meagre warming trend, along with a few limp crocuses, cannot hold a candle to the botanical splendour of Lotus Land.

VANCOUVER

Toronto has always comforted itself, when suffering by comparison to Vancouver's magical (and lengthy) spring, with talk of culture, ours of course being vastly richer than theirs. The most important culture is the kind you put in your mouth, and with the already acknowledged exception of sushi, Vancouver has always been assumed to offer food that was inferior to Toronto's.

Eat Italian or French or Cal/Ital/Nouvelle in Vancouver, and you'll wish you'd never left the East. But Chinese food is another matter: Vancouver *becs fins* have a tradition of defending their Chinese food against ours, on the grounds that a) they are closer to the sea and therefore to the source of so many important Chinese ingredients and b) their greater Chinese population ensures a higher quality of Chinese restaurant.

Nice if it were true. The differences between Vancouver and Toronto Chinese food are interesting to the aficionado, but on rather close examination, I think I found as many greasy overcooked eastern abominations in Vancouver as one can find in Toronto. There are more Chinese restaurants in Vancouver, and more of them are elegant. We are driven to Richmond Hill or Woodbridge for the high-born Chinese experience.

In Vancouver it's different: downtown is full of upscale Chinese restaurants. For example, the Imperial Seafood Restaurant, a splendid two-storey dining room with tall, beautifully curtained windows overlooking Burrard Inlet. Eating dim sum at lunchtime and watching ships in the sparkling harbour is the sort of aesthetic experience that makes a person awfully glad to be alive. Some of the dim sum at Imperial are exceptional: the pot-sticker dumplings are delicate, unlike the usual petrified skin effect of pot-stickers on these parts. There is an entertaining shrimp dumpling clothed in a thin scrambled egg blanket and local black cod with sweet corn sauce. But otherwise Imperial's thrill is by and large environmental.

Inori

Crystal Lodge, Whistler (formerly Nancy Greene Lodge)
604 932-2221
Expensive. All major cards.
HOURS: Mon.-Fri. 7 a.m.-10:30 a.m. and 6 p.m.-10 pm., Sat.-Sun. 7 a.m.-1:30 p.m. and 6 p.m.-10 p.m.
Wheelchair accessible. Licensed. Allergy aware.
Reservations recommended.

Is the sushi in Vancouver better because of its proximity to the sea? That helps when you're eating black cod and Dungeness crab, but the sweet shrimp and the yellowtail are certainly not local to BC. Vancouver sushiphiles have the Oriental *consciousness* of their city to thank, not to mention the yen. Perched on Canada's western edge looking ever eastward, Vancouver is much influenced and educated by the Pacific Rim.

The sushi mavens of Vancouver have Tokyo to thank for their edible joys. The many business travellers from Japan support Vancouver's plenteous sushi bars with their generous expense accounts. Immigrants from the East help too. The sushi bars of Vancouver are an ongoing unofficial Japan-Canada trade mart.

Vancouver's fixation with sushi is such that even when

Vancouverites leave home for their nearby ski resort, they must have sushi. While Ontarians are roughing it on chili and dogs, the Whistler ski resort has (count 'em!) *four* Japanese restaurants. One of them, Inori, has a sushi bar so long it has to bend (36 seats at the sushi bar alone). Inori is elegantly done in etched glass with triangular motifs (à la mountain shape) and dark stained red wood accents. Everybody's wearing après-ski clothes, but they're paying $100 a couple to suck on sea urchin and raw shrimp. The sushi is no better than we get in Toronto, but if Inori were in Collingwood there'd be mass orgasm. Welcome to Lotus Land.

Maple Garden Hot Pot Restaurant

4260 No. 3 Road, Richmond

604 273-3202

Moderate. All major cards.

Wheelchair accesible. Licensed.

Reservations recommended.

Vancouver is hot for Chinese hot pots these days. In a hot pot restaurant, patrons sit in front of a copper pot that is sunk into a table or counter and has a burner under it to bring the stock in the pot to a boil. You order the chicken or the seafood or the combination meal. The

Inori

server brings a large platter of raw ingredients: shrimp, oyster, scallop, squid, beef, bok choy, rice noodles, shiitake mushroom, tofu, salmon and seafood balls and more. You cook each bit as you wish in your very own hot pot, dip it in spicy sesame soy chili sauce and eat. All for $9.95.

The hottest hot pot restaurant is Maple Garden in Richmond. (This is Vancouver's equivalent to Thornhill, although Richmond makes Thornhill seem exciting.) Maple Garden is done in dusty rose with halogen and a lot of windows. Hot pot is pleasant food, but it's not lighting any gastronomical fires.

Sun Sui Wah

4810 Main Street (Near 32nd)

604 872-8822

Moderate. All major cards.

HOURS: All-day menu daily 11 a.m.-11 p.m.

Open all holidays.

No wheelchair access. Licensed. Allergy aware.

Reservations necessary.

Sun Sui Wah is as ordinary looking as you get in Vancouver; it's in a stripmall in the middle of nowhere, Main Street near 32nd. But even here, where the cachet is subzero, there are tanks for live Dungeness crab, rock cod and lobster, and the yuppie colours of dusty blue and dusty rose have been installed. From the classy lighting to the white tablecloths, you get the idea: downmarket Chinese has been redefined.

Sun Sui Wah serves two exceptional dishes: $28 buys barely poached geoduck, which cooked resembles the sweetest and most delicate steamed clam. Its second signature is roast squab, wherein the small pigeons have been roasted so cleverly that their flesh overflows with juice but their skin is crispy crackly. Hail to cooking magic. Otherwise Sun Sui Wah is as disappointingly ordinary as downtown Toronto's Chinese restaurants. The grass may be greener there, but the frozen shrimp are just as tasteless as they are here.

Tojo

202-777 West Broadway (Near Willow)
604 872-8050
Expensive. All major cards.
HOURS: Dinner Mon.-Sat. 5 p.m.-11 p.m.
Closed Sun.
Wheelchair accessible. Licensed. Allergy aware.
Reservations recommended.

Tojo-san puts his palms together and leans forward in the smallest possible bow. Every move he makes is like that: quiet, deliberate and delicate. Several years ago, one of Vancouver's good sushi restaurants, Kamei Sushi, offered Tojo Hidekazu $10,000 to train their sushi chefs, but he refused, because he feels their philosophy differs from his.

Vancouver is full of fine fish-cutters, but there is

Sun Sui Wah

only one Tojo, the shaman of sushi, the man who fixes you with his eye as he passes you the barbecued eel sushi, and instructs: "No soy sauce." With three words he assures the precious balance of things, which is more important to him than all the money a high-living tourist from Toronto might spend.

Tojo's barbecued eel is unlike any barbecued eel to be eaten at a Toronto sushi bar. Hereabouts that creature is served cold, pre-cooked so that it resembles sweet and sour soggy cardboard. Pleasant flavours, nebishy texture. Tojo brings the eel fresh from the grill, moistly oozing sweet and sour sauce into the sushi rice. We are pleased to honour his injunction against soy sauce.

There are few cooking artists who rise to the challenge of a customer who says: "Feed me. I am yours." Most chefs, when spoken to thus, will reply with the daily special or whatever else they're trying to get rid of. Tojo, on the other hand, when faced with a compliant gourmand sitting at his sushi bar, replies with an edible dream that unfolds in careful sequence.

First he whets the appetite with raw tuna chunks tossed with soy, *wasabi* (Japanese green horseradish), sesame oil, green onions, sake and *mirin* (Japanese sherry). We are overwhelmed by the richest, butteriest tuna ever tasted. Then begins the serious sushi foreplay: a paper-thin egg wrapper enfolding raw yellowtail and scallops, with tiny green cress stems at the centre, and a scattering of orange smelt eggs for colour.

Tojo-san goes in for the kill with a breathtaking sequence of moves: spicy marinated tuna sushi topped with a tiny hill of pureed pickled *daikon* (Japanese white radish) and smelt eggs. Again, an injunction: "No soy sauce." He climaxes with an inside-out roll (his trademark): the centre is asparagus with fresh lobster, which is wrapped in a lettuce leaf, then *nori* (sushi seaweed), then smoked salmon.

After the climax comes the dénouement, the change of pace, the edible breather: Tojo passes us a small plate of local steamed black cod on a light sweet and sour sauce, with marinated mushrooms. We sigh, we are his forever. But the master is not yet finished with the supplicants. The parade of sushi pleasures resumes.

Tojo-san's face has a look of fierce concentration as he leans forward to assemble a plate of lobster sushi just so: lobster shell, hill of snowy shredded daikon and the sushi. Then he fast-cooks the small local scallops (fresh and complete with roe) on their shells with a drizzle of teriyaki sauce.

He looks at us now? Can we handle more pleasure or are we sushi small-fry? Can he take us higher? For Tojo has more up the sleeve of his kimono, much more, if we can go the distance. He will do a bewildering variety of hand-rolled cone sushi, served instantly after rolling so that the seaweed will not lose its precious crispness.

His fast fingers roll steamed asparagus, avocado spears, sushi rice and wasabi into a fat seaweed cone. On top of this bouquet are a few fragments of raw scallops and a sprinkle of dazzling orange smelt roe to crackle on the tongue. Another Tojo cone has a raw quail egg on top. There is a cone with spears of barbecued salmon skin. There is Tojo's rainbow sushi, striped on the outside with salmon, omelette, green radish sprouts and red snapper. Inside out California rolls. Paper thin slices of raw red snapper with citrus, soy, daikon and chili sauce.

Tojo was born 44 years ago in a village in southern Japan. He apprenticed five years in Osaka to become a sushi master. There he learned above all to prize the

Tojo

freshness of fish. Better a local fresh fish, he believes, than a less than fresh "correct" one from far away.

Nothing, not money, not production convenience, comes between Tojo and fresh sushi. When people who sit at the sushi bar leave Tojo's, they do not merely pay and depart. "Thank you, Tojo-san," they say, sated and grateful for the master's ministrations.

Victoria

1088 Melville Street (In Royal Center Mall)
604 669-8383
Moderate to expensive. All major cards.
HOURS: Lunch daily 11 a.m.-2:30 p.m.
Dinner daily 5 p.m.-10 p.m. Open all holidays.
Wheelchair accessible. Licensed. Allergy aware.
Reservations recommended, necessary
on weekends.

The Victoria, on the ground floor of the glamorous Royal Center mall, is a downtown Vancouver big name. Victoria is the Chinese restaurant with French service, where waiters whisk away your plate after it's tainted with the smallest speck of food, and where an appetizer of raw sliced geoduck (the giant Vancouver clam whose body resembles an elephant's private parts) goes for more than $25.

Victoria, like the Imperial (aptly named), is more interesting in social than gastronomic terms. Eating raw (or poached) geoduck is a transcendental experience denied to sinophilic Torontonians. But you can find this sweet-fleshed clam at most Vancouver Chinese and Japanese restaurants. Going the way of the *haute bourgeoisie* isn't necessary.

Vancouver Chinese food is interesting primarily in terms of its ambience and what that foreshadows for Toronto. From the Victoria on down, everything Chinese in Vancouver is upscale compared to Toronto's Chinese food.

Victoria